Numbers and Narratives

This volume argues for a more quantitative, economic and theoretical approach to sports history. The author notes that sport can have peculiar economics as in no other industry do rival businesses have to cooperate to produce a sellable output. He also demonstrates, via a case study of early gate-money football in Scotland, that sports producers were not always seeking profits, and often put winning games and trophies ahead of making money. Another analysis examines how industrialisation affected sport, how sport became an industry in its own right and how the workplace became a major provider of sports facilities. A look at third sector economics highlights how the popularity of football provided an ideal vehicle for charity fund-raising. The book observes that most sports participants are amateurs but at the elite level the paid player has a key role, and this is assessed through case studies of the jockey and the golf professional. Finally, the author discusses and evaluates various theories relating to the historical development of the sports club.

This book was originally published as a special issue of *Sport in Society: Cultures, Commerce, Media, Politics.*

Wray Vamplew is Emeritus Professor of Sports History at the University of Stirling and Visiting Research Professor at Manchester Metropolitan University, UK. His research has gained awards from the North American Society for Sport History and the Australian Sports Commission. He is currently working on an international economic history of sport.

Sport in the Global Society – Contemporary Perspectives
Series Editor: Boria Majumdar

The social, cultural (including media) and political study of sport is an expanding area of scholarship and related research. While this area has been well served by the *Sport in the Global Society* series, the surge in quality scholarship over the last few years has necessitated the creation of *Sport in the Global Society: Contemporary Perspectives*. The series will publish the work of leading scholars in fields as diverse as sociology, cultural studies, media studies, gender studies, cultural geography and history, political science and political economy. If the social and cultural study of sport is to receive the scholarly attention and readership it warrants, a cross-disciplinary series dedicated to taking sport beyond the narrow confines of physical education and sport science academic domains is necessary. *Sport in the Global Society: Contemporary Perspectives* will answer this need.

DIY Football
Edited by David Kennedy and
Peter Kennedy

A Social and Political History of Everton and Liverpool Football Clubs
The Split, 1878–1914
Authored by David Kennedy

Football Fandom in Italy and Beyond
Community through Media and
Performance
Authored by Matthew Guschwan

Numbers and Narratives
Sport, History and Economics
Authored by Wray Vamplew

Sex Integration in Sport and Physical Culture
Promises and Pitfalls
Edited by Alex Channon, Katherine Dashper, Thomas Fletcher and Robert Lake

A Social and Cultural History of Sport in Ireland
Edited by David Hassan and
Richard McElligott

Football and Health Improvement: an Emergent Field
Edited by Daniel Parnell and Andy Pringle

A Social and Cultural History of Sport in Ireland
Edited by Richard McElligatt and
David Hassam

The Containment of Soccer in Australia
Fencing Off the World Game
Edited by Christopher J. Hallinan and
John E. Hughson

The History of Motor Sport
A Case Study Analysis
Edited by David Hassan

The Making of Sporting Cultures
John E. Hughson

Numbers and Narratives
Sport, History and Economics

Wray Vamplew

LONDON AND NEW YORK

First published 2017
by Routledge
2 Park Square, Milton Park, Abingdon, Oxon, OX14 4RN, UK

and by Routledge
711 Third Avenue, New York, NY 10017, USA

Routledge is an imprint of the Taylor & Francis Group, an informa business

© 2017 Taylor & Francis

All rights reserved. No part of this book may be reprinted or reproduced or utilised in any form or by any electronic, mechanical, or other means, now known or hereafter invented, including photocopying and recording, or in any information storage or retrieval system, without permission in writing from the publishers.

Trademark notice: Product or corporate names may be trademarks or registered trademarks, and are used only for identification and explanation without intent to infringe.

British Library Cataloguing in Publication Data
A catalogue record for this book is available from the British Library

ISBN 13: 978-1-138-63507-4

Typeset in Minion Pro
by RefineCatch Limited, Bungay, Suffolk

Publisher's Note
The publisher accepts responsibility for any inconsistencies that may have arisen during the conversion of this book from journal articles to book chapters, namely the possible inclusion of journal terminology.

Disclaimer
Every effort has been made to contact copyright holders for their permission to reprint material in this book. The publishers would be grateful to hear from any copyright holder who is not here acknowledged and will undertake to rectify any errors or omissions in future editions of this book.

Contents

Citation Information		vii
Preface		1

Part I: Introduction

1.	Count me in: reflections on a career as a sports historian	3
2.	The power of numbers: a plea for more quantitative sports history	19

Part II: Sport, economics and the economy

3.	Scottish football before 1914: an economic analysis of a gate-money sport	27
4.	Sport, industry and industrial sport in Britain before 1914: review and revision	46
5.	'It is pleasing to know that football can be devoted to charitable purposes': British football and charity 1870–1918	62

Part III: The sports professional

6.	Still crazy after all those years: continuity in a changing labour market for professional jockeys	84
7.	Successful workers or exploited labour? Golf professionals and professional golfers in Britain 1888–1914	106

Part IV: Developing theory

8.	Empiricism, theoretical concepts and the development of the British golf club before 1914	131
9.	Playing together: towards a theory of the British sports club in history	161
	Index	177

Citation Information

The chapters in this book were originally published in *Sport in Society: Cultures, Commerce, Media, Politics*, volume 19, issue 3 (April 2016). When citing this material, please use the original page numbering for each article, as follows:

Preface
> *Preface*
> *Sport in Society: Cultures, Commerce, Media, Politics*, volume 19, issue 3 (April 2016), pp. 295–296

Chapter 1
> *Count me in: reflections on a career as a sports historian*
> *Sport in Society: Cultures, Commerce, Media, Politics*, volume 19, issue 3 (April 2016), pp. 297–312

Chapter 2
> *The power of numbers: a plea for more quantitative sports history*
> *Sport in Society: Cultures, Commerce, Media, Politics*, volume 19, issue 3 (April 2016), pp. 313–320

Chapter 3
> *Scottish football before 1914: an economic analysis of a gate-money sport*
> *Sport in Society: Cultures, Commerce, Media, Politics*, volume 19, issue 3 (April 2016), pp. 321–339

Chapter 4
> *Sport, industry and industrial sport in Britain before 1914: review and revision*
> *Sport in Society: Cultures, Commerce, Media, Politics*, volume 19, issue 3 (April 2016), pp. 340–355

Chapter 5
> *'It is pleasing to know that football can be devoted to charitable purposes': British football and charity 1870–1918*
> *Sport in Society: Cultures, Commerce, Media, Politics*, volume 19, issue 3 (April 2016), pp. 356–377

CITATION INFORMATION

Chapter 6
Still crazy after all those years: continuity in a changing labour market for professional jockeys
Sport in Society: Cultures, Commerce, Media, Politics, volume 19, issue 3 (April 2016),
pp. 378–399

Chapter 7
Successful workers or exploited labour? Golf professionals and professional golfers in Britain 1888–1914
Sport in Society: Cultures, Commerce, Media, Politics, volume 19, issue 3 (April 2016),
pp. 400–424

Chapter 8
Empiricism, theoretical concepts and the development of the British golf club before 1914
Sport in Society: Cultures, Commerce, Media, Politics, volume 19, issue 3 (April 2016),
pp. 425–454

Chapter 9
Playing together: towards a theory of the British sports club in history
Sport in Society: Cultures, Commerce, Media, Politics, volume 19, issue 3 (April 2016),
pp. 455–469

For any permission-related enquiries please visit:
http://www.tandfonline.com/page/help/permissions

Preface

Wray Vamplew

The introductory section reflects on my career as a sports historian and the use of quantification as the dominant methodology that I have employed in my work. It argues for an increased use of statistics as a means of strengthening arguments by providing a statistical basis for historical assertion; by allowing more effective comparisons to be made; and by enabling the testing of hypotheses.

Section Two looks at some of the relationships between sport and economics. The first article was an early venture of mine into the peculiar economics of elite sport. Sport was one of the economic success stories of the late nineteenth century, yet in the commercial sector the motivations of sports promoters and organizers varied from profit maximization (as in conventional business) through to utility maximization where winning trophies takes precedence over revenue raising. This is discussed in the context of Scottish football. The second article turns to the broader question of sport and industry. It examines how industrialization in the economy affected sport; how sport became an industrial sector in its own right; and how the workplace became a major provision of sports facilities to the population. The final article enters the field of third sector economics. This sector is differentiated from the private (business) one in that revenue is not an end product but a resource and from the public (government) one as it cannot forcibly raise revenue via taxation. It is differentiated from both in that its sources of support include volunteer time and donations of money. The popularity of sport at participant and spectator level has provided an ideal vehicle for charity fundraising and this is looked at via football in England and Scotland.

Section Three considers that minority among sports participants: the professional. Paid players existed before industrialization. Sports labourers learned early that they could make money from sport not only from winning prizes, but also by securing a patron, giving tuition and exhibitions, and selling instruction books, portraits, and memorabilia. It is likely that some jockeys, pedestrians, and pugilists developed as sportsmen out of their servant tasks of messengers and bodyguards, while cricketers found employment as estate workers because of their bowling skills. However, amateurs dominated elite sport in the Victorian era and professionalism itself used to be a concept concerned more with class than payment for play. In both the sports examined here, golf and horseracing, the paid performer became superior to the amateur.

The final section applies theory to two aspects of the club in sports history. First the development of the golf club, the institution behind one of the fastest growing recreational activities of late nineteenth- and early twentieth-century Britain and the first participant sport to expend and invest large sums of money, is considered via the application of varying concepts of capital – physical, financial, cultural, social, and human. Secondly theoretical explanations of the sports club more generally are discussed in the context of the origins of the club; various levels of associativity; capital formation particularly that involving social capital; conviviality; the life cycle of the club; and aspects of third sector theory, the economics of the firm and invention and innovation.

I am grateful to the executive academic editor of this journal, Dr Boria Majumdar, for the invitation to present my ideas to a wider audience. Several of the articles are original, the others, as indicated, are either expanded or amended versions of previously published works.

Count me in: reflections on a career as a sports historian

Wray Vamplew

ABSTRACT
This article outlines my work as a sports historian and the people and events that have influenced my research and career. On route, I outline some of my thoughts, opinions and prejudices about academic life.

Early years

Figures have always fascinated me. Sad child that I was, I voluntarily took arithmetic books home from primary school. At Hemsworth Grammar School, an institution that provided educational opportunity for working-class kids from coalmining villages, I discovered economic history, a topic pioneered in the curriculum by Don Hudson, a man who demonstrated that enthusiasm for your subject was a vital cog in teaching – something that I tried to bear in mind in my later lecturing and tutoring. A new world opened as I found that statistics was applicable to the humanities. My A levels (do they still exist?) were in Mathematics, Further Mathematics and History. Heeding my headmaster's advice, I opted to go to university at the other end of the country to study a new degree, a BSc in Social Sciences at Southampton. There, courses in accountancy (which I had intended as a profession- sad again), sociology, economics, econometrics and history, all stood me in good stead as I ventured into an academic career. I represented the University at athletics, rugby union and soccer (at the time when I was suspended by the local RFU for playing rugby league alongside professionals) but the only history I did was that of the Chartist movement. Eric Clapton, the guitarist, took his trousers off in my room but that's another story!

In my training, as an economist, I was taught positive rather than normative economics, the branch of the subject in which value judgements are not supposed to impinge on analysis. Hence, my aversion to those sports academics, generally of left wing persuasion (as I am myself) who are guilty of what I term 'reverse research' in which they know what they want to conclude so they search solely for evidence that will support this. Or those who draw the conclusion even if it is not fully backed up by the empirical data collection.

I was also schooled in the use of theory which I believe is central to understanding the social science of sport. As an economist, I have always used theory both implicitly and explicitly. In his seminal work, Booth takes sports historians to task for a failure to engage more extensively with theory and criticizes those who simply gather facts to tell a story (Booth 2005). Yet Booth can be too harshly judgemental and appears unwilling to accept that approaches other than his own can still be useful. Although (very) few sports historians openly discuss theoretical issues, many implicitly use theory, or more precisely, theoretical concepts, to help them frame questions. Booth later acknowledged that theoretical structures such as modernization, hegemony, feminism, discourse and textualism have been embraced in this way (Booth 2010, 12–13). Yet I worry that these concepts are being applied uncritically. The concept of the 'body' pervades a corpus of writing by sports historians but how many of them are clearly aware of the subtleties and complexities of Foucault's work on the knowledge-body-power trilogy? Moreover, Booth plays down the possibility that the theory being applied could be erroneous. However, no theory is immutable. If the facts do not fit the theory then the historian should check the facts again and, if still convinced they are correct, then the theory should be modified. Historians must not only be prepared to use theory, they also must be prepared to adapt it. Until substantiated by evidence, theories are just competing hypotheses. They might aid our understanding but they do not explain a situation completely. Empirical support is a necessary concomitant for accepting any hypothesis. I see no place in sports history for those who accept a theory in its entirety and then slavishly and uncritically apply it with a 'one theory fits all situations' mentality.

Edinburgh

On finishing my degree, I was offered a tutorship in economics and economic history at the Australian National University under Professor GSL Tucker, but turned it down in favour of a place at Nottingham University to qualify as a teacher of history. So much for plans to be an accountant. Then, out of the blue, the Dean of Social Sciences at Southampton asked if I would be interested in doing a Ph.D. in the Department of Economic History at Edinburgh University. 'They need an opening bat' he said. The unbeaten fifty that I had scored in a staff vs. student cricket match had been remembered. A scholarship followed and away I went across the border to work on a history of the relationship between railway development and the Scottish economy. This was a study in counterfactual history. The basic notion of which is that if it is alleged that fact A led to result B, one way to show this is to argue that if A had not happened then B also would not have occurred. In my case, I attempted to remove the railways from Scotland and assess what would have happened to its industries if there had been no railway demand for coal, iron and engineering products, and transportation would have been dependent on a version of what already existed in the form of canals, roads and shipping. The thesis involved many thousands of computations all done on a hand-wound, mechanical calculator: thank goodness for the development of the computer and statistical packages. Much depends on the logic of the assumptions made as to what developments might have occurred: Napoleon might have won at Waterloo had he had nuclear weapons is not an acceptable counterfactual. In my thesis, I ruled out an earlier invention of the automobile but accepted that the canal network might have expanded as might coastal shipping facilities, thus avoiding, I hope, the criticism of counter-factual history by Eric Hobsbawm (1974, 376) and others as being 'if my grandmother had had wheels she might have been a greyhound bus' history!

Later I took an element of counterfactual history – 'what if history' – when I explored what might have happened to British sport in the absence of greater leisure time, increased disposable income and the growth of towns and cities, factors which promoted the development of mass spectator sport, widespread commercialism and professionalism within sport and the ensuing problems of corruption and sharp practice consequent upon the influx of money into the sector. I argued on the basis of empirical evidence that neither of the realistic alternatives – pre-commercialized sport and contemporary amateur sport would have been problem-free (Vamplew 1988, 6–8).

After two years, as a Ph.D. student and one concurrently as a part-time zero-hours contract teaching assistant, I was offered a lectureship in the Department. Although I continued my doctorate and began to publish on railway history, I commenced my research in sports history. It is probably new to the Leicester School with whom I have had several academic skirmishes, that I also did some voluntary sports sociology teaching. The sociologists at Edinburgh encouraged my new interest and asked me to participate in a sampler short course collection for students finishing their first year. Frank Bechhofer was particularly supportive, even when I so bored one of his dinner guests that, looking at what was then my small frame, she asked if I was a jockey!

The results of my research were published as *The Turf: A Social and Economic History of Horse Racing* in 1976 to mixed reviews (Vamplew 1976). I explained the development of horseracing in economic terms along the lines that it originated from a combination of wealth, lack of spending opportunities and competitive instinct. It was a prime example of conspicuous consumption in which match races between two owners demonstrated an ability and willingness to risk money. Racing has been a dynamic product and clearly, even by 1900, was a different sport from that of 1700. The pre-modern version was predominantly rural, highly localized and was free to watch but two centuries later it had national rules and many courses were enclosed and charging gate money. What happened was a combination of commercial widening (more fixtures), commercial deepening (new revenue sources), product improvement (modifying the original sporting competition) and product development (changing the nature of racing).

The most critical review came from Roger Longrigg in the *Times Literary Supplement* who felt that mine was 'a classic example of history rewritten by preconception' (hoisted by my own petard?), though he acknowledged that my efforts to find evidence to support my ideas were 'ingenious'. The broadsheets were more easily satisfied: the *Sunday Times*' reviewer said it was 'never dull or unduly sociological' and that of the *Irish Times* thought it 'thoroughly researched and well-argued'. The *Economist* praised the 'high quality analysis' (*Times Literary Supplement*, 23 July 1976; *Sunday Times* 30 May 1976; *Irish Times*, 5 June 1976; *Economist*, 5 June 1976). As might be expected, most academic reviewers found something to criticize. Although James Walvin stated it to be 'a notable contribution', both 'perceptive' and 'original', Tony Mason felt that I had been cavalier with my source material and John Walton, though accepting that it was 'the first serious history of an important business enterprise', did not appreciate the 'frothy frivolity' of my writing style and felt that I failed to bring together the threads of my twentieth-century analysis. Jack Dowie saw it as 'a good book, well-researched and written, simultaneously entertaining and informative, always asking sensible questions' but followed Walton's line via a racing metaphor in which he compared the work to 'watching the Cesarewitch on a misty October day at Newmarket … [where] … it is a long time before it is clear what exactly is (and has been) going on', especially when I 'finished the race a few furlongs from the spectators' (*New Society* 27 May 1976 [Walvin]; *Victorian Studies*, 20 (1977/1978), 105–106 [Mason]; *Business History*, 19 (1977), 103 [Walton]; *Economic History Review*, 30 (1977), 356–357 [Dowie]. Nevertheless, even with its shortcomings, it became a standard citation in horseracing and sport history literature.

By the time the book came out, I had left Scotland. Edinburgh University operated a ratio of senior to junior staff which worked against the Faculty of Social Sciences, a new grouping in a university dominated by long-established faculties of Medicine, Law and Divinity. Hence, with promotion unlikely, in 1975, I immigrated to Australia to take up a lectureship in economic history at the Flinders University of South Australia. This came about via a chance meeting with Eric Richards, a professor of history at the Flinders. There was no interview, just the submission of a CV. This time I decided to go. Michael Flinn, one of the professors in the Edinburgh department, had an old colonial view of the empire and felt I should only move to a chair, something I never achieved in my 18 years in Australia. In passing I should note that at the time I had less respect for Flinn than the other professors in the department, Berwick Saul and Christopher Smout. They, I felt, were real researchers whereas Flinn had moved into synthesis, something which as a Young Turk, I felt, was not what chairs should be doing. Some years on I realized that synthesis can be true scholarship: Michael, a belated apology.

Another reason for leaving was disillusionment with a country in which the lights were off half the time and there was a running political sore in the shape of Northern Ireland. In 1974, I did a stint teaching at Queen's University in Belfast which gave me an abhorrence of organized religion and its consequence for civil society. I had never lectured before where the Catholics and Protestants sat at opposite sides of the theatre and a tutorial argument had sectarian undertones and this was to be the next generation of influence! One of my economic history colleagues was later murdered by Loyalist paramilitaries. I spent most of my free time working through old copies of the *Journal of the Royal Statistical Society* to produce a reappraisal of the operation of the Corn Laws (Vamplew 1980).

Australia

Flinders was an institution in its first decade of operations and open to ideas. There, along-side my conventional economic history teaching, I was allowed to develop a multidiscipli-nary course in Sport and Recreation with sports philosopher Bob Paddick. I also developed an honours course on sports history from which emerged Daryl Adair with whom I later co-authored a debated history of sport in Australia (Adair and Vamplew 1997).[1]

In 1977, Richard Cashman and Michael McKernan organized the first Sporting Traditions Conference at the University of New South Wales.[2] From this emerged the Australian Society for Sports History which, despite some initial friction between those trained in physical edu-cation and those with a history background, became a progressive force for the development of sports history. I was the foundation editor of its associated journal, *Sporting Traditions*. In those pre-personal computer days everything had to be typewritten and duplicated on a Xerox machine. I became President of the Society in 1989 and was honoured with its first life membership when I left Australia.

Whilst in Australia, my penchant for quantitative work led to an invitation to write a major statistical history of South Australia to commemorate the state's 150th anniversary (Vamplew 1986). This gained me a place on the state's heritage committee where I was instrumental in saving the scoreboard at the Adelaide Oval. It also produced an approach to edit *Australians: Historian Statistics*, one of the collections in a multi-volume set of reference works commemorating the Australian Bicentennial (Vamplew 1987). Within that volume, I put together data on sport and recreation with a concentration on crowd attendances. Years later, when visiting my son in Ballarat, we took a Sunday afternoon trip to a bookshop in a nearby rural community. There in the window was a mint, second hand copy of the volume. When told that I was the editor the proprietor insisted that I autograph the book, destroying its pristine nature but, in his opinion, increasing its value. I suspect it will still be there on my next visit! A useful spin off from this project were several statistical monographs and the *Australian Historical Statistics Bulletin*, both of which enabled useful quantified sporting material to gain an audience.

I continued work on British sports history and in 1988 produced my seminal work, *Pay Up and Play the Game: Professional Sport in Britain, 1870–1914*. This was to be published by Leicester University Press but when they insisted on cutting its length, I sent the manuscript to Cambridge University Press who accepted it in its entirety. Leicester was miffed but academics should not allow publishers to dictate everything in what is often a one-sided relationship. One thing that was missing from *The Turf* was any real theoretical underpinning. I first attempted to rectify this in *Pay Up and Play the Game* in which I applied the concepts of profit and utility maximization, cartelization and economic rent to several sports including racing. The objective of the work 'was to produce a quantified economic and slightly social history of commercialized sport by the application of comprehensible economic theory to hard, empirical data' (Vamplew 1988, xiv). This was fortunate enough to win the inaugural North American Society for Sport History (NASSH) Book Award.[3] I was appreciative of the fact that an American society had given its prestigious award to a book on British sport by a Yorkshireman living in Australia, especially when there was an outstanding book on American college football also on the shortlist.

Given the distance of Australia from my basic source materials, the book could not have been written without the aid of grants from the Australian Research Grants Committee, the Carnegie Trust and Flinders University. I have been fortunate in my career to obtain grants to aid my research, over $300,000 in Australia and over £150,000 in Britain, so hopefully what I say now will not be construed as sour grapes. Scholars today are forced by their employers to apply for grants, not to pursue scholarship but to be measured as part of a research quality exercise. Yet grants reflect only the quality of the proposal not the quality of the research which still has to be done. Grants are an input not an output. It is simply easier for the bean counters to add up the amounts received and use them as a proxy measure rather than attempt to effectively measure the quality and impact of the actual research undertaken. Another trend in grants that should be condemned is the concentration of awards into support of large projects. Do not believe all the guff about this encouraging collaboration and inter-disciplinarity. It may do that, but the underlying reason is to reduce the administrative burden. Small grants with which historians can do a lot are proportionately more expensive to deliver. Not those historians are getting many grants these days as increasingly they go to STEM subjects (science, technology, engineering and mathematics). I simply note that although sport historians will never cure cancer, nor will they produce chemical weapons, or algorithms that helped plunge the western world into a financial crisis.

As stated above, Australia is a long way from the rest of the world and for Australian academics, especially in the pre-internet years, the international conference was a vital cog in progressing a career. Certainly they are part junket but they are very useful for young ambitious academics to make contacts and to mark out their territory. In 1983, I was invited to one on 'More than a Game: The Importance of Sports' in St Louis organized by Chuck Korr, where I became infamous for accusing an NBL coach who demanded an unquestioning acceptance of his authority of wanting players who would have made train drivers to Auschwitz. I have never been convinced by the public school rhetoric about the character-building nature of team sport. The assumption is that it will create good character but why should it? Manliness can easily spill over into brutality; *esprit de corps* can result in confrontation; and there is a fine line between courage and foolhardiness. Earlier in 1982, Chuck had gained me a Weldon Springs Fellowship to the University of Missouri-St Louis to assist him in the final preparation of his book on West Ham United (Korr 1986). I ended up on local television debating the ethics of sponsorship with a former Olympic athlete, a CIA agent and the mascot of the St Louis Cardinals!

Following some high profile player brutality and crowd disturbances, I was asked by the Australian Sports Commission in 1991 to investigate crowd and player violence in Australian sport (Vamplew 1991). The report led the Australian Soccer Federation to nominate me for the ASC Sports Science Education Award which, despite adverse comments on a satirical television sports programme, I received. Not all my recommendations were implemented though I still stand by one that was not: players should have to pass a test on the rules before they can be selected. I returned to this topic some years later when I led a group at Stirling to examine the development of sporting conduct codes throughout the world in an endeavour to find best practice for the UK Sports Commission to implement (Vamplew and Dimeo 2004). I have to declare that where sports violence and other forms of cheating are concerned, I believe in original sin. All my historical research suggests that pure sport has been a rare occurrence.

During my tenure at Flinders, the University brought in a policy that only Heads of Departments could have a professorial title. An opportunity arose when Gus Sinclair opted to return to Melbourne but two strong internal candidates led to the appointment of an outsider. I was angry. The issue was not that of being overlooked but the way that I found out via a circular to staff saying who the next Head of Department would be without the courtesy of being informed privately in advance. Professor Ray Brown of the Department of Social Welfare calmed me down and counselled that how I reacted would be noted. He also donated me a large set of pigeon holes that accompanied me on all my succeeding appointments. I thank him on both accounts. Nevertheless, I determined to leave and was offered a Dean's position at Launceston Institute of Technology. I decided not to accept but the offer must have fed through to the Vice-Chancellor at Flinders and shortly afterwards I was asked to become Pro-Vice-Chancellor, essentially number three in the academic administration pecking order.

My portfolio at Flinders included the recruitment of overseas students. Do not believe anything that universities say about wanting to internationalize their campuses and their concern for international students. At every university I have been involved with the bottom line is to collect international student fees. This has led, though no university is willing to acknowledge it, to some very unsuitable admissions, not all I will stress from Asia. Money has become the leitmotif which, as my work in sports history has shown, inevitably has led to problems.

I also achieved perhaps a unique distinction in, as part of an anti-bureaucracy drive that I instigated, persuading a university committee to disband itself. As an administrator and argumentative academic, I have always tried to reduce the level of bureaucracy which detracts from the real tasks of academe. Of course, newcomers will not have known a life when bureaucracy was less intensive and intrusive and will accept it as part of the job. Fortunately, advances in computer technology and web access have speeded up the research process and to some extent offset the adverse productivity effects of excessive form-filling.

As PVC, I also counted as a triumph that I merged the Faculties of Nursing and Medicine, against the wishes of some senior medics. Ultimately, they outwitted me by voting that a nurse should become the first Dean of the new grouping in the belief – a self-fulfilling prophesy perhaps – that she would not cope with the situation, leaving her successor as a medical man. Where I was successful was in insisting that potential doctors go on the wards during their first year as a medical student so as to experience inter-relations with patients. At that time, South Australia operated a numerical scoring system in its matriculation and those with the highest aggregate totals almost automatically enrolled for the high status degrees of either law or medicine, even when they were palpably unsuited for those professions. My innovation enabled such students to come to terms with this and opt instead for a career in science or medical research.

The merging of faculties was part of a major restructuring of the University which I oversaw when the whole of tertiary education in the state was being reorganized. I had to set up a new School of Engineering with the newly created University of South Australia and oversee the merging of Sturt College of Education into Flinders. One consequence was that my old department had disappeared and been merged into History. With my term as PVC coming to an end, I faced the option of moving back to my ex-Department with its loss of independence and some disgruntled staff or moving on.

Leicester

I was realistic enough to accept that I did not have sufficient influential non-academic contacts to contemplate becoming a Vice-Chancellor but felt that my administrative skills could still be useful. I was also ready to return to the UK following a bout of home-sickness after attending a football research conference in Aberdeen at a time when the daffodils were blooming. I gained an interview for the position of Research Director at the University of Central Lancashire but was told that I had to pay my own fare over from Australia! De Montfort University proved more generous and following an interview at the Institute of Directors in London (the Vice Chancellor much preferred the capital to Leicester) I became Head of the School of Arts and Humanities. The University was also generous with removal expenses which even covered bringing a car over from Adelaide. Only on arrival did I discover that the money had come from the School budget which was already substantially in deficit. The job was a challenge, not least because my predecessor had left me six months mail to deal with. De Montfort was in transition from polytechnic to university status and had little experience of non-industrial research. The School operated on several campuses: two in Leicester, two in Bedford, one in Lincoln and another in Milton Keynes. It also included an art school and a drama department whose staff were certainly different from the pragmatic, hard-nosed medicos at Flinders.

As Head of School, I was eligible for a personal chair and, after due process, became the first Professor of Sports History in Britain. Huw Richards did a decent interview with me for the *Times Higher*, but most other journalists sought to test me on sports facts, presumably so that they could claim that the sports history professor knew nothing about his subject. Although the press can help academics communicate their ideas to a wider audience (possibly useful as a measurement of impact these days), the relationship can be fraught. Journalists are looking for the quote not the explanation. In Australia, one piece of my research was summed up in the headline 'University Lecturer Says Gambling is Good For You'. There are some excellent journalists with whom it is worth cultivating a relationship but too many are lazy, preferring to free ride on our egos and expertise.

I turned the School into one with a research culture which gave us some rating (and monetary reward) in the 1996 RAE, but I was less happy with other aspects of the job which included dealing with student suicides, staff accused of rape and pressure from several PVCs, all full of ambition for themselves rather than the institution. I coped but at the expense of my personal research. However, coping is not what academic leadership should be about. I suspect the Vice-Chancellor was aware of my feelings and, to his credit, he welcomed a business plan from me to establish a centre of excellence in sports history so that we could build upon our relative success in the RAE. This led to the establishment of the International Centre for Sports History and Culture. I deliberately did not tie the centre down to a particular sport, used 'culture' as a weasel word to cover all manner of things, and tagged everything 'international' for marketing purposes.

One rule that was laid down was that the Centre had to become financially viable. This meant that we had to seek consultancy and knowledge transfer earnings. When, at Edinburgh, I had obtained contracts to write the history of a major whaling and shipping firm and also a merchant bank (Vamplew 1975). The latter never saw the light of day as I discovered that the firm had been funding German rearmament in the 1930s, a fact that they did not wish to publicize. At Flinders, I continued to pursue consultancy work and became involved in a sports history consultancy enterprise in which I helped prepare reports on the Australian Sports Medicine Federation, betting in Australian rugby league, and junior and school rugby league in New South Wales (Vamplew 1989; O'Hara and Vamplew 1990; Cashman and Vamplew 1991). Along with a few fellow sports historians, I also became involved with a television company who paid for a brainstorming weekend in a luxury hotel on the beachfront at Manly. The resulting series did not mention us, nor did the accompanying book: but we received our money. By the time I arrived at De Montfort in 1993, I had changed my mind as to the participation of staff in paid consultancy work; or at least as to the proportion of money they should receive if they were working on university time. So when I obtained contracts for the International Centre to write the histories of the Professional Golfers Association and the UK Physical Education Association, to give assistance to a sporting art exhibition at the National Portrait Gallery and to investigate the prospects for Newcastle United Football Club to leave St James's Park, much of the money went to pay the Centre's bills though I also used some of the cash to fund a Ph.D. scholarship (Vamplew 1997; Bailey and Vamplew 1999; Holt, Lewis and Vamplew 2002).

Supervising research students has been a rewarding experience intellectually. Over my career, I have been involved in the supervision of 17 at masters and 22 at doctorate level. Not all have been successful though the failures generally have been self-selective in not giving the thesis priority in their lives: this is not a criticism merely an explanation.

De Montfort was an institution that appointed professors with a view to them scaling the heights but it was reluctant to back them with the resources to achieve this. I suspect it was hoped that a few would become stars and that this justified the failure of the others. That said it gave me free rein to establish the International Centre and for that I am grateful. However, I rebelled against the minutiae of quality control paperwork. Clearly I was in an institution where nobody was trusted. This came to a head when De Montfort insisted on a full quality inspection of two European partners with whom the Centre was planning to launch a Master's degree under the aegis of FIFA. As both institutions had much more academic status than De Montfort I refused to submit the morass of information required. The writing was on the wall (it was certainly not on the forms!) and I decided to leave.

Stirling

I was encouraged to apply for a readership at the University of Stirling with the promise (one that was kept) that I could later make a case for a personal chair if I got the position. It may have helped that I was a member of the RAE Panel for sports-related subjects, thanks to a nomination from the British Society of Sports History (BSSH). So, in 2001, I became Director of Research in the Sports Studies Department and later also Associate Dean for Research in the Faculty of Management, in which Sports Studies lay at one end of the spectrum and Computer Science at the other. Additionally, I took on the task of teaching research methods to honours sports studies students and developed sports ethics courses for physical education students and taught Master's course. Sports history alas only featured as examples in these. However, we were able to host both the Silver Jubilee Conference of the BSSH, in 2007 and one for the International Society for the History of Sport and Physical Education (ISHPES), the only truly international sports history organization, in 2009. My own research progressed via AHRC and Leverhulme grants to examine the development of the golf club as a social institution, though administrative duties delayed the writing up and publication of the results.

In my later years at De Montfort, I began to work with Scottish-based sports historian Joyce Kay, research that was progressed even more when I moved to Stirling. Our first joint piece was a chapter on Scottish racing which showed the historical paucity relating to the sport north of the border (Kay and Vamplew 2000). Our major joint work was the writing, not editing, of the *Encyclopaedia of British Horseracing* published as part of a Routledge sports reference series, in 2005 (Vamplew and Kay 2005). It had a chequered history in that it was first commissioned by ABC Clio who then, via a policy change instituted by their American management, opted out of the contract. Frank Cass picked up the reins but was swallowed by sports publishing giants Routledge before the work appeared. The latter had to be persuaded that, despite the loss of visual impact, the authors were not prepared to stand the cost of illustrations. It also nearly ended in disaster when one author – the technologically challenged one – lost the final version of the manuscript somewhere in the internet ether. We tried to avoid recycling old material and examined some previously neglected areas such as the link between racing and the arts, the church and alcohol. We looked at the social, economic and political forces that shaped the development of the sport and emphasized the historical duality of continuity and change. Like *The Turf*, before it, the *Encyclopedia* was translated into Japanese.

As I noted earlier, in this article theory is not immutable and I have always argued that if the facts do not fit the theory, first check the facts and then, if they are correct, change the theory. This is what Joyce and myself suggested when we attempted to assess the relevance to horseracing of Allen Guttmann's (1986) famous seven-stage model of modernization in sport (Vamplew and Kay 2003). By the 1830s, racing was a major British sport, organized at local level the length and breadth of the country; the Classics and other major races had been established; and large crowds were attracted, reputedly over 100,000 at Doncaster, Epsom and a few other venues. However, using Guttmann's criteria, racing did not appear to be modernized at this time. We went on to suggest that Guttmann's model failed to give sufficient attention to the roles of gambling, professionalization and commercialization, all of which might change the view of how modernized racing was before Victoria became monarch.

At times my administrative workload as Pro-Vice-Chancellor at Flinders, Head of School and the International Centre for Sports History and Culture at De Montfort, and Director of Research at Stirling undermined my output as a researcher in that it prevented me from having long stretches of uninterrupted research time. Hopefully I took my research skills into my administrative work when I prepared reports or investigated problems. This lack of sustained research time was one reason for my venturing into encyclopaedia territory. In Australia, I helped to produce the *Oxford Companion to Australian Sport* and back in Britain several volumes for the ABC Clio/Cass/Routledge series of sporting encyclopaedias (Vamplew et al. 1992; Cox, Jarvie, and Vamplew 2000; Cox, Russell, and Vamplew 2002; Collins, Martin, and Vamplew 2005).

My main task at Stirling was to prepare the Department for the forthcoming Research Assessment Exercise, on which depended our government research funding for the foreseeable future. We gained first place in the RAE for Scotland and fifth in the UK by dint of what was described by one of my senior colleagues (tongue in cheek I hope) as a submission that belonged on the fiction shelves of the University library. This was somewhat unfair to the members of staff who had done high quality research work. The success in the RAE contributed to Stirling becoming Scotland's University for Sporting Excellence.

One way in which I helped us gain our accolade was to encourage joint publication of work in order to demonstrate both collaboration (a buzz word in the 2008 RAE) and increased productivity. This was common in sports science but less so in sports social science. However, I had long practised this myself as I believed there was symbiosis and synergy in joint authorship because of the varying approaches taken by the respective researchers. Hence, I published with, amongst others, Joyce Kay, a geographer and economic historian, Jane George with a background in Scottish history, Tony Collins, a cultural historian, museum director Peter Lewis, social historians Daryl Adair, Keith Sandiford and Richard Holt, and with my Ph.D. students, John Tolson and Iris Middleton who had become the experts in their chosen fields.

Nearing the end of my career, I returned to editorial work. An appeal by the NASSH led me to apply for the position as Editor of the *Journal of Sport History*. I wanted to put something back into the profession from which I had gained so much. An interview followed at the NASSH Conference held at Glenwood Springs in Colorado. The hotel boasted the largest outdoor natural hot springs pool in the world – it seemed to be the size of two soccer pitches – and that scenes for *The Omen* had been filmed there! An omen for me was that there was a tiny settlement nearby called Wray. It was a big step for NASSH to appoint their first non-North American editor. Perhaps they were desperate as the journal was more than a year behind in publication. It took time but not only did hard work from the editorial team get us back on schedule, but we also regained our place in the Scopus Database.

My time at Stirling ended unhappily. For several years, the administration had asked the Department for a post-RAE business plan. This had been supplied on a regular basis but clearly had never been read, not even the executive summary (again supporting my view of the unnecessary and unproductive paper chase demanded by those wanting to cover their backs). A key element of the plan was the retention of two major researchers for a couple of years on a part-time basis while the Department was reconfigured to support the University's claim to be the Scottish University for Sporting Excellence. Neither of us was retained; nor was there any discussion about it. Worse still, to my mind, was the brusque letter from the Vice Chancellor wishing me a happy retirement but with no thanks for anything that I had done for the University. I now realize that she too was being forced to retire. The University did grant me emeritus status (not Emirates as one senior administrator mistakenly called it, though free flights would have been nice) and I was allowed to keep my library card and email address. For a while, I retained the use of an office but this was culled when a new Head of School (once again, as appears the case in many institutions, a new CEO restructures what has just been restructured under the previous incumbent and the Department had now become a School) arrived with a mission to de-social science the department and to challenge the big boys in sports science. I note with a degree of schadenfreude that Stirling fell to 19th in the 2014 REF. I had intended to donate my books to the University library but instead they went to the research collection of the National Football Museum which, although it had relocated to Manchester, had retained a research arm in Preston. I had become involved with the Football Museum when I discovered it held a full set of the Football Association Minute Books which made my research into charity and football much easier than trying to gain access via the Football Association itself.

Post-Stirling

I was not ready for full retirement, for intellectual rather than financial reasons, and I circulated my CV to potential employers around Britain. At one stage, it seemed likely that I would be made an offer by Northumbria but this fell through when that university too opted out of sports history. Then, came an approach from John Hughson, many years ago a doctoral candidate, whom I had examined but now a research professor at the University of Central Lancashire. Ironically, the institution that had once suggested I pay my own interview costs now offered me a Visiting Professorship in the International Institute for Football Studies. As the 2014 REF approached, this appointment was manipulated to make my research eligible but at the expense of lessening the length of the contract. As I became older and even grumpier, I elected not to seek a renewal of the contract in July 2014 as I was sick of the incessant form-filling: nonetheless, I had to fill in a form to activate my retirement. To my surprise, I received a redundancy payment when my employment ceased. I remain an Honorary Visiting Professor. I have recently accepted an invitation to become a Visiting Research Fellow at Manchester Metropolitan University assisting Dr Dave Day's research group.

Whilst *in situ* as *JSH* editor, I received an email from Jonathan Manley of Routledge asking for my views on the state of the *International Journal of the History of Sport* and whether I could recommend anyone to become Managing Editor of that publication with the imminent departure of Foundation Academic Editor, Professor Tony Mangan. My choices were Patricia Vertinsky and/or Brian Stoddart, but, unknown to me Jonathan had solicited advice from others and I was offered the position. It was a challenge but one I relished. I inherited a situation in which the refereeing process was opaque, the page budget was not adhered to, authors of many submitted articles had not been informed of acceptance/rejection with some taking a year to be reviewed, commitments to publish were inadequately documented and the backlog of articles was unknown, the editorial structure was over-heavy, convoluted and without job specification, forward planning was insufficiently detailed, old articles and even books, were being republished, and the journal website was out-of-date (over two years in some instances) and contained submission instructions geared to a non-electronic age. My initial job parameters were to re-establish its academic credibility in the light of the previous Executive Academic Editor's use of the journal for self-aggrandizement, develop a system for receiving and peer-reviewing submissions to the journal, streamline the cumbersome editorial and advisory structure, and set up a fully documented forward publishing schedule. Over the following four years, actions were taken to obviate the failings of the previous regime by establishing editorial teams and a new editorial board with job specifications; developing forward planning with detailed publication schedules; adopting guidelines for guest editors; updating the journal website including new instructions to authors; enforcing an electronic-only submissions and refereeing policy; and, after clearing the backlog, focussing only on articles. In June 2014 when I handed over to Rob Hess, the journal was ranked 21st in the History category of Thomson- Reuters Journal Citations Rankings. An alternative measure provided by GoogleScholar listed *IJHS* in the top ten of the most influential journals in history and Scimago placed it in the top quartile for history journals. I also established a relationship with ISHPES and one issue a year is now devoted to papers from their conference. Throughout my tenure was plagued by attempted interference from the previous Managing Editor (though he had given himself a more grandiose title) and eventually the publishers had to formally sever ties with him. That aside I enjoyed the position. I relinquished the job six months early as a new team had taken over responsibility for the journal at the publishers and it seemed sensible for this to correspond with editorial team changes. Although I have no desire to be looking over the shoulder of the new incumbent, I have accepted his proposal to become Special Projects Editor with a role in devising special issues of the journal and am currently planning one on methodology in sports history.

More recently, I have used my editing experience to produce a four-volume collection of readings for Routledge (Vamplew 2014). My working agenda was that each piece selected had to fulfil at least one of the following criteria: show ways of doing sports history; demonstrate the global development of the subject and a geographical spread including some non-western contributions; reflect a big debate in sports history or set the agenda for future research; illustrate an essential theme; or provide information on one country that has relevance for other nations. The selections were not always necessarily the best in the field - that is a subjective judgement - but they were representative of sports history as it has been practised. I am currently involved in producing a similar collection for Sage with Mark Dyreson as co-editor (Vamplew and Dyreson 2016). The project will reflect the major debates that have occurred in the subject, include articles that were original, agenda-setting and have had impact and demonstrate the different approaches to doing sports history.

In my 'retirement', I have been honoured by having a special issue of *Sport in History*, the journal of the BSSH, published in my honour, in 2009; having an article of mine in that journal listed as one of the most significant of the past 30 years; having two articles in the *International Journal of the History of Sport* rated the best in their year; being named 2011 ISHPES Award winner for my contribution to sport history; and being awarded a BSSH Fellowship, in 2011. I am grateful that my peers have acknowledged the value of my work. No academic can ask for more.

Final reflections

Sports history is no longer a marginal academic subject. It has now been recognized that sport is a significant cultural activity that matters to millions of people and ought to be studied by academic researchers, including historians who can seek to explain its development. Correctly practised, sports history is a counter to nostalgia, myth and invented tradition. It can be considered the sports memory of a nation: without sports history there is sporting amnesia. It can set straight the sporting record but also it can explain why some things changed and why continuities also occurred. History's great contribution to sports studies is the time dimension. As Swedish novelist Henning Mankell, creator of Inspector Wallander, has noted, history is not something that is behind us, it follows us into the future. If we want to know where sport is heading, it is useful to know where it has been. It provides the benchmarks for measuring progress and change (or the lack of it). The sporting past has shaped the sporting present as all sports have some inheritance from the past be it rules, governing bodies, styles of play, competitions or equipment. Good sports history looks at more than the ludic: it contextualizes events by placing them in a wider social, political, economic or cultural environment.

I have always argued that a major duty of a sports historian is to set straight the sporting record, and in particular, prevent myths becoming conventional wisdom. Obviously, this has not gone down well with that branch of practitioners who deny the authenticity of historical 'facts' and give equal billing to any, and anyone's, version of history. More constructive a criticism of my views has come from a young North American scholar who suggested that what might be asked is 'why those myths took hold, what political purpose they served, whether those principles have changed over time and how we might reconcile their persistence in the present' (Schultz 2010, 50–51).

I maintain that empiricism is basic to sports history. In the absence of evidence there is no history. Reasoned based on fragmentary evidence, with or without theoretical underpinning, is one thing; assertion solely by the application of theory when there is no evidence is quite another. Nevertheless, I stress that reasoned speculation is not an historical truth; it is a hypothesis awaiting testing by further evidence. This, of course, is the nature of much historical revisionism.

Facts can change. Even basic sportifacts such as scores and results can be amended years past the original occurrence as when Lance Armstrong's Tour de France titles were taken away after he admitted long-term drug use or the reallocation of Olympic medals for similar misdeeds that came to light long after the original presentation ceremony. More common is change due to new information coming to light or new theory being applied to existing information which reveals possible alternative explanations. Three examples will suffice to make this point.

First, sometimes the sports historian can correct sins of omission rather than commission. Until the 1980s, the official list of Olympic gold medallists was one short: the records did not include Donald MacKenzie's victory in pigeon shooting at the Paris Olympic Games of 1900. Diligent research by Howell and Howell (1988) for their study of Australian Olympians, however gave MacKenzie his rightful place in Olympic history. One reason for his win being forgotten was his event. The pigeons he shot were live ones and over time the killing of birds for competitive sport (rather than for sport as hunting) fell into disfavour and, at the Olympics, pigeon shooting disappeared from the programme until revived in the more humane form of clay pigeon shooting in 1952.

A second example of facts being changed comes from classical sport. The idea that the ancient Greeks sought to achieve both intellectual and bodily excellence had become a common belief, often cited with the rubric 'mens sana in corpore sano'. The research of Young (2005), however, has shown that although the phrase did originate in Classical times, it was Roman not Greek and had nothing to do with the Olympics or even athletics. It was in fact a direction by the satirist Juvenal as to what people should pray for: a sound mind in a sound body. It was a call neither to academic nor sporting excellence but to mental and physical health. It only became associated with athletic endeavour in mid Victorian Britain and then only because of a false interpretation of the original statement.

Another, more recent, example relates to new sources of evidence being mined. Several decades of research had produced a conventional narrative of European sports history in which modern sports were seen as a consequence of Britain's industrialization which were then diffused from Britain to the continent. This is now being subjected to serious revision, partly, as a result of greater access to non-English language research findings. Another Young, Christopher this time and Alan Tomlinson (2011) accept that Britain incubated many athletic pursuits, but they maintain that others had no connection with Britain and were a product of the diverse movement cultures extant in Europe. They examined 22 significant sports and suggested that only six or seven can be considered as having uniquely British origins. They went further and identified four clusters of sport development within Europe alone: not just the British but also German, Soviet and Scandinavian versions.

Any regrets? I try not to do 'shoulds' and 'oughts' but I wish I had had the time to take a doctorate in sports history. But I did not prioritize this so I cannot complain. More irritating was that, despite *Play Up and Play the Game*'s many citations, no-one seemed to read my early chapters which outlines the early economic history of Britain and how sport and leisure fitted into this. I put substantial effort into this and I thought at the time that it was an innovative outline of relevance to both economic and sports historians. But you cannot make people appreciate your work. One thing is certain: I am glad I gave up accountancy.

I started my career as a scholar but somewhere along the line transmogrified, not totally reluctantly, into a small businessman. Now I intend to concentrate on academic matters for which my enthusiasm is unabated. For my last research, I have set myself the task of retooling in economic theory and writing a world economic history of sport. This will not be a narrative synthesis of the economic history of sport in different countries, but will focus on a set of economic issues and questions about sports history and whether the solutions have been similar around the globe. I doubt it will find a publisher but I will enjoy researching and writing it.

Disclosure statement

No potential conflict of interest was reported by the author.

Notes

1. For a review symposium with contributions from John Nauright, Tara Magdalinski, Rob Hess and Douglas Booth see *Sporting Traditions* 13. 2 May 1997, 99–115 and for a response by Daryl Adair see *Sporting Traditions* 14. 1 November 1997, 111–134.
2. For memories of this see Cashman (2007) and McKernan (2007).
3. As an award winner it later featured in the Test of Time series of the *Journal of Sport History* in which the impact and influence of the first decade of winners was assessed a couple of decades on. See Hardy (2014).

References

Adair, D., and W. Vamplew. 1997. *Sport in Australian History*. Melbourne: Oxford University Press.

Bailey, S., and W. Vamplew. 1999. *100 Years of Physical Education 1899–1999*. London: PEAUK.

Booth, D. 2005. *The Field: Truth and Fiction in Sport History*. Abingdon: Routledge.

Booth, D. 2010. "Theory." In *Routledge Companion to Sports History*, edited by S. W. Pope and J. Nauright, 12–33. Abingdon: Routledge.

Cashman, R. 2007. "A Most Memorable Conference." *Sporting Traditions* 23 (2): 1–4.

Cashman, R., and W. Vamplew. 1991. *Junior and School Rugby League in N.S.W.* Sydney: New South Wales Rugby League.

Collins, T., J. Martin, and W. Vamplew, eds. 2005. *Encyclopedia of Traditional British Rural Sports*. Abingdon: Routledge.

Cox, R., J. Jarvie, and W. Vamplew, eds. 2000. *Encyclopedia of British Sport*. Oxford: ABC Clio.

Cox, R., D. Russell, and W. Vamplew, eds. 2002. *Encyclopedia of British Football*. London: Cass.

Guttmann, A. 1986. *From Ritual to Record: The Nature of Modern Sports*. New York: Columbia University Press.

Hardy, S. 2014. "Counting the Ways: Wray Vamplew's Pay up and Play the Game and Its Importance to Sport History." *Journal of Sport History* 41 (1): 117–128.

Hobsbawm, E. 1974. "Labor History and Ideology." *Journal of Social History* 7 (4): 371–381.

Holt, R., P. N. Lewis, and W. Vamplew. 2002. *The Professional Golfers' Association 1901–2001*. Worcestershire: Grant.

Howell, R., and M. Howell. 1988. *Aussie Gold*. Albion: Brooks Waterloo.

Kay, J., and W. Vamplew. 2000. "Horse-Racing." In *Sport, Scotland and the Scots*, edited by G. Jarvie and J. Burnett, 159–173. East Linton: Tuckwell.

Korr, C. P. 1986. *West Ham United: The Making of a Football Club*. London: Duckworth.

McKernan, M. 2007. "Making Sporting Traditions." *Sporting Traditions* 23 (2): 5–8.

O'Hara, J., and W. Vamplew. 1990. *Report on On-Course Betting in Rugby League*. Sydney: New South Wales Rugby League.

Schultz, J. 2010. "Leaning into the Turn: Towards a New Cultural Sport History." *Sporting Traditions* 27 (2): 45–59.

Tomlinson, A., and C. Young. 2011. "Towards a New History of European Sport." *European Review* 19 (4): 487–507.

Vamplew, W. 1975. *Salvesen of Leith*. Edinburgh: Scottish Academic Press.

Vamplew, W. 1976. *The Turf: A Social and Economic History of Horse Racing*. London: Allen Lane.

Vamplew, W. 1980. "The Protection of English Cereal Producers: The Corn Laws Reassessed." *The Economic History Review* 33 (3): 382–395.

Vamplew, W. 1986. "South Australians 1836–1986: A Statistical Sketch." In *South Australian Year Book*, edited by G. C. Sims, 1–88. Adelaide: South Australian Government Statistical Office.

Vamplew, W., ed. 1987. *Australians: Historical Statistics*. Sydney: Fairfax, Syme and Weldon.

Vamplew, W. 1988. *Pay up and Play the Game*. Cambridge: Cambridge University Press.

Vamplew, W. 1989. *A Healthy Body: The Australian Sports Medicine Federation 1963–1988*. Canberra: ASMF.

Vamplew, W. 1991. *Violence in Australian Sport: Its Extent and Control*. Canberra: Australian Sports Commission.

Vamplew, W. 1997. *Newcastle United Football Club: An Economic Impact Statement*. Leicester: ICSH&C.

Vamplew, W., ed. 2014. *Sports History: Critical Concepts in Sports Studies*. Abingdon: Routledge.

Vamplew, W., and P. Dimeo. 2004. *Sporting Conduct Initiatives: An International Perspective*. London: UK Sport.

Vamplew, W., and M. Dyreson, eds. 2016. *Sports History: Issues, Debates and Challenges*. New York: Sage.

Vamplew, W., and J. Kay. 2003. "A Modern Sport? 'from Ritual to Record' in British Horseracing." *Ludica* 9: 125–139.

Vamplew, W., and J. Kay. 2005. *Encyclopedia of British Horseracing*. Abingdon: Routledge.

Vamplew, W., K. Moore, J. O'Hara, R. Cashman, and I. F. Jobling, eds. 1992. *The Oxford Companion to Australian Sport*. Melbourne: Oxford University Press.

Young, D. C. 2005. "Mens Sana in Corpore Sano ? Body and Mind in Ancient Greece." *The International Journal of the History of Sport* 22 (1): 22–41.

The power of numbers: a plea for more quantitative sports history

Wray Vamplew

ABSTRACT

By drawing on examples, this article outlines the contribution that a statistical approach can make to sports history. It suggests that this has become neglected as sports historians have become increasingly influenced by the cultural turn. It argues that counting can strengthen arguments by providing a statistical basis for historical assertion; by allowing more effective comparisons to be made; and by enabling the testing of hypotheses. Finally it suggests several major sports history projects that could be undertaken using large-scale quantified research.

'What are you going to count?' Allegedly this was a common remark of mine to research students at De Montfort University (Cronin 2009, 393). It is only partly apocryphal as I certainly emphasized the importance of numbers to, among others, Middleton (2000) who was researching the history of early horseracing in Yorkshire and the late Tolson (2000) who was working on railways and horseracing. Iris's work was a follow up to my argument that racing was Britain's first national sport, albeit one generally practised at the local and regional level. It was also an acceptance of the challenge by Huggins that my 'initial hypotheses' and 'generalisations' needed to be tested at the local level, away from the major meetings which, by virtue of their dominance, could present a different, even distorted, picture (Huggins 1987, 89). Iris and I then published a piece in *Northern History* which set the pattern of Yorkshire horseracing into the work/leisure calendar of an agricultural society (Middleton and Vamplew 2003). Using documented evidence from newspapers, early versions of racing calendars, and diaries and correspondence of persons involved in racing, we showed in quantified detail that the timing of race meetings within the year was influenced by holidays and fairs, the seasonal work patterns of a largely agrarian community, and the dates of the Assizes. John opted to challenge my view that 'it is no exaggeration to say that the railways revolutionised horseracing' (Vamplew 1976, 33). John and I published an early paper on the topic in 1998 and then a later one revisiting the subject after his thesis was completed (Tolson and Vamplew 1998, 2003). What we demonstrated, with quantitative evidence, was that the railways had an important role in the transformation of British racing but they were not the driving force. Although the speed and convenience of the railways eased travel for the distant spectator, thousands of whom took advantage of the racing specials, racing was a significant spectator sport before the railway network emerged. Indeed, it was not until 1930s that the railways carried as many passengers to the Derby as had attended a century before without the aid of the locomotive. In order to follow their occupation, jockeys too had to travel but the increase in the miles they travelled over time owed more to the expansion of fixtures than to the railway. Using trains meant that horses could travel in a matter of hours what had previously taken them days or even weeks to walk and by the end of the nineteenth century, the railway was the standard method of getting racehorses any distance. Yet there is no evidence that this led to horses racing more often or travelling greater distances to compete. As for railway company sponsorship of race meetings, even at its height it totalled less than 5% of all sponsorship. Jockey Club regulations on prize money and its restrictions on the opening of new courses were far more important in shaping the structure of the racing industry than anything to do with the railways.

Numbers are important. To my mind, the most useful history is that which enables generalization. This is why I do not fully appreciate qualitative history. At best such history supplies examples with which to illustrate an argument; at worst it provides the personal experience of one person without noting its typicality. The great contribution of quantifiers is to help determine what is typical. When the first game of golf was played in Scotland is not that important; much more significant is know when the game became a common recreational activity. Staying with golf, a biography of Harry Vardon, the Tiger Woods of his day, contributes to the understanding of a champion golfer troubled by tuberculosis and marital difficulties (Howell 1991). This is interesting but more useful as sports history if it is contextualized into asking if tuberculosis was an industrial disease of professional golfers and whether the marriage problems emanated from the time away from home making a living as an elite professional designing courses and playing in championships.

Why else do I advocate the use of counting in sports history: indeed in any history? Numbers are important for several academic reasons. First, they can add strength to an argument by providing a statistical basis for historical assertions. Measurement can allow historians to be more precise in their answers. Sport is full of statistics but to batting averages and record times should be added such things as the proportion of players from a particular ethic background or the gender balance of sports club membership. Two examples can illustrate this point. By creating a database of 4794 jockeys, Barbezat and Hughes (2014) were able to show that in 1880 African-American riders were over-represented in the jockey profession (22%) relative to the proportion they occupied in the general population (13%) and that the decline in African-American jockeys over time was less precipitous than has been conventionally assumed. It was also meticulous counting by Hunt (2009) of the occupations of 500 players from the first two decades of the Gaelic Athletic Association using census returns, land valuations, trade directories and other sources that destroyed the foundation myth that it comprised mainly landless labourers.

Second, counting allows more effective comparisons to be made. Without Dixon, Garnham, and Jackson's (2004) quantitative analysis of the shareholders' registers combined with an identification trawl through the 1901 Census, not only could no generalizations be made about the nature of shareholding and especially shareholders in North-East football clubs, comparisons could not be made with other clubs, sporting or otherwise. In my own work, counting enabled the charity donations of football clubs to be put in perspective against the other sources of income of the charitable institutions and the relative dangers of flat and jump racing to be compared via rates of injury (Kay and Vamplew 2010; Vamplew 2000).

Third, the collection of statistical data enables hypotheses to be tested. In a recent issue of *Sporting Traditions,* the conventional wisdom in Australian sport that there was a cultural divide reflected by a preference between Australian Rules and Rugby football which corresponded geographically with South-Western and North-Eastern Australia was tested statistically. By examining television ratings for 2297 fixtures, Fujak and Frawley (2013) were able to confirm this and show that the Australian Football League had failed in its efforts to make its sport the 'national' game. In my own studies, a statistical approach allowed me to test my hypothesis that golfers were in a better economic position than their fellow professionals in football, cricket and horseracing, a view that otherwise could only be speculated upon. If you study 3000 professional golfers, you are able to say something about the average and age at appointment and retirement, the length of career, the degree of mobility between clubs and the modal level of earnings (Vamplew 2008).

Finally, Steve Hardy argues that numbers, even simple ones, have an undue influence of public policy. In this sense, quantitative work can be seen as leading to applied sports history, though this does suggest the existence of policy-makers who respect evidence.

Nevertheless, the *Routledge Companion to Sports History* includes but a single reference to quantification in its index (Pope and Nauright 2010). If quantification is so useful why has it been so neglected by sports historians? One reason of course is that some topics are not suited or relevant to a statistical approach. Numbers are the essence of that history which looks at collective experiences such as sports crowds or groups of professional players, but this quantification might be seen as less necessary by those researchers more concerned with the experience of the individual. In seeking to generalize, aggregation can marginalize those who do not fit the standard pattern, those who are in effect statistical outliers. Even in my own work, one of my most cited articles is a piece on sports museums which has become a standard reference in the field without a statistic in sight! Similarly, my article on the development of rules in sport has no reliance on figures (Vamplew 1998, Vamplew 2007).

Another reason for rejecting a quantitative approach is that intellectual climate change has affected academic research. There has been a turn away from quantification to the qualitative in both epistemology and methods in a host of academic fields. As Cronin (2009, 393) notes by the mid-1990s, the history profession – and some sports historians – had participated in the 'cultural turn' where they looked not to 'hard facts but for "texts" that could be "read". There was no truth, only a variety of discourses, power dynamics and a welter of culture that had to be decoded'. Put more simply by Hardy (2014, 121): 'numbers had lost their lustre as icons of knowledge'.

Yet another reason perhaps is that quantitative work is not seen as exciting. I remember my postgraduate history tutor at the University of Edinburgh arguing that not even Lord Macaulay, doyen of Victorian historians, could make statistics interesting. Yet, to the numerate, the revealing of information as the figures emerge is comparable to the excitement of the phrenologists as election results are declared. I still recall the mounting anticipation as, club by club, my analysis of Scottish football clubs revealed an unusually high percentage of working-class shareholders. Or the joy when an old book in the library of the Royal & Ancient Golf Club listed the members of Hawick complete with their occupations. Each to their own I suppose!

It may also be a lack of confidence in their ability to manipulate numbers in a meaningful way that deters some sports historians from venturing into the quantitative jungle. At one end of the statistical spectrum, there are simple tables which bring together aggregates totalled from individual figures. At the other are more complicated measures such as the dynamic and static measures of equality that I produced for my article on Scottish football reproduced in this volume and later for several sports in *Pay Up and Play the Game* (Vamplew 1982, 2004). As one whose spatial dysfunctionalism inhibits him from moving furniture through a door, I can accept that some sports historians will have difficulty in coping with higher order statistical operations. Nevertheless, knowing whether the mean, mode or median is the most appropriate calculation to make should not be beyond most of us.

Another answer to why quantification does not figure high in the sports historian's repertoire is that too many sports historians have preferred the easier (which is not the same as saying 'easy') qualitative methodologies. Qualitative sports historians are not intellectually lazy – their works can buzz with ideas – but perhaps not many of them are prepared to undertake what Cronin (2009, 395) has acknowledged as the 'hard work' associated with empirical, statistical methodology. Quantification has a high research time/word output ratio: counting can be a laborious, time-consuming, often 'tedious' process with hours of work resulting in just one table or even a mere sentence (Hardy 2014, 121). The previously mentioned database of American jockeys created by Barbezat and Hughes (2014, 19–20) involved, firstly, working through the 1880 US population census, as digitized by the North Atlantic Population Project, using the coding for 'athlete', then following up the entry at the transcription level for each of the 2589 individuals identified and reducing the figure to the 558 men listed as a jockey or something similar. This could not be done for subsequent censuses as they did not allow for occupations to be searched for electronically, so the rest of the database was constructed by listing all known jockeys riding at any time between 1885 and 1930, using information gleaned from jockey license listings, turf publications, national and local newspapers, census enumeration sheets, passport applications and First World War draft registration cards. Elaboration on how this was done can be found in the article. How much easier would it have been simply to rely on impressionistic sources and hypotheses of racialism and the rise of Jim Crow laws, migration away from the south and increased legal impediments to racing to explain the decline in African-American jockeys. In a similar way that academe tends to distinguish between the hard sciences (STEM) and the soft ones (social sciences), perhaps it is time to distinguish between the hard (quantitative) and soft (qualitative) sports history.

All that said, it should be noted that even non-quantifying sports historians sometimes implicitly use statistics, often in a cavalier manner. In his work on poetry, public schools and militarism, renowned educational historian Mangan (1996a, 150) rightly accepts, 'it is impossible to assess with certainty the influence of the rhetoric' though, against all statistical reasoning, he then maintains 'it may have been, and probably was, deeply influential'. Elsewhere, despite noting that the impact of the poets 'cannot be measured with any precision', he claims their influence was 'extraordinary and extensive' (Mangan 1996b, 165). More generally, every time historians make a claim of 'many' or 'most' they are implying (usually erroneously) that they have done some counting. Too often a few examples have shown something and it is seized on as being typical without the additional spadework necessary to justify the statement. As elsewhere in the social sciences, argument by example is no substitute for the use of hard, quantified data. Isolated examples can offer support but no reputable scientist or social scientist would accept results based on one or two tests so similarly sports historians should not use a handful of examples make sweeping claims. Ultimately, the calculations may back up the initial idea … but they may not. Numbers enable us to get beyond impressions.

Associated with this dubious use of implicit statistics is the use of correlations without numerical backup. It has become conventional wisdom is that Britain's educational institutions for the upper and middle classes used sport in a way that its practitioners could easily and effectively adopt for military purposes. The logical chain runs as follows: public schools played sport in a particular way; this way of playing encouraged certain characteristics that could be transferable into warfare; many military officers attended public school; ergo public school sport was helpful to the war effort. Yet, statistically we do not know what proportion of public schools adopted an educational policy that formally encouraged the development of athleticism with its compulsory games and associated character building or what proportion of military officers were educated at public school. The answers may be 'the vast majority' but this needs to be shown not assumed. The view has become accepted without being appropriately tested. It has been recycled not researched. Where is the real evidence that this occurred? That many army officers attended public school and that games were played at those schools is a possible correlation but not a proof.

There are sports historians who would reject all statistical evidence as being manufactured and untrustworthy. Such historians are allied with those post modernists who accept virtually no evidence as being accurate. There is a school of post-modernist thought that would reject almost any evidence, particularly, one suspects, that involving numbers. There is a danger here of putting the sports history discipline on to an inclined plane to academic oblivion. The closer you move to nihilism, the nearer you get to the abandonment of any meaningful social science. To argue that everyone is so different from anyone else that mass behaviour cannot be predicted is to undermine the basic premise of economics, social psychology, political science or even social, economic and sports history.

Booth (2005, 19), an acknowledged expert on historical method, dismisses quantitative history noting that 'while quantitative research appears in economic, political and social history, in sports history quantitative expositions usually fall into the realm of "elementary descriptive statistics" that "identify the most important features of the data through rearrangement and presentation"' (Hudson 2000, 53) and was 'not convinced that a quantitative paradigm warrants greater attention than traditional narrative'. Had he himself ventured into quantitative history his subjectivity-high *One Eyed* would have been more soundly based on evidence than on value-laden emotion, though that may be the type of history that he prefers (Booth and Tatz 2000). Without quantification, the degree of discrimination in sport cannot be ascertained only asserted. In maligning counting, Booth may have been looking at poor examples of quantification. Maybe he has experienced sports history where statistics have been abused and misused; or maybe Booth never looked at all as he failed to cite any pieces.

Often even when some sports historians do count they do not tell us what proportion of the total cases examined the examples represented, what proportion of possible cases were examined at all, and whether the sample was random, stratified or just what was available. Although, I have respect for much of his work, I felt Malcolm (2002) came to grief in his efforts to show that cricket used to be a violent and dangerous sport. Comparative levels of violence in pre-modern and modern cricket can only be effectively ascertained by statistical means. Malcolm makes no real attempt to do this, though he does provide some quantified material in his list of 29 cricket-associated fatalities 'from the earliest records' to 1897 which he argues show 'the relative acceptability of such accidents'. These all come from the same source, a collection of *Curiosities of Cricket* by an 'Old Cricketer' and no attempt is made to check their validity or veracity, admittedly not an easy task when no specific dates are attached to the material. Here, Malcolm's interpretation of evidence can be questioned. Assuming that his data cover a century and a half, it is not a high death rate, particularly when those fatalities not directly due to the nature of the game are removed from the total. Two deaths from heart disease, two from over exertion, one from snake bite, another by being crushed between railway trucks while recovering the ball and one from falling over a cliff whilst following the ball are not in the same category as those from being hit by the ball, collisions with other players or falling on a stump. Moreover, no attempt is made to calculate deaths in more modern cricket.

Sometimes too much is claimed from the statistics presented. Harvey's (2004, 175) argument for widespread mass spectator sport by the 1840s is undermined by an inability to present any systematic figures for sports crowd attendance. He does produce a table representing attendances of over 1000 on an annual basis for the 1840s, but as this averaged less than 45 such crowds a year, less than one a week, it is scarcely evidence of sufficient effective demand for these to be more than sporadic occurrences.

Quantified evidence is no different from any other form of historical data in that it has to be evaluated for rigour and validity. As with good qualitative sports history, the quantitative practitioners must also critique their potential source material in order to decide whether its use is warranted. It is poor academic practice to simply use any statistical information without assessing its veracity and what its employment could bring to any argument. For some years, historians accepted an 1882 newspaper estimate of the total number of New Zealand rugby players as being 50,000, a number that gave substantial clout to the claim that the game was the country's national sport at that time. At least among sports historians that should have raised queries. As Ryan pointed out, there were only 300 known teams at the time so the figure must have been erroneous. It was the typist who prepared the honours thesis which first cited the newspaper estimate who had hit one key too many thus multiplying the original 5000 players 10-fold! (Daley 2010, 21–22).

Historians should always ask three major questions of any primary source material. When was it produced? What was the authority of the person producing it? Why was it produced? An excellent example of how to do this is Kay's (2009) review of the *Racing Calendar* in which she dissects the pros and cons of utilizing the data presented in what is the longest unbroken run of any sporting periodical. She concludes that

> there is no reason to suppose that its official lists ... or its record of 'approved' race meetings are in any way flawed. It may have increasingly spread the gospel according to the Jockey Club from the middle of the nineteenth century and its omissions may present a rather distorted picture of racing for the ordinary punter but its statistical evidence probably offers the most comprehensive view of British horseracing over a period of 200 years. (Kay 2009, 359)

She goes on to use the data to look at female participation in horseracing and present an overview of international aspects of the sport. The point to emphasize is that potential problems with the data are discussed overtly – an open sandwich in contrast to the often unfathomable contents of a sausage – so that others can also make a judgement.

There are major gaps in our sports history knowledge which large-scale quantified research could close. Allied to his interest in the sports industry, Hardy (2014, 120) has suggested 'we might benefit from a quantitative-comparative analysis that aggregates data on the variety of people who worked in the sport industry as it developed in the last two hundred years'. Another suggestion is for a comparison of 'women's experiences across time, place, class and race' (Hardy 2014, 124).

Cronin (2009, 394) adds the middle class to the research agenda:

> time has to be spent so that we know who these middle classes were in terms of their occupations, their property status, social and associational lives, their habits and customs, religious affiliation, political affiliation and level of education. What do we mean by the term, who was included and excluded, how did people move in and out of the middle classes and how did that group come to connect with sport. Put simply: we have to count.

My suggestion is a quantitative study of British sports clubs in an attempt, first to assess the extent and expansion over time of the basic unit of sports organization in Britain, and, second, membership levels to aid in estimates of sports participation at the associational level by sport, location and, possibly class.

Hardy (2014, 125) concludes his assessment of the influence of *Pay Up and Play the Game* and my 'insistence on the power of numbers' by emphasizing that 'numerical data do not provide any readier access to "truth" than paintings or photographs or old interviews or any other kind of credible evidence. But they do seem to have a compelling power. Wray Vamplew's *Pay Up and Play the Game* reminds us that a quantitative and comparative approach forces us to pursue different source material and think in different ways. Not better ways but different way'. But I would add, as a confirmed hacker on the golf course, I believe that, as in golf itself, it is the number that matter. It is not important how elegant the swing is (qualitative and subjective); it is the score at the end of the round that counts (quantitative and objective).

Disclosure statement
No potential conflict of interest was reported by the author.

References
Barbezat, D., and J. Hughes. 2014. "Finding the Lost Jockeys." *Historical Methods: A Journal of Quantitative and Interdisciplinary History* 47 (1): 19–30.
Booth, D. 2005. *The Field: Truth and Fiction in Sport History*. Abingdon: Routledge.
Booth, D., and C. Tatz. 2000. *One-eyed: A View of Australian Sport*. Sydney: Allen & Unwin.
Cronin, M. 2009. "What Went Wrong with Counting? Thinking about Sport and Class in Britain and Ireland." *Sport in History* 29 (3): 392–404.
Daley, C. 2010. "The Refs Turned a Blind Ear": The Cultural Paradigm and New Zealand's Sport History. *Sporting Traditions* 27 (2): 15–27.
Dixon, P., N. Garnham, and A. Jackson. 2004. "Shareholders and Shareholding: The Case of the Football Company in Late Victorian England." *Business History* 46 (4): 503–524.
Fujak, H., and S. Frawley. 2013. "The Barassi Line: Quantifying Australia's Great Sporting Divide." *Sporting Traditions* 30 (2): 93–109.
Hardy, S. 2014. "Counting the Ways: Wray Vamplew's *Pay Up and Play the Game* and Its Importance to Sport History." *Journal of Sport History* 41 (1): 117–128.
Harvey, A. 2004. *The Beginnings of a Commercial Sporting Culture in Britain, 1793–1850*. Aldershot: Ashgate.
Howell, A. 1991. *Harry Vardon*. London: Stanley Paul.
Hudson, P. 2000. *History by Numbers*. London: Bloomsbury.

Huggins, M. 1987. "Horse-racing on Teesside in the Nineteenth Century: Change and Continuity." *Northern History* 23: 98–118.

Hunt, T. 2009. "The GAA: Social Structure and Associated Clubs." In *The Gaelic Athletic Association, 1884–2009*, edited by M. Cronin, W. Murphy and P. Rouse, 183–202. Cork: Irish Academic Press.

Kay, J. 2009. "Still Going After All These Years: Text, Truth and the Racing Calendar." *Sport in History* 29 (3): 353–366.

Kay, J., and W. Vamplew. 2010. "Beyond Altruism: British Football and Charity, 1877–1914." *Soccer and Society* 11 (3): 181–197.

Malcolm, D. 2002."Cricket and Civilizing Processes: A Response to Stokvis." *International Review for the Sociology of Sport* 37: 37–57.

Mangan, J. A. 1996a. "Games Field and Battlefield: A Romantic Alliance in Verse and the Creation of Militaristic Masculinity." In *Making Men: Rugby and Masculine Identity*, edited by J. Nauright and T. Chandler, 140–157. London: Cass.

Mangan, J. A. 1996b. "'Muscular, Militaristic and Manly': The British Middle-class Hero as Moral Messenger." *The International Journal of the History of Sport* 13 (1): 28–47.

Middleton, I. M. 2000. "The Developing Pattern of Horse-racing in Yorkshire 1700–1749: An Analysis of the People and the Places." PhD thesis, De Montfort University.

Middleton, I. M., and W. Vamplew. 2003. "Horse-racing and the Yorkshire Leisure Calendar in the Early Eighteenth Century." *Northern History* 40: 259–276.

Pope, S. W., and J. Nauright, eds. 2010. *Routledge Companion to Sports History*. Abingdon: Routledge.

Tolson, J. 2000. "The Railway Myth: Flat Racing in Mainland Britain 1830–1914." PhD thesis, De Montfort University.

Tolson, J., and W. Vamplew. 1998. "Derailed: Railways and Horse-racing Revisited." *Sports Historian* 18 (2): 39–49.

Tolson, J., and W. Vamplew. 2003. "Facilitation not Revolution: Railways and British Flat Racing 1830–1914." *Sport in History* 23: 89–106.

Vamplew, W. 1976. *The Turf*. London: Allen Lane.

Vamplew, W. 1982. "The Economics of a Sports Industry: Scottish Gate-money Football, 1890–1914." *Economic History Review* XXXV.4: 549–567.

Vamplew, W. 1998. "Facts and Artefacts: Sports Historians and Sports Museums." *Journal of Sport History* 25: 268–292.

Vamplew, W. 2000. "Still Crazy After all Those Years: Continuity in a Changing Labour Market for Professional Jockeys." *Contemporary British History* 14 (2): 115–145.

Vamplew, W. 2004. *Pay Up and Play the Game*. Cambridge: Cambridge University Press.

Vamplew, W. 2007. "Playing With the Rules: Influences on the Development of Regulation in Sport." *The International Journal of the History of Sport* 24: 843–871.

Vamplew, W. 2008. "Successful Workers or Exploited Labour? Golf Professionals and Professional Golfers in Britain 1888–1914." *The Economic History Review* 61: 54–79.

Scottish football before 1914: an economic analysis of a gate-money sport

Wray Vamplew

ABSTRACT
On the basis of data collected at club level, it can be suggested that most Scottish elite football teams were not profit-maximizers. The lack of price competition, the existence of free entry for some spectators, the playing of uneconomic friendly and minor cup fixtures, the relative under-utilization of ground facilities, and the employment policies and wage structures of clubs point to utility taking precedence over profits. Even if the clubs had been profit-maximizers, this would have required collusion at the Scottish Football League (SFL) level in order to produce uncertainty of results at both match and championship level, but the members of the SFL seem to have been willing to tolerate a high degree of inequality in playing success.

Comment

This article first appeared in the *Economic History Review*, second series, vol. XXXV No. 4, November 1982, pp. 549–567. It was that journal's first article on sport and a pioneering attempt by myself to apply quantitative methods and economic theory historically to a sector of the sports industry, in this instance Scottish gate-money football. It brought the concepts of peculiar economics, static and dynamic equality of competition, economic rent, and profit- and utility-maximization into the world of sports history.

Whereas competing firms in the normal economy do not need to collaborate to make a product, this is not true of football teams who need a rival to play for any output to occur. Moreover, the ultimate aim of those running the football firms may be to maximize utility (the winning of matches and trophies) rather than profit; so, whereas a conventional business would be concerned with controlling the margin between outlay and revenue, the utility seeker could be willing to spend on players – sometimes at the risk of insolvency – to try and produce a winning team.[1]

At the time of writing, work on Scottish football was limited but since then a multitude of works, many of them focussing on the sectarian rivalry between Rangers and Celtic, the Glasgow duo often referred to as 'the old firm' because of the economic significance of their sporting, religious and tribal antagonism.[2] The increased productivity has been helped by the establishment of the Scottish Football Museum at Hampden Park in 1994 which has enabled a significant archive of research material to develop including runs of nine-teenth-century sports journals and the minute books of the Scottish Football Association (SFA) and the Glasgow Charity Cup Committee. None of the new work has weakened the argument advanced in the original article. However, what can be emphasized now is the key role that Scotland played in the development of gate-money and professional football. Soccer, the world's most popular sport, began in Britain but its history there has been dom-inated by English perspectives partly because of inadequate historical research on football in Scotland. The SFA has never had its story told; the Scottish Football League (SFL) has, but in an unreferenced work (Crampsey 1990). There are many club histories, generally hagiographical, but none in detail of the pioneers who formed the SFA except for Queen's Park. Academic work has tended to focus on sectarianism or aspects of national identity. Few have written academically for Scotland as they have in England on the diffusion of the game into different areas, the emergence of professionalism, the role of the public schools and certainly no overall view. Yet Scotland was in some respects at the centre of the game before 1914. The SFA, founded in 1873, was the second oldest national football administra-tive body in the world, developed its own rules for the game, and was an influential member of the panel that determined the international playing rules. Scotland pioneered charity football matches and the Glasgow Charity Cup, the largest such competition in the world, was adopted as a model by Sheffield, Birmingham and London, the three largest regional associations in England (Kay and Vamplew 2010). Scotland was a major supplier of talent to the English game; indeed, it was the flow of Scottish 'professors' to Lancashire teams that highlighted the development of illegal professionalism in England. Moreover in the Edwardian era, Scotland had the three largest football stadia in the world with consequent record crowds (Goldblatt 2006).

Some of the economics references are out of date now, but they were pioneering at the time. The ensuing three decades have seen significant developments on the economic theory of sport; particularly recommended is the work of Szymanski, an economist with a sense of history (Szymanski 2003a, 2003b, 2004; Szymanski and Késenne 2004). Useful synopses of the current lines of thinking can be found in edited books by Késenne (2014) and Andreff and Szymanksi (2006), as well as the textbook by Downward, Dawson and Dejonghe (2009).

I am grateful to Flinders University and the Australian Research Grants Committee for financial assistance, to the SFA for access to their records and to John Hutchinson for permission to use material from his unpublished work on the Heart of Midlothian F.C. I am especially grateful to the late Peter Bilsborough for the unselfish provision of data from his graduate research. Useful comments came from Owen Covick, Chuck Korr, and the discussants at the 1980 Conference of the Australian and New Zealand Economic History Association, Canberra. All references to club prospectuses, financial statements and shareholders are based on information filed at the Companies Registry, Edinburgh for live companies and the Scottish Record Office, Edinburgh for defunct enterprises.

Introduction

In 1708 the 'common people of Scotland' were described as being 'addicted' to the game of football (J. Chamberlayne, *Magnae Britanniae Notitia: or the Present State of Great Britain* (1708), 524, cited in Magoun (1931), 8). Two centuries did little to change their attitude, and a knowledgeable commentator, writing in 1906, maintained that 'the enthusiasm of the Scot for the Association game is without parallel in any race for any particular sport or pastime' (Connell 1906a, 45). Football itself, however, had changed. The earlier game had been unorganized, violent, wide-ranging in time and space, and held irregularly. By the late nineteenth century, two authorities, the SFA and the SFL, were organizing the game and setting rules as to its conduct, and matches were being played regularly on defined pitches with a prescribed time limit. The main difference, though, was that the earlier folk football had been essentially for the participants whereas the new football was, at its highest level, geared towards the paying spectator: Only twenty-two were allowed to play, but there could be thousands watching them. Football had become part of the mass-entertainment industry. As one sports journal put it: 'Scottish football cannot be described as anything else than a big business' (*Scottish Sport*, May 14, 1894).

A study of Scottish football in this later period can contribute to two major debates. One is the controversy over the standard of entrepreneurship in the late nineteenth-century Britain. Although British entrepreneurs have been criticized for failing to develop new industries sufficiently, the critical literature rarely mentions the emergence of the leisure industries.[3] Yet, the post-1870 years witnessed a significant increase in sports spectatorship. A substantial rise in working-class spending power, growing urbanization and a concentration of free time into Saturday afternoons all encouraged the marketing of gate-money sport. Indeed, commercialized sport for the masses was one of the economic success stories of late Victorian Britain throughout the nation, in cycling, rugby, cricket, soccer, horse-racing, athletics, boxing and other sports, grounds were enclosed, stadiums built, and gate-money charged.[4]

One possible reason for the neglect of the sports industries in the entrepreneurship debate lies with the major issue to be discussed in this article, the question of whether profits were the ultimate objective of gate-money sports clubs: if they were not overtly profit-maximizers, then their development may not be a true test of entrepreneurship. Most studies of modern North-American sports clubs have accepted that they were profit-maximizers,[5] but in Britain many clubs, particularly those in football, have exhibited long-term operating losses (Wiseman 1977, 30), which suggests that some other goal had priority over profits. It has been argued that utility-maximization was such a target in that, subject to financial viability or a minimum security constraint, clubs sought to win as many matches and championships as they could (Sloane 1970). Although winning may produce profits, it is commonly accepted by sports economists that consistent winning does not maximize them. Profit-maximization, with given costs, requires the maximization of entertainment value so as to attract as many spectators as possible, and it is generally argued that attendances will be higher where the outcome of an event is uncertain than where the result is predictable (Dabschek 1975, 53; Davenport 1969, 7; Jones 1969, 3; Neale 1964, 2; Noll 1974, 156; Rottenberg 1956, 51; Sloane 1980, 25; Wiseman 1977, 36). This is true both in the short-term at match level and in the long-run at championship level. Sustained success may keep open the prospect of victory for a club in a prolonged competition, but simultaneously, it reduces such prospects for other teams and may dissuade their fans from attending, thus reducing not only aggregate league attendances but also those at matches involving the runaway champions.[6] Consistent winning, i.e. successful utility-maximization, is therefore a second-best profit policy. This article adds a historical dimension to the debate by assessing whether Scottish gate-money soccer clubs before 1914 were profit- or utility-maximizers. The issue is examined first by studying individual club data and then by looking at the economic system within which the clubs operated.

Evidence from the clubs

Clearly clubs played to win: the football authorities would not tolerate any other action. However, winning could also be a way to make money. A good run in the Scottish Cup could be very rewarding financially: so much so that the SFA was led to comment on 'the number of clubs who have been lifted from poverty to affluence during the past few years through the agency of the Scottish ties' (SFA Annual Report 1903/04). It is probable that winning league matches could also be lucrative. Unfortunately, few of the available accounts separate league from cup revenues and only one covers years with sufficient change in a club's league position for a comparison to be made: in the three seasons beginning 1906/7 Hearts finished 9th, 11th and 12th and the club's share of gate receipts averaged £127 per game, whereas in 1912/13 and 1913/14, when third place was obtained, the average was £210.

Nevertheless, as winning did not necessarily maximize profits, which had priority, cups and championships or money? Apart from Celtic, who were established in 1888 specifically to raise money for a Glasgow Catholic charity, it is doubtful whether initially many clubs were primarily interested in attracting spectators (Handley 1960, 13–15). Certainly club advertisements in the *Scottish Football Annual* were concerned with recruiting playing members. However, such advertising had ceased by 1885 and possibly around that time gatemoney took on greater significance.

It was hoped that clues to the clubs' attitudes could have been obtained from the prospectuses issued when they adopted company status, a movement begun by Celtic in 1897 and followed by over twenty major clubs before 1914. Unfortunately, only twelve prospectuses survive at the Company Registry and this limited sample gave ambivalent results. Four clubs specifically mentioned possible future financial achievements and two concentrated upon the football triumphs which were to come. Apart from one, which went limited to purchase a ground of its own, it is not clear why the remainder became companies. A similar ambivalence is found in the very few surviving company annual reports. They usually emphasized the playing record of the club, but profits and losses were also commented upon, particularly losses, with explanations advanced for the financial performance.

Possibly, the actual commercial practice of the clubs can throw light on the situation. Admittedly, results do not always conform to intentions, but over two and a half decades some coincidence could be expected. A starting point here is that, for any given home match, most costs can be regarded as fixed. All capital expenditure has already been incurred; players' wages have been decided beforehand, often at the start of the season; and ground-staff, administrators and clerks have to be employed anyway. Possibly, the only short-run variable cost would be stewards and police, and frequently, the former would be volunteers. In such circumstances, revenue-maximization could be equated with profit-maximization, and possibly both with spectator-maximization.

What, then, could clubs do to maximize attendances? Although it might seem that the development of a winning team would be a useful policy, as such sides generally attract larger crowds than losing ones (Noll 1974, 155; Sloane 1980, 29), as stated above there is general agreement among sports economists that, for a given quality of game, the spectator demand will be higher the more equally balanced are the competing sides. The creation of such uncertainty, however, is not within the ambit of a single club: as discussed later, such a development requires collusion between clubs.

Clubs tried to attract spectators by making access easy and by providing stands to combat the weather and to make viewing more pleasant. Every prospectus stressed the tram and railway facilities which were available and the special arrangements which had been negotiated with the transport companies. Moreover, there was substantial investment in building stands. Table 1 shows that around 10% of a club's income could stem from stand receipts and those clubs which failed to erect them viewed their absence as detrimental to revenue (Annual Report of East Stirlingshire 1911/12).

There was no attempt to compete for spectators by price. Certainly from the early 1890s, all advertisements and references, apart from an occasional cup tie, are to a basic ground-charge of six pence with a similar common policy of reduced rates for children and free admission both to women and to uniformed servicemen.[7] Whether this price maintenance was a cartel arrangement is not clear: nothing has been found in the SFA records, but the SFL may have set minimum charges.[8] If so, then possibly this was designed to prevent clubs competing with each other for spectators. The scheduling of games could serve this purpose to some extent, though, with five teams in Glasgow, this had its limitations. A second possibility is that, if price competition was excluded, then clubs would have to compete in the product market and this might serve to raise the general standard of play. Finally, there could be equity reasons for the policy: if a home team gambled incorrectly on the price elasticity of demand it would be unfair to the visiting side, who would obtain less revenue than they had anticipated. Prices were raised above the minimum for stands

Table 1. Sources of income of Scottish football clubs.

		Gate		Stands		Season tickets		Transfers		Other		Total
		£	%	£	%	£	%	£	%	£	%	£
Celtic	1892/93	2687	66.2	414	10.2	158	3.9	–	–	802	19.7	4061
	1895/96			[5390	76.0]	187	2.6	40	0.6	1474	20.8	7091
	1896/97			[4530	73.1]	313	5.1	145	2.3	1209	19.5	6197
Clyde	1896/97			[1016	86.8]	95	8.1	60	5.1	–	–	1171
East Stirling	1913/14			[646	71.9]	34	3.8	195	21.7	24	2.7	899
Hamilton	1907/08			[1829	93.4]	112	5.7	–	–	18	0.9	1959
Hearts	1906/07	5807	80.9	816	11.4	299	4.2	1	–	267	3.7	7180
	1907/08			[4940		96.1]		1	–	201	3.9	5142
	1908/09			[4145		78.5]		1056	20.0	79	1.5	5280
	1912/13			[8180		89.6]		866	9.5	85	0.9	9131
	1913/14			[7726		76.8]		2215	22.0	120	1.2	10061
Hibs	1910/11			[2932	80.1]	105	2.9	617	16.8	8	0.2	3662
	1912/13			[4446	94.5]	118	2.5	40	0.8	101	2.1	4705
Rangers	1895/96			[3580	83.2]	306	7.1	–	–	415	9.6	4301
	1896/97			[7090	86.1]	353	4.3	–	–	795	9.7	8238
	1897/98			[7136	88.4]	310	3.8	–	–	623	7.7	8069
	1912/13			[13024		92.0]		34	0.2	1106	7.8	14164
St J'stone	1910/11	437	66.6	72	11.0	75	11.4	55	8.4	17	2.6	656
	1911/12	701	71.8	88	9.0	144	14.7	–	–	44	4.5	977
St Mirren	1913/14			[4357	84.3]	400	7.1	400	7.1	88	1.5	5644
3rd Lan'k	1891/92			[1078	88.6]	139	11.4	–	–	–	–	1217
	1892/93			[1412	90.8]	143	9.2	–	–	–	–	1555
	1895/96	2172	85.3	75	2.9	141	5.5	–	–	158	6.2	2546
	1896/97	2037	74.7	356	13.1	163	6.0	–	–	171	6.3	2727
	1897/98			[3314	86.6]	170	4.4	135	3.5	207	5.4	3826

Source: Pre-1900: *Scottish Sport*; post-1900: annual financial statements.

and other semi-exclusive areas. The reason for this was that ground entry fees were shared with the opposition, but additional charges for the stands were retained by the home club.

At the match level, the lack of price competition and the availability of free entry weaken the argument for profit-maximization. The case is further undermined if the season as a whole is considered. Although the SFA imposed a close season in the interests of both the players and summer sports, within the open period teams appear to have played as many games as they could, even arranging friendlies when they had no cup or league fixture (SFA Annual Report 1893/94). Moreover, they seem to have entered a number of competitions in addition to the Scottish Cup and League. This could be interpreted as profit-maximizing behaviour as they were perhaps trying to distribute fixed costs over more output, but costs were fixed to a much lesser extent over the season than at individual games. Players had to be paid for extra matches, and more ground maintenance would be required. Of course, as long as marginal revenue exceeded marginal costs, playing extra games could still be profit-maximizing. There are, however, grounds for suggesting that receipts would not be large at non-League and non-SFA Cup games. First, spectators were not that interested in friendly matches. Prior to the formation of the SFL when most games were friendlies, the SFA commented that 'on the majority of their matches clubs actually lose money – the profit coming from the few-and-far-between big gate' (*Scottish Football Annual*, 1888/89, 35). Admittedly both Rangers and Celtic did well financially out of 'friendlies' with leading English clubs but no doubt nationalistic fervour gave these games a competitive edge (Handley 1960, 30; *Scottish Sport*, June 19, 1891). There is some later evidence in Hamilton Academical's complaint of 'unprofitable' friendly matches in 1907/8 and in Heart's profit-and-loss account for 1912/13, which shows a total revenue of only £8 5s. 7d. from friendly matches. Second, most other cup games would be of a lower standard than either Scottish cup or league matches because non-league clubs would often be involved. Finally, many of these games were played on mid-week afternoons; but time-off during the week was not the privilege of many supporters.

If clubs were profit-maximizers, it might have been expected that their stadia would have been used for non-football activities, particularly in the close season.[9] All clubs took powers to do this, and in the 1890s Rangers, Celtic, and Queen's Park organized many cycling and athletic meetings with at least eight other clubs also establishing cycle tracks. Those clubs which possessed superior facilities could also hire their grounds to the SFA as venues for representative fixtures. The data in Table 1 show that before 1900 clubs obtained on average 8.8% of their income from such activities. After the turn of the century, however, there was a decline in public demand for cycling and athletics and the clubs were either unwilling or unable to find a substitute. Direct comparisons cannot be made because different teams were generally involved, but the available data show that outside sources produced only 2.6% of total income.

Whether a club was a profit- or utility-maximizer would also have implications for its employment policy. Dabscheck has argued that the behaviour of the utility-maximizer in the labour market will differ significantly from that of the profit-maximizer (Dabscheck 1975). The profit-maximizer will be willing to redistribute playing talent in order to equalize sporting competition, whereas the utility-maximizer will be concerned to obtain and retain the best players. Hence, the latter will be more inclined to endorse a restriction-free labour market in which those with the money secured the most talented workers, while the former might be willing to impose limits to players' wages and mobility.

NUMBERS AND NARRATIVES

Maximum wages might also be accepted by the profit-maximizer as a means to profit via cost-reduction. The utility-maximizer, however, will be more willing to pay the star player his economic rent. This is not to say that he is unconcerned with costs: in fact, he will try to minimize his costs, but within a given wages fund. Having decided what can be afforded for labour he will spend that amount, but will practise wage discrimination so as to maximize the playing efficiency of the team. Dabschek hypothesizes that the effective utility-maximizer will develop a tripartite wage structure in order to satisfy this objective. First, players will receive a guaranteed income over a period of possibly three to five years, and this income will vary with the perceived skill of the player.[10] Secondly, the team will be paid by results and will receive additional income in the form of uniform – to emphasize the team effort – bonuses for winning matches. Finally, individual players will obtain bonuses for their part in the team's performance, though these will be paid at the end of the season when their relative contribution can be more clearly assessed.

As the utility-maximizer wishes to secure the services of the best players, he will seek to enlarge his wages fund so that he can compete effectively for them. He will thus look to supplement gate receipts from other sources. The larger the wages fund the more will be spent on players: in individual wages so as to obtain the best talent and to encourage it to perform at a high level; in aggregate wages so as to expand the labour force and provide adequate reserve coverage as well as to keep players from joining rival clubs; or in transfer fees so as to purchase better players from other teams.

Although not fully replicated in Scottish soccer, indications of Dabscheck's ideal-type utility-maximizer can be found. No restrictions were placed on competition for new players and, even though contracted players were tied to their club, their employers could sell their services to another team. There was no maximum wage, and it is clear that the most successful teams paid the highest wages: indeed, Rangers' second team earned more than Partick Thistle's first team (Crampsey 1978, 7). Moreover, wage discrimination was operative within teams: although Hearts' first team wages in 1902 ranged between only £3 and £4 a week, payments when not playing through injury widened to between £1 10s and £4, and close season earnings varied from £1 to £3 per week (Heart of Midlothian Wage Books: courtesy of John Hutchinson). The three-tiered wage structure can also be identified: income was guaranteed for a season at a time, including summer wages for the better players; win and draw team incentives were paid, as were end-of-season bonuses for winning cups and championships (Allison 1966, 208; Handley 1960, 37; Heart of Midlothian Minute Books, *passim*); and, although no individual seasonal bonuses have come to light, after five years or so a star player might be awarded a benefit match from which he retained the surplus after the deduction of costs.

The weakest application of Dabscheck's thesis to Scottish football is in regard to the clubs' efforts to maximize their wages funds. Summer sports and ground hirings made little contribution after 1900 and gate-money dominated club revenues, though even here pricing policies were not designed to maximize revenue or profit. Nor was there much resort to external funds unless shareholding or some early loans are viewed in this light, but they were not used, at least not overtly, for either player payments or transfer fees. Nevertheless, it is still possible that the concept of the wages fund was employed. Unfortunately, there are insufficient data available to examine any club in detail, but 22 observations covering 11 clubs yielded a rank-order correlation of +0.91 between revenue and current wage bills

NUMBERS AND NARRATIVES

Table 2. Net profits of Scottish football clubs (£).

	1906/7	1907/8	1908/9	1909/10	1910/11	1911/12	1912/13	1913/14	Average
Celtic			1753	−1501	555[a]	−715[a]	4221[a]	3131	1241
Hibernian	894	781	25	736	517	398	194	743	536
Partick Thistle				−325[a]	198	958	696	588	423
Hearts	394	−477	−198	−202	−245	1196	1374	1440	421
Motherwell				491[a]	[−246[a]]		507[a]	981[a]	297
Falkirk		1510	−366	−1128[a]	−481[a]	1352[a]	935[a]		292
St. Mirren			−30	−50	−146	44	−147	372	7
East Stirlingshire					38	17	−6	−26	−10
Hamilton		−112	280	181	−127	597	−213	−739	−19
St Johnstone					−32	−176	40	51	−29

Source: Annual financial statements.
Notes: Profit figures given in the statements have been adjusted to allow for expenditure on revenue account which conventionally would be classified as investment.
[a]Indicates that insufficient detail was available for this to be done and thus profits may be understated in that year.

and 10 observations for 6 clubs revealed a correlation of +0.84 between revenue and the wage bill of the following season.

Whether or not cups and championships were put before profits, in practice, if the limited data in Table 2 are any guide, several clubs made profits large enough to justify substantial dividends. Yet, despite the absence of any official limitation on dividends – unlike the situation in England where the FA imposed a 5% maximum (Green 1953, 152; *Athletic News*, December 27, 1909). – relatively few shareholders appear to have received direct returns on their investment. Although the sample is small, of all the teams whose financial statements could be traced, apart from Celtic only Falkirk (10% in 1907/08 and 1912/13) and St Mirren (5% in 1909/10) paid dividends. Celtic was a major exception as it paid 20% in its first year, followed by seven successive 10% (Handley 1960, *passim*). Certainly, no Edinburgh club ever distributed any profits to its shareholders (Mackie 1959, 118). Yet, the ratio of net tangible assets per share was generally too low to offer much protection to shareholders should the club cease trading. In such circumstances, it might have been expected that shareholders would demand at least some dividends as compensation for their capital being at risk. No evidence has been found, however, to suggest that shareholders objected to not receiving dividends. Indeed, the one major row that has come to light was a revolt by many Celtic shareholders when dividends were declared in preference to donations to charity (McNee 1978, 94–95).

The solution to this paradoxical situation may lie in the occupational composition of the shareholders. Table 3 contains an analysis of both soccer club shareholders and of those in a sample of more definitely profit-oriented sports companies. A comparison reveals a significantly larger proportion of working-class shareholders in the football clubs. Possibly many of these saw a small shareholding as merely an extension of their role as supporters. Others were already members of the clubs and thus were likely candidates for shares when company status was adopted. Working-class shareholdings were generally small – in most clubs the mode ranged between 10 shillings and one pound – which suggests that a claim for a season ticket at a reduced price, psychic income from belonging to the club, or possibly a vote at the A.G.M., were stronger motivations than financial returns. Many of these shareholders could well view the club as a voluntary cooperative association

NUMBERS AND NARRATIVES

Table 3. An occupational analysis of shareholders in major Scottish football clubs and in Scottish sports companies before 1916.

	Football clubs[a]				Sports companies[b]			
	Shareholders[c]		Shareholdings[d]		Shareholders[c]		Shareholdings[d]	
	No.	%	No.	%	No.	%	No.	%
Aristocracy and gentry	5	0.2	320	0.9	46	10.3	11,647	24.5
Upper professional	85	3.7	1624	4.8	61	13.6	6958	14.6
Lower professional	117	5.0	1,768	5.3	30	6.7	2628	5.5
Proprietors associated with the drink trade	262	11.3	10,496	31.2	30	6.7	4,570	9.6
Other proprietors and employers	309	13.3	6906	20.5	167	37.2	18,024	38.0
Managers and higher administrators	84	3.6	1,284	3.8	26	5.8	1,380	2.9
Clerical	318	13.7	2,872	8.5	48	10.7	792	1.6
Foremen, supervisors, and inspectors	44	1.9	278	0.8	4	0.9	112	0.2
Skilled manual	8	37.5	6,424	19.1	33	7.4	1,226	2.6
Semi-skilled Manual	183	7.9	1,475	4.4	3	0.7	132	0.3
Unskilled Manual	44	1.9	154	0.5	–	–	–	–
Totals	2321	1000	33,611	100.0	448	100.0	47,469	100.0
Untraced or unspecified	157		1285		177		8051	

Source: Club date from shareholders registers held by Scottish Record Office, West Register House, Edinburgh for defunct companies and by the Registrar of Companies, George Street, Edinburgh for existing companies.
Notes: [a]Clubs covered were Aberdeen, Airdrieonians, Ayr United, Celtic, Clyde, Cowdenbeath, Dumbarton, Dundee Football & Athletic Club, Dundee, Dundee Hibernian, East Fife, East Stirlingshire, Falkirk, Hamilton Academicals, Heart of Midlothian, Hibernian, Kilmarnock, Motherwell, Partick Thistle, Rangers, Saint Bernards, Saint Johnstone, and Saint Mirren.
[b]Companies covered were Ayr Racecourse Syndicate, Edinburgh Cycling Academy, Edinburgh Ice Rink, Glasgow Indoor Bowling and Recreation Co., Glasgow Real Ice-Skating Palace, Hamilton Park Racecourse and Lanark Racecourse.
[c]At the time that shares were first issued.
[d]At the time that the shares were first issued. Converted into £1 units.

rather than as a capitalistic enterprise. To them, shareholding was more consumption than investment.[11]

Most money was raised from the business community. This group also provided the bulk of the club directors, over 40% of those traced in 1914, and at this time, directors determined both the playing and the financial tactics of the club. Here, there was a possibility of commercial motivation in the form of contracts, particularly for building and refreshments. Although Aberdeen and Dumbarton specifically excluded directors from contracting with the club, no other articles of association included such a restriction, and certainly at Hearts, many contracts went to committee men and directors (Heart of Midlothian Minute Books, June 17, 1897, July 19, 1901, May 26, 1905, October 31, 1906, April 27, 1907). Moreover, there were indirect monetary benefits to be had if a successful football team was established in an area. Several clubs stressed the regular influx of several thousands of potential customers when they endeavoured to sell shares to local businessmen.[12] One group in particular could benefit and this may account for the remarkable proportion of shares held by those involved in the drink trade – hoteliers, publicans, licensed victuallers, brewers etc. What concerned these, and to some extent the other businessmen who held shares, was home attendance: the size of the gate at away matches was immaterial to their business receipts. In such circumstances, their policy as directors might be to promote a winning team rather than one which maximized the profits derived from the entrance fees at home and away matches.

If it was not distributed to shareholders what did happen to the money made by the clubs? Some went to charity: indeed, the SFA claimed that 'many institutions depend so largely on football for a helping hand' (SFA Annual Report 1894/95). However this was mostly from pre-season practice or friendly matches, for which the SFA refused to let clubs retain the proceeds, or from special competitions organized to assist various city charities. Relatively little money went to charity directly from the club accounts. Of 37 profit and loss accounts covering 12 clubs only six clubs made donations, with contributions averaging less than 1% of net profits.

Clubs generally used their profits to build up reserve funds. Even in the limited sample, only one club did not run at a loss for at least one season and thus reserves had to be accumulated in order to ensure the maintenance of operations without severe financial pruning. If wages plummeted too far following a poor financial year players might not be willing to try and improve their productivity in terms of match results. Thus, reserves were used to cushion the impact of financial losses upon wages. Acting in this way is not inconsistent with the wages-fund hypothesis as it is not necessary to spend all the cash on hand. Indeed, the accumulation of reserves could be seen as part of a wages-fund policy in that money would need to be readily available for transfer fees should a suitable player come on the market. Profits were also used to finance ground improvements. Although from the balance sheets to hand only Celtic and Hibernian used reserves for this purpose, all clubs except Hearts, Hamilton and East Stirlingshire had physical assets valued well in excess of share capital, which suggests that profits were being ploughed into spectator and playing facilities.[13] Using profits to finance ground and playing improvements can be seen as a device for attaining further profits, but for what purpose? Ultimately, apart from the few clubs which paid dividends, strengthening or maintaining the team seems to be the answer. Profits for most clubs were a means to an end, rather than an end in themselves.

Nevertheless, no matter how suggestive it might be, none of the preceding discussion proves that clubs were not profit-maximizers. Clubs may have appeared to have adopted an overt policy of trying to win as many matches as they could because, as individual clubs, they had no option but to do so. The dilemma facing any profit-maximizing club is that if it wins every game it could undermine its profitability, but if it did not play to win it would face trouble from both its supporters and from the football authorities. Short of refusing to sign the best players available to it or deliberately transferring star players to weaker clubs, there is little that the individual club could do to equalize playing ability between teams. Action, however, could be taken by the clubs in aggregate at the level of the league, which can be viewed as a cartel within which members can make collusive arrangements to maximize joint or even individual profits. This possibility is examined below.

Concerted action and interdependence

Until the formation of the SFL in 1890, Scottish clubs played mainly friendly matches and a varying number of cup-ties, depending upon their playing success. Cups gave teams something more than just honour to play for, and consequently became very popular with both clubs and their supporters: the Scottish Cup was established in 1873 and by 1890 there were many other cup competitions in Scotland, generally organized on a regional basis.[14] However, after the SFA banned Scottish clubs from the English Cup in 1887, there was only one major trophy to compete for at anything more than regional level, and it was quite feasible for two leading clubs to meet each other at the very beginning of the competition. The major clubs grew increasingly dissatisfied with this situation and possibly influenced by the successful inauguration of the Football League in England, organized a similar league in Scotland, which from the 1890/91 season scheduled regular competitive matches between top-level Scottish clubs (Connell 1906b, 269). Initially composed of 11 teams, by 1914, the League had expanded to a first division of 20 clubs. A second division commenced in 1893.

If the constituent clubs of a league believe that its maintenance is in their interests, then they may have to take concerted action to attain their objective. Any long-term dominance of the league by a few clubs could lead to a decline in aggregate attendances and profitability, and the long-run losers, both financially and in play, might leave. However, since clubs exhibit mutual interdependence in that they have to combine to produce saleable output, they require the survival of a number of clubs of reasonable standard: in sporting product markets, unlike most business, oligopolists have no desire to become monopolists. Yet, clubs could not deliberately set out to lose games in order to reduce their dominance: neither their fans nor the football authorities would condone such behaviour. Hence, collusive arrangements might be necessary to keep the league viable. Efforts could be made to equalize sporting competitiveness by imposing restrictions on the labour market so that the richer clubs could not monopolize the best playing talent. Failing this, some form of income redistribution could be undertaken to try to ensure the economic survival of the weaker members of the league: the money received could, of course, be used to strengthen the team (Dabscheck 1976a).

Before discussing the policies adopted by the SFL it should be noted that the League did not exert sole authority over its members. The SFA ruled Scottish football as a whole and made decisions which had implications for League teams on matters such as the length of the playing season and the disciplining of players and clubs. Moreover, it should be emphasized that the SFA was not a mouthpiece of the League clubs as its committee was composed predominantly of non-League representatives.

As much of the quality of a team is directly attributable to the talent of its players, restrictions on the free operation of the labour market could influence the relative sporting competitiveness of teams in a league. Such regulations have included recruiting zones allocated to specific teams, drafting mechanisms to distribute playing talent, and limitations on wages, bonuses and signing-on fees paid to players and on transfer fees paid to clubs (Dabscheck 1976a, 1976b; Sloane 1976). Neither the SFL nor the SFA did much in this direction save for a rule which tied a player to the League club for which he first signed. Once he had joined a club, he was no longer a free agent. If he was dissatisfied with the terms offered he had the right to appeal to either the League Management Committee or the SFA, but he had no right to change clubs. If his employers refused to transfer him or if he refused to accept the conditions of his contract, his only option was to quit Scottish League football. At one time, he could have headed south to English soccer, but in 1898, the English and Scottish Leagues agreed to recognize each other's registrations (Sutcliffe, Brierley, and Howarth 1939, 13). Within Scotland, the alternative was lower-quality, lower-paid, football.

However, as there was no maximum wage nor any zoning restrictions on recruitment, the richer clubs were able to offer the highest wages and signing-on fees to talented new entrants to League football. Moreover, clubs were allowed to transfer players and, as there was no limit to the transfer fee, the greater a club's financial resources, the more it could afford to offer in the auction for a particular player. There was thus little to prevent the gravitation of player-talent to a few wealthy clubs.

Whether this occurred is examined in Table 4 by defining high-quality players as current Scottish internationals. The significant discontinuity in the proportion of caps going to Rangers, Celtic and Hearts after 1895/6 is due to SFA policies of not selecting Scots who

Table 4. Distribution of Scottish international caps, 1890/91–1912/13.

		(1)	(2)	(3)	(4)			
Period	No. of Caps Awarded	To English-based players	To Scottish-based players	To Scottish League players	To players from Celtic, Rangers, and Hearts	4 as % of 1	4 as % of 2	4 as % of 3
1890/91– 1895/96	198	3[a]	195	95	59	29.8	30.3	62.1
1896/7– 1901/02	198	22	176	126	101	51.0	57.4	80.2
1902/03– 1907/08	198	61	137	135	90	45.5	65.7	66.7
1908/09– 1913/14	198	49	149	149	98	49.5	65.8	65.8

Source: Calculated from data in Vernon and Rollin (1978, 709–720).
[a]There was a policy of selecting only home-based Scots until 1895/96.

were playing for English clubs till that season and of picking totally different teams for each of the three annual home internationals until 1893/94 (*Scottish Football Annual* 1878/79, 81; SFA Annual Report 1895/96). The later fall in the share of caps going to Scottish League players which went to the three major clubs is partially a function of the expansion of the League: the percentage of caps to Scottish-based players going to Rangers, Celtic and Hearts actually rose. Two major conclusions can be drawn. First, within Scotland, the League was eventually able to recruit the best talent: the last non-League cap awarded was in 1903/04. Second, although there was no significant increase in the concentration of the best players in the three leading clubs after 1907/08, the talent was very concentrated with two-thirds of all caps to Scottish-based players going to these teams.

As the labour market was not tightly controlled, there was little likelihood of equality of sporting competition being attained. Table 5 measures the static equality of competition by showing the standard deviations of winning percentages within the League each season from 1890/91 to 1914/15: the higher the standard deviation, the less equal are the teams.[15] It would appear that the Scottish League was generally an unequal contest, especially when a comparison is made with the English League, where there was some influence from the imposition of a maximum wage in 1901 and a limit to signing-on bonuses from 1891 (Green 1953, 408; Sutcliffe, Brierley, and Howarth 1939, 113). In no season was the competition more equal in Scotland than in England, and the mean Scottish standard deviation of 18.31 was higher than that of any single season south of the border. Although there was a trend towards more equal competition – in successive quinquennia the mean Scottish standard deviations were 22.25, 21.72, 17.84, 15.40 and 14.32 – nevertheless in a situation where the winning percentages must average 50.00, even the later standard deviations are significantly large.

Although the competition within each season was unequal, it is possible that different teams were dominant at different times. However, an examination of top League positions and Scottish Cup Finals clearly demonstrates the dominance of Celtic, Rangers, and, to a lesser extent, Heart of Midlothian. Only in three seasons of the first quarter-century of the League's operation did they fail to fill at least two of the top three positions and on six occasions they obtained all three places. Neither Celtic nor Rangers ever finished lower than fifth and that on only three occasions between them. Similarly, in the 24 cup-finals up to 1914, these three clubs provided a finalist in all but three years and, including the abandoned final of 1909, won the trophy 17 times.

NUMBERS AND NARRATIVES

Table 5. A measure of the static equality of competition in the Scottish and English first divisions.

	Scottish		English	
	No. of teams	Standard deviation of winning percentages	No. of teams	Standard deviation of winning percentages
Season				
1888/89			12	18.04
1889/90			12	15.61
1890/91	10[a]	28.36	12	12.44
1891/92	12	22.02	14	16.61
1892/93	10	19.02	16	11.35
1893/94	10	20.42	16	12.37
1894/95	10	21.45	16	12.37
1895/96	10	19.40	16	12.85
1896/97	10	22.69	16	10.91
1897/98	10	16.84	16	9.33
1898/99	10	27.15	18	8.20
1899/00	10	22.54	18	10.91
1900/01	11	17.85	18	9.02
1901/02	10	17.56	18	5.56
1902/03	12	19.28	18	8.51
1903/04	14	19.09	18	10.60
1904/05	14	15.40	18	12.90
1905/06	16	15.60	20	8.33
1906/07	18	13.83	20	9.24
1907/08	18	17.02	20	6.30
1908/09	18	15.95	20	7.13
1909/10	18	14.60	20	9.67
1910/11	18	15.26	20	9.75
1911/12	18	11.04	20	7.65
1912/13	18	13.65	20	12.03
1913/14	20	16.28	20	7.09
1914/15	20	15.39	20	7.75

Source: Calculated from data in *Scottish Football Annual* (1899), *Scotsman passim*, *Evening Times Football Annual* (1915) and Sutcliffe, Brierley, and Howarth 1939.
[a]Initially there were eleven teams but Renton were expelled from the S.F.A. for playing a match against Edinburgh Saints, in reality St Bernards who had been suspended by the S.F.A. for professionalism (S.F.A. Annual Report 1890/91). Renton had played five league matches and these results were cancelled. Golesworthy (1976, 183).

Long-term rank-order correlations between league positions in different seasons would have enabled something to have been said about performance over time of all teams, not just the top performers. Unfortunately, the change in both the number and composition of the teams in the League virtually restricted the use of this coefficient to one-year and three-year intervals. The average for the one-year measures was +0.64 and for the three-year correlations +0.62, with a figure of +0.58 when season 1906/07 was ranked against that of 1912/13. This suggests that even lower down the League there was some consistency in the relative performance of teams over time.

Support for this view comes from Table 6, which measures the dynamic equality of competition by showing the average winning percentages of all teams which participated in the Scottish first division before 1915. Although the mean of individual club standard deviations is 12.2, which suggests some disparity in any particular team's performance over time, there was no discernible trend for individual standard deviations to vary with the overall mean winning percentage: teams at the top experienced similar fluctuations in performance as teams at the bottom. Hence, most clubs could anticipate that their winning percentage could vary significantly from year to year, but not so much that positions in the championship would become totally unpredictable over a period of time. What is very clear

NUMBERS AND NARRATIVES

Table 6. A measure of the dynamic equality of competition in the Scottish first division, 1890/91–1914/15.

Team	No. of seasons in first division	Period[a]	Mean winning %	Standard deviation	Highest %
Celtic	25	1890/91–1914/15	74.9	8.7	91.7
Rangers	25	1890/91–1914/15	73.3	10.4	100.0
Hearts	25	1890/91–1914/15	60.0	14.9	86.1
Falkirk	10	1905/06–1914/15	58.9	11.8	76.4
Hibernian	20	1895/96–1914/15	54.3	12.2	84.1
Airdrieonians	12	1903/04–1914/15	53.8	9.0	63.3
Ayr United	2	1913/14–1914/15	53.3	14.0	63.2
Dumbarton[c]	6	1890/91–1895/96	51.0	27.7	84.1
Clyde[b]	9	1906/07–1914/15	50.9	13.0	70.6
Aberdeen	10	1905/06–1914/15	50.7	9.5	70.6
Third Lanark	25	1890/91–1914/15	50.0	10.0	82.7
Dundee	22	1893/94–1914/15	49.7	14.4	70.6
Saint Mirren	25	1890/91–1914/15	46.2	8.0	55.6
Morton	15	1900/01–1914/15	42.0	14.1	71.1
Kilmarnock	16	1899/00–1914/15	41.3	7.3	50.0
Partick Thistle	20	1895/96–1914/15	40.8	14.6	61.8
Saint Bernards	7	1893/94–1899/00	40.5	12.5	63.9
Dumbarton[c]	2	1913/14–1914/15	40.1	6.1	44.7
Motherwell	12	1903/04–1914/15	40.1	8.5	54.4
Hamilton	9	1907/07–1914/15	39.7	6.8	50.4
Cambuslang	2	1890/91–1891/92	39.2	23.3	55.6
Raith	5	1910/11–1914/15	38.4	2.6	42.1
Leith Athletic	4	1991/92–1894/95	37.6	17.5	56.8
Renton	3	1891/92–1893/94	33.5	19.6	47.7
Queen's Park	15	1900/01–1914/15	33.2	8.8	44.1
Port Glasgow Athletic	8	1902/03–1909/10	31.3	8.8	41.2
Abercorn	4	1890/91–1896/97	27.7	13.4	38.6
Clyde[b]	8	1891/92–1899/00	27.2	13.4	45.6
Vale of Leven	2	1890/91–1891/02	21.0	13.6	30.6
Cowlairs	1	1890/91–1890/91	16.7	–	16.7

Source: Calculated from data in *Scottish Football Annual* (1899); *Evening Times Football Annual* (1915); *Scotsman*, *passim*.
[a]The period covers the range from first to last appearance. However, if a team was out for over four years a separate entry was made.
[b]Clyde withdrew in 1900 and did not return till 1906.
[c]Dumbarton withdrew in 1896 and did not return till 1913.

from the Table is the dominance of Celtic and Rangers. Not only did they win three points out of every four played for, but the best seasonal performances of 23 of the other 28 clubs ranked below their average percentage. Moreover, Celtic's worst performance, only 58.3% in 1890/91, topped the best performance of 15 clubs, and Ranger's poorest season, 54.5% in 1891/92, was better than the best attempts of 12 other clubs.

It could be argued that, as the League took little action to create sporting equality, either within a season or over time, it was not interested in profit-maximization. Was the objective of the league then simply survival, to keep itself viable in order that its members would have a recognized major championship to play for? Such a policy might require income redistribution between clubs so as to keep the constituent members financially afloat. As early as 1880 the SFA decided that gate-money at cup-ties should be shared equally between the clubs, but the SFL had a two-thirds: one-third arrangement in favour of the home club. Not till 1905 did the SFL adopt the SFA policy and, well before then, once-famous clubs such as Renton, cup-winners in 1885 and 1888, Vale of Leven, cup-finalists seven times, and Dumbarton, winners of the first two League championships, had fallen out of the League.

Their almost village populations could not match the gates of the city clubs and provide the finance to compete successfully in the labour market. Even pooling match receipts favoured those clubs with the largest aggregate home support. Moreover, all that was shared was the basic gate-money; stand receipts were retained by the home club. This, of course, was to the advantage of those sides which could afford to provide such spectator facilities.

It has been suggested that a failure to subsidize the unremunerative enterprises in a league could lead either to fewer teams or to poorer quality teams, both of which could reduce aggregate league revenue (Sloane 1970, 127). Much will depend on whether adequate substitutes are forthcoming. Prior to 1901, the ten new entrants to SFL's first division performed creditably with an average winning percentage of 46.1 in their first season – 50.3 if Abercorn's disastrous 8.3% is discounted. In such circumstances more equitable income redistribution may have been viewed as unnecessary: there would always be another good team coming along to replace any which fell by the wayside. Indeed, many of the newcomers succumbed themselves, only five surviving into the twentieth century. After 1901, an expansionist policy saw the league increase progressively from ten to twenty clubs. The fourteen new clubs up to 1914 averaged a winning percentage of only 37.7 in their first season. However, all but two survived in the League and one of those returned. Possibly, a contributory reason was the change in policy over gate-sharing in 1905.

League expansion was a way of ensuring the survival of the League. If there are too many teams outside a league which can offer a comparable product for sale, then their games might undermine those of the league as attractions for spectators. Ultimately, a rival league might emerge. Bringing additional teams into the group headed off this potential problem by reducing the quality of the rival product and possibly increasing that of the SFL. As far as the better teams in the League were concerned, expansion would increase the likelihood that talent would win out by reducing the importance of an occasional upset of form. For the rest, more entrants meant more competitive matches and possibly more victories.

Before concluding that the League was not a profit-maximizing cartel several caveats must be made. First, the SFL was a closed competition with no automatic promotion or relegation. Each year the bottom team in the first division had to apply for re-election. After 1901, this was generally forthcoming, possibly because an expansionist policy could accommodate them without detriment to potential new entrants. However, in the first decade of the League, several sides failed to secure re-election. Whether the Dumbartonshire clubs were pushed out because they could not offer sufficient gate-money to satisfy the other teams is a matter for conjecture, though both Vale of Leven and Dumbarton had two poor playing seasons before they left and Renton's last season winning percentage of 11.1 was the third-worst in League history: the worst, Abercorn's 8.3, also resulted in no re-election, but not Dundee's 9.1 which, on the basis of their other performances, seems to have been an aberration. Secondly, profits are based on the scissor blades of revenue and costs, and could be made by lowering the latter, though conceivably this would be risking a long slide to football oblivion. Thirdly, transfers were a way of redistributing income between teams. In England, several clubs remained viable only through recruiting, training and then transferring players. While there is no evidence that this was the case in Scotland, it remains a possibility (Bassett 1906, 162). By selling their best players, however, such clubs would lessen their chances of making profits at the gate.

Conclusion

Scottish football clubs were not uninterested in profits; clearly some level of profit was necessary to playing performance or to survival. Nevertheless, on the basis of the data collected at club level, it can be suggested that most of the teams were not profit-maximizers in the sense that they put money before winning matches. The lack of price competition, the existence of free entry for some spectators, the playing of uneconomic friendly and minor cup fixtures, the relative under-utilization of ground facilities, and the employment policies and wage structures of clubs point to utility taking precedence over profits. Even if the clubs had been profit-maximizers this would have required collusion at the League level in order to produce uncertainty of results at both match and championship level, but the members of the SFL seem to have been willing to tolerate a high degree of inequality in playing success.

Two aspects of the market for soccer, coupled with the desire to survive, help to explain this situation. One was that each club was supplying two different markets with the same product: the demand of the partisan supporter was for a winning team; the demand of the less-committed was for a close, high-quality, encounter. Both were likely to withdraw their support if the team lost too frequently so the production of a winning team was a reasonable policy objective. It was also more within the ambit of the individual club than was the creation of uncertainty. Admittedly if a team won too easily too often, this could also result in a falling demand from the football connoisseur, but at least the club fan would be retained. Much, of course, would depend on the proportion of committed followers that a club had. This is unknown, though it can be hazarded that the sectarian rivalry of Rangers and Celtic fans provided these two clubs with a strong hard-core allegiance. Winning can then be seen as a second-best profit policy, but it was less risky than trying to profit-maximize by creating uncertainty. Uncertain results can go either way; too many in the wrong direction could undermine a team's long-term viability. Hence, clubs preferred to attempt to maximize their playing efficiency and risk too successful a season and diminishing financial returns rather than try to profit-maximize and risk losing too many matches.

A second feature of the product market was the degree of competition between the clubs. If the clubs were competing against each other for spectators then one team's increase in attendance could merely be at the expense of a rival. Uncertainty of results can raise aggregate football attendances only if additional spectators are attracted from other leisure activities. In Scotland, the spatial dispersion of football grounds meant that the market for soccer was fragmented, but to a lesser degree than in England because of the concentration of clubs in the Central Lowlands belt and particularly in Glasgow. There is no way, of course, in which the matches of Rangers and of Celtic can be considered as substitutes for each other, but it is conceivable that developments in intra-city transportation enabled them to draw support away from other Glasgow teams. On the other hand, railway specials allowed these, and other leading teams, to take some of their vast support with them to away matches, thus making an important contribution to the finances of the clubs visited. From this viewpoint, the very success of Rangers, Celtic and, to a lesser degree, Hearts, which gave them their huge followings helped keep the other clubs viable.

It should also be stressed that there was no absolute barrier to sporting success in Scottish soccer. Although Rangers, Celtic and Hearts dominated the League and Scottish Cup honour board, they did not invariably make a clean sweep. Of the twenty clubs in the first division in 1914/15, only eight had not finished in the top three positions sometime, and of these only four had never reached a Scottish Cup Final. Running close to the big three may have become accepted as a criterion of success by the weaker clubs, with survival at League level being their over-riding objective. Moreover, there were other trophies to be won, and any club playing first division football regularly should have had the quality to win a city, county or local charity cup from time to time.[16] Thus, in effect, they maximized their utility outside the major competitions.

The late nineteenth century was a period of rapid commercialization of sport in Britain. As has been shown, however, not all the entrepreneurs involved were motivated primarily by the profit motive. Whereas it is clear from their prospectuses that many companies concerned with cycling, horse-racing and ice-rinks were looking to deliver dividends to their shareholders, the committeemen and directors of most Scottish soccer clubs changed their sports organizations into business enterprises and adopted company status with the intention of winning matches and championships rather than making money. Whether utility-maximization was more common to team than to other sports remains to be investigated. Recent research has suggested that cricket also belongs to the utility end of the motivational spectrum (Vamplew 1981b; Vamplew and Sandiford 1986).[17] Why the degree of profit/utility mix varied both between and within sports is also a subject for future research, though the work on Scottish football suggests that the occupational composition of the shareholders and directors may have had a role to play (Vamplew 1981a).

Notes

1. For a simplified discussion of this see Vamplew (2012).
2. For a bibliography of recent work on aspects of Scottish football see McDowell (2012).
3. For contemporary bibliographies on the debate see Saul (1969) and Payne (1974).
4. Other entertainment industries which developed at this time include the music hall and the seaside holiday. On these, see Bailey (1978), Walvin (1978) and Walton (1981).
5. E.g. Noll (1974, 415), Jones (1969), Demmert (1973); Skully (1974), Davis (1974, 381) accepts general profit-maximization but suggests that a minority of owners were not particularly profit motivated, and El Hodiri and Quirk (1971), whilst acknowledging that owners are not always motivated solely by profits, found that the evidence supported their hypotheses based on profit-maximization. Davenport (1969), 8 suggests that owners of baseball teams are frequently 'just as interested' in winning championships as in making profits.
6. Knock-out cup competitions are somewhat different in that the end of the tournament brings together the unbeaten teams in the competition, whereas end-of-season league games, even those involving leading clubs, may have no bearing whatsoever on the championship. Similarly, there is a quality aspect to any individual game in that a close contest between teams at the top of the league is likely to attract a larger crowd than an equally close contest at the foot of the table.
7. Free admission for women was in vogue by 1888 and did not cease till 1918 (*Scottish Sport*, November 6, 1888; Crampsey 1978, 19). The rationale is not known. Servicemen were given free entry on the supposition that if necessary, they would help to control the crowd.
8. Access was not granted to the records of the SFL so this, and matters discussed below, remain areas for speculation.
9. Information in this paragraph courtesy of Peter Bilsborough.
10. No reason was given for the choice of time period. Possibly, a few seasons are necessary to integrate a group of players fully into a team.
11. These issues are discussed in more detail in Vamplew (1981a).
12. See, for example, the prospectuses of Hearts, Ayr, and St Mirren.
13. Hearts, however, had £6,000 cash on deposit at the bank and Hamilton had taken out a £1,000 loan to pay for improvements and had established a sinking fund.

14. Thirty seven such competitions were deemed important enough to warrant a mention in the *Scottish Football Annual* of 1890/91.
15. The terms static and dynamic equality of competition are borrowed from Daymont (1975, 91).
16. Unfortunately, results are to hand only prior to season 1899/1900, but in that first nine years of the SFL, the following clubs all won major regional trophies while their league performances were moderate: St Mirren (30.6), St Bernard (38.9), Dundee (38.9), Dumbarton (18.5), Abercorn (38.6). Figures indicate winning percentages in the SFL in the season in which they won the trophy.
17. Schofield (1982) argues that county cricket clubs in the twentieth century acted as a profit-maximizing cartel though with a desire to retain the traditions of the game acting as a brake on its actions. Most of his evidence is post 1945.

Disclosure statement

No potential conflict of interest was reported by the author.

References

Allison, W. 1966. *Rangers: The New Era*. Glasgow: n.k.
Andreff, W., and S. Szymanski. 2006. *Handbook on the Economics of Sport*. Cheltenham: Edward Elgar.
Annual Report of East Stirlingshire. 1911/12. *Document held in Companies Register*. Edinburgh: Registry House.
Bailey, P. 1978. *Leisure and Class in. Victorian England*. London: Routledge and Kegan Paul.
Bassett, W. I. 1906. "Big Transfers and the Transfer System" In *The Book of Football*, edited by C. Leatherdale. London: Amalgamated Press.
Connell, R. M. 1906a. "The Association Game in Scotland." In *The of Book Football*, edited by C. Leatherdale. London: Amalgamated Press.
Connell, R. M. 1906b. "The Scottish Football League and Its History." In *The Book of Football*, edited by C. Leatherdale. London: Amalgamated Press.
Crampsey, R. 1978. *The Scottish Footballer*. Edinburgh: Blackwood.
Crampsey, R. 1990. *The Scottish Football League: The First 100 Years*: Glasgow: SFL.
Dabscheck, B. 1975. "The Wage Determination Process for Sportsmen." *Economic Record* 51: 52–65.
Dabscheck, B. 1976a. "Labour Market Versus Product Market Control." *Journal of Industrial Relations* 17: 174–190.
Dabscheck, B. 1976b. "Sporting Equality: A Reply." *Journal of Industrial Relations* 18: 85–86.
Davenport, D. S. 1969. "Collusive Competition in Major League Baseball: Its Theory and Institutional Development." *American Economist* 13: 6–30.
Daymont, T. H. 1975. "The Effects of Monopsonistic Procedures on Equality of Competition in Professional Sport Leagues." *International Review for the Sociology of Sport* 10: 83–99.
Davis, L. E. 1974. "Self-regulation in Baseball, 1909-71." In *Government and the Sports Business*, edited by R. G. Noll, 349–386. Washington, DC: Brookings Institute.
Demmert, H. G. 1973. *The Economics of Professional Team Sports*. Lexington, KY: Heath.
Downward, P., A. Dawson, and T. Dejonghe. 2009. *Sports Economics: Theory, Evidence and Policy*. Abingdon: Rouledge.
Goldblatt, D. 2006. *The Ball is Round: A Global History of Football*. London: Viking.
Golesworthy, M. 1976. *The Encyclopedia of Association Football*. Newton Abbot: Hale.
Green, G. 1953. *The History of the Football Association*. London: Naldrett.
Handley, J. E. 1960. *The Celtic Story*. London: Stanley Paul.
El Hodiri, M., and J. Quirk. 1971. "An Economic Model of a Professional Sports League." *Journal of Political Economy* 79: 1302–1319.
Jones, J. C. H. 1969. "The Economics of the National Hockey League." *The Canadian Journal of Economics* 2: 1–21.)
Kay, J., and W. Vamplew. 2010. "Beyond Altruism: British Football and Charity, 1877–1914." *Soccer and Society* 11 (3): 181–197.
Késenne, S., ed. 2014. *The Economic Theory of Professional Team Sports*. Cheltenham: Edward Elgar.
Mackie, A. 1959. *The Hearts*. London: Stanley Paul.
Magoun, F. P. 1931. "Scottish Popular Football, 1424–1815." *The American Historical Review* 37: 1–13.

McDowell, M. L. 2012. *A Cultural History of Association Football in Scotland, 1865–1902.* Lampeter: Edwin Mellen.

McNee, G. 1978. *The Story of Celtic.* London: Stanley Paul.

Neale, W. C. 1964. "The Peculiar Economics of Professional Sports: A Contribution to the Theory of the Firm in Sporting Competition and in Market Competition." *The Quarterly Journal of Economics* 78 (1): 1–14.

Noll, R. G. 1974. "Attendances and Price Setting." In *Government and the Sports Business*, edited by R. G. Noll, 115–157. Washington, DC: Brookings Institute.

Payne, P. L. 1974. *British Entrepreneurship in the Nineteenth Century.* London: Macmillan.

Rottenberg, S. 1956. "The Baseball Players' Labor Market." *Journal of Political Economy* 64: 242–258.

Saul, S. B. 1969. *The Myth of the Great Depression, 1873–1896.* London: Macmillan.

Schofield, J. A. 1982. "The Development of First-class Cricket in England: An Economic Analysis." *The Journal of Industrial Economics* 30 (4): 337–360.

Scottish Football Association (SFA). *Various Years. Annual Reports.* Hampden Park, Glasgow: Scottish Football Museum.

Skully, G.W. 1974. "Pay and Performance in Major League Baseball", *American Economic Review*, LXIV: 915–930.

Sloane, P. J. 1970. "The Economics of Professional Football: The Football Club as a Utility Maximizer." *Scottish Journal of Political Economy* 18: 121–146.

Sloane, P. J. 1976. "Sporting Equality: Labour Market Versus Product Market Control – A Comment." *Journal of Industrial Relations* 18: 79–84.

Sloane, P. J. 1980. *Sport in the Market.* London: Institute of Economic Affairs.

Sutcliffe, C. E., J. A. Brierley, and F. Howarth. 1939. *The Story of the Football League, 1888–1938.* Preston: Football League.

Szymanski, S. 2003a. "The Economic Design of Sporting Contests." *Journal of Economic Literature* 41: 1137–1187.

Szymanski, S. 2003b. "The Assessment: The Economics of Sport." *Oxford Review of Economic Policy* 19 (4): 467–477.

Szymanski, S. 2004. "Professional Team Sports Are Only a Game: The Walrasian Fixed-supply Conjecture Model, Contest-nash Equilibrium, and the Invariance Principle." *Journal of Sports Economics* 5 (2): 111–126.

Szymanski, S., and S. Kesenne. 2004. "Competitive Balance and Gate Revenue Sharing in Team Sports." *Journal of Industrial Economics* 52: 165–177.

Vamplew, W. 1981a. "Ownership and Control in Gate-Money Sport: Scottish Football before 1915", *Canadian Journal of History of Sport and Physical Education.* XII: 56–83.

Vamplew, W. 1981b. "L.B.W. or L.S.D.: The Economics of English County Cricket before 1914". Paper Presented to the Third Sport and History Conference, La Trobe University, Melbourne.

Vamplew, W. 2012. "Economic Approaches to Sports [and Cultural] History" In *Cultural Histories and Cultural Politics*, edited by Eisenberg C and A. Gestrich, 110–123. Berlin: Arbeitskreis Deutsche Englandforschung.

Vamplew, W., and K. Sandiford. 1986. "The Peculiar Economics of English Cricket before 1914." *British Journal of Sports History* 3 (3): 311–326.

Vernon, L., and J. Rollin. 1978. *Rothmans Football Yearbook, 1977/78.* London: Brickfield.

Walton, J.K. 1981. "The Demand for Working-class Seaside Holidays in Victorian England", *The Economic History Review*, 34, 249–265.

Walvin, J. 1978. *Beside the Seaside.* London: Allen Lane.

Wiseman, N. C. 1977. "The Economics of Football." *Lloyds Bank Review* 123: 29–43.

Sport, industry and industrial sport in Britain before 1914: review and revision

Wray Vamplew

ABSTARCT
This article focuses on three aspects of the historical relationship between sport and industry. First, it will assess the view that modern sport was a lagged by-product of the Industrial Revolution which then was exported round the world from the first modernized economy. Second, it will consider sport as an industry in its own right examining the early commercialization associated with sport, the nature of the sports product and the often neglected issue of entrepreneurship. Finally, it will turn to workplace sport which demands attention not only due to the sheer scale of its extent but also for the apparent approach to some form of gender equality in the provision of sports facilities.

Comment

In 1988, I published a book chapter which became the standard interpretation of the relationship between sport and industrialization in Britain (though my study at the time was limited to the English situation) (Vamplew 1988). Thirty years on I was asked to contribute another chapter on industrialization to the *Oxford Handbook of Sports History* (Vamplew, forthcoming). This stimulated me to revisit and modify some, but not all, of my earlier views. In particular, I discovered that there has been significant research done on workplace sport since my earlier contribution.

Sport and the Industrial Revolution

In the mid-eighteenth century, the English economy began an accelerated structural transformation in which industry came more into prominence. In turn, this industrialization had an impact on popular sport as it called for new work patterns. Before the Industrial Revolution, when agriculture dominated the economy, work was much more intermittent than it was to become and there was substantial recreational time available to the working man.[1] In industry, particularly factory industry, the pressure was less seasonal and more unrelenting. What was required in the factories was regular hours and, above all, long hours. Unit overhead costs could only be reduced if the growing volume of machinery and other capital equipment was intensively employed. Even in relatively unmechanized industries, economies could be obtained by task specialization and the division of labour. In such situations, there was much to be gained from the synchronization of labour with all members of a production team working the same hours.

It was no easy task to persuade a labour force to accept the new work disciplines. Not only was working from dawn to dusk for six days a week virtually throughout the year alien to traditional work patterns, but also the location of industry meant that, for many, industrial employment would involve not only occupational but also geographical mobility. Hence, in the early stages of factory industry, employers faced a labour shortage which lessened the effectiveness of disciplinary measures such as fines or dismissals. Even where successful, such methods served only to obtain a minimum performance: they did not necessarily change the labour force's attitude to work. A possible longer term solution lay in the increased earnings which could be obtained for working longer hours. Certainly, the cash stimulus appeared to work for agricultural labourers at harvest time when long hours of unremitting toil would be put in, but this lasted for only a few weeks and, to the labouring poor, could make all the difference between basic subsistence and a more comfortable living. Whether it would work all the year round was less clear, especially as many contemporaries suggested the existence of a backward sloping supply curve of labour, as epitomized in agricultural economist, Arthur Young's (1771, 391) famous dictum that 'everyone but an idiot knows that the lower classes must be kept poor or they will never be industrious'. Yet possibly the supply of labour problem was really a supply of goods problem. Unless the workers' consumption horizons could be stretched, the labour force would exhibit a preference for leisure which would lead to an output below that desired by their industrial employers. An increased range of consumer goods was vital as a demonstration of the better material life which hard work could bring. Increased imports, the emergence of the products of the Industrial Revolution and the shop window effect of the company store served to instil the consumption habit in the workforce. Once the workers had accepted that they wanted higher consumption standards, not only were wage incentives rendered more effective, but the way was open for the use of fines and dismissals as a disciplinary threat to those standards (Vamplew 2004, 33–35).

The acceptance by the workforce that leisure cost them money enabled working hours to be extended, but inevitably there was a limit to the trade-off between less leisure and more income. Even for those workers with low leisure preference, Sundays were generally free from labour and, despite increasing pressure, numerous holidays were still recognized. What their workers did in this free time was of concern to many industrial and commercial employers, since certain leisure activities could be detrimental to productivity: injuries from violent sports could keep workers away from their desks or machines; excessive drinking could result in absenteeism and hangovers; and gambling could undermine the work ethic. They saw the violent human and animal sports of rural Britain, the ploughing matches and hedge-laying contests that demonstrated agricultural skills, and the folk football matches played over extensive areas of land as incompatible with industrial society, industrial location or industrial work patterns. Employers thus supported the more general middle-class move to impose its own morality on a society in which the aristocracy and working class were united in their drunkenness, profaneness, sexual indulgence, gambling and love of cruel sports. The traditional way of life was to be discredited and the importance of work upgraded: the idle rich and the idle poor were both to be condemned. Respectability was to be the aim of all society. Hence, a campaign was mounted against drink, idleness, bad language, popular customs, holidays and sports (Vamplew 2004, 36–37). Encouragement and exhortation were strengthened by legislation at national level to outlaw many blood sports and ban Sunday entertainments and at urban level to prohibit street football.

The first generation of historians who looked at sport in Britain believed that the Industrial Revolution thus had a negative impact on sporting activity (Malcolmson 1975; Cunningham 1980). However, since their work, the growing interest in sports history and the consequent detailed examination of the early industrialization period has shown that many traditional sports continued to be played into the later nineteenth century and that there was apparently no leisure vacuum to be filled. Indeed Adrian Harvey's (2004) intensive study of eighteenth- and nineteenth-century newspapers and sporting periodicals led him to suggest that during the first half of the nineteenth century, a commercial sporting culture developed to serve a mass public. He also argues that there was a major expansion in sporting activity in Manchester, the cotton capital of Britain. In other words, there was a chronological coincidence between industrialization and the expansion of sporting activity.

The conventional view now is that modern sport originated in the nineteenth century as a direct consequence of Britain's industrialization, epitomized in Neil Tranter's (1998, 29) axiom that

> … as a general rule, the more industrial and commercial the economy the greater the extent of organised sport and the earlier its inception. It was no accident that Britain, the first country to industrialise, was also the first country to introduce a codified, institutionalised and highly commercialised sporting culture.

Or, put more succinctly by European scholars Bourg and Gouguet (2005, 4): 'modern sport was born in England at the time of the industrial revolution' and even more recently by Irish sports historian Cronin (2014, 30) 'sport in its modern sense was initially a product of the British industrial revolution'.

However, there is a danger that the pendulum has been swung too far. The role of industrialization as a driver of modern sport is too often taken as a chronological correlation without the causal relationship being fully specified. It is hard to see how early industrialization could have impacted positively on sport. Possibly the mindset that encouraged venture capitalists to risk investment in industry was of the same ilk that persuaded wealthy gamblers to promote sport as a means to wager (Guttmann 2004, 59–60). The version of team sports that emanated from the public schools may have emphasized qualities of use for the industrialist – teamwork, obeying orders and discipline – but this should not be exaggerated: such sport encompassed the idea of chivalry (fair play) rather than that of industrial capitalism and, as can be seen from Newbolt's famous poem *Vitai Lamparda*, sport taught the virtues of war not of commerce (Vamplew 2014, 2298–2301). Moreover, little evidence has yet been discovered of industrialists actively promoting sport until the last third of the nineteenth century.[2]

Even if a link between industrialization and sport can be identified, we have to consider another historical revision which disposes of the idea that there was an industrial *revolution* in Britain. Instead, it has been recognized that the process of industrialization was a drawn out one which only accelerated significantly with the widespread application of steam power in the second quarter of the nineteenth century. The first factories were little more than a bringing together of handicraft workers under one roof. Even when power was adopted for mechanization, it was limited to areas where water flow was fast. The cotton works on the hillsides of Lancashire had neither a significant influence on national economic production nor any real impact on leisure patterns of workers generally or even in the county itself. Nationally even by the mid-nineteenth century, 5.5 million of the 7.25 million industrial workers were employed in non-mechanized industry and agriculture was still the largest employment sector (Vamplew 2004, 42, 48). There was still plenty of time and space for traditional sport and recreation to continue (Collins, Martin, and Vamplew 2005).

Only when steam became the driving force for mass production did factories become less geographically determined and did industry *begin* to change the environment in which sport took place as increased urbanization, concomitant upon industrialization, began to lessen the open space available. The real contribution of industrialization to the development of sport lay in the increased incomes and increased leisure time that productivity brought: despite some precursors in particular trades, this was a product of the late rather than even the mid-nineteenth century and certainly not before then (Vamplew 2004, 44–50). Increased productivity enabled employers to concede to demands to lessen the working week for their labour force and to pay them higher wages. This had two major consequences for sport. First, it helped create a mass market for spectator sport by setting Saturday afternoons free of work, thus providing a time slot into which gate-money sport could fit. Second, for those who preferred to be active rather than watch others play, the increase in disposable income allowed the purchase of bicycles and other sporting equipment. By this time, the middle-class attitude towards sport had changed and they now accepted that, if appropriately controlled, it could be a force for good in creating healthier citizens, rejuvenating labour and building character. In the words of Dennis Brailsford (1991, 48), what they had seen as an economic vice now became an economic virtue.

Tomlinson and Young (2011) suggest that modern sports emerged from developments in the early modern era rather than as a by-product of industrialization. They argue that many modern traits are evident from as early as 1450: sport became increasingly institutionalized by the creation and codification of rules; dedicated sport spaces were being built; a European-wide trade in sports equipment existed; and a professional class of athletes, coaches and officials had emerged. They also note that from the Renaissance onwards, the sportification of military exercises and the rise of spectator sports as popular entertainment are observable. What is not clear is whether the examples discovered are precursors rather than initiators, a typical rather than commonplace and further research is needed before full support can be given to their view that 'the weight of current evidence indicates that the threshold for the beginnings of modern sport – at least in some social classes in some regions – could be moved back before 1800' (Tomlinson and Young 2011, 10).

What can be argued is that some of the preconditions for the emergence of modern sport originated before widespread industrialization but that its actual take-off required further stimuli. Guttmann (2004, 85) in his seminal work on the modernization of sport saw preconditions emerging before industrialization as he views modern sport as a (long-delayed?) by-product of the scientific revolution of the European enlightenment. Szymanski (2008) too sees the European enlightenment as a starting point as the roots of modern sport can be seen in the new forms of associativity created at that time, specifically, the club which is the fundamental unit of modern sport.[3] Yet none of this demonstrates that modern sport existed on any significant scale prior to the late nineteenth century. Mass spectator sport did exist before this time though it was intermittent, often annual at best. Harvey's claim for widespread mass spectator sport by the 1840s is undermined by an inability to present any systematic figures for sports crowd attendance. He does produce a table representing attendances of over 1000 on an annual basis for the 1840s, but as this averaged less than 45 such crowds a year it is scarcely evidence of sufficient effective demand for these to be more than sporadic occurrences (Harvey 2004, 175).[4] The market was not yet ready for regularly scheduled sports events. It was not until the economic benefits of industrialization filtered down to the mass of the population that a large and regular paying clientele could be relied upon for sports events.

In examining the development of sport, it is important to differentiate the interrelated but semi-independent concepts of industrialization, urbanization and commercialization. Industrialization contributed to the commercialization of sport but many aspects of sport were commercialized long before industrialization. Cricket, pedestrianism (professional athletics), prize-fighting, rowing and especially horse racing had 'a long history of mass spectating, profit-seeking promoters, paid performers, stake-money contests and gambling' (Tranter 1998, 14–15). However, although some spectators paid to watch from grandstands or to be close to the action, generally much of the commercialization of the time was associated *with the sport* – beer and food stalls, itinerant entertainers, etc. – rather than being *of the sport itself*. Indeed Harvey's study of commercialization in British sport before 1850 uses a wide definition of commercialization which includes not just gate money but also participants' meals purchased as a condition of entry, competitors direct entry fees, spectators' refreshments and additional associated entertainments such as balls and theatrical shows.

Mass markets for sport required not only spending power and time in which to spend it, but also a concentration of population *and* ease of access to the venues. This came with urbanization and the development of inter-town but especially intra-town transportation, a requirement not fulfilled by early urbanization. Moreover, although much urbanization was a consequence of industrialization either directly (manufacturing centres) or indirectly (ports and distribution centres), other forces were at work such as population growth, immigration and agricultural change, not all of which can be totally attributed to the coming of industry.

Sport as industry

This leads into a consideration of sport as an industry. Sport can be regarded (and measured) as an industry in its own right in several ways: as spectator gate-money events, as drivers of demand for sports apparel and equipment, and as employers of labour.

Any work here must use Stephen Hardy's (1986, 17–19) model of 1986 as the starting point. He postulates three aspects to be looked at: the game form itself which becomes a commodity once spectators are prepared to pay to watch it; services ancillary to the game form such as creating stadiums to hold the paying public and the media which advertise the events; and the production of the equipment required to participate in the sport.

There are several inherent differences between the sports product and more conventional consumption goods. Sport is *non-predictable* and is thus a product where result or quality cannot be guaranteed. There is no script, no template and no identical replication. There is no homogeneity about sport. Even a replay of a cup tie with the same line-ups of players as in the original match is a different output. No sports result be predicted with total certainty. Indeed 'uncertainty' is the selling point of the sport product: a maxim of sports economists is that the more unpredictable a contest the greater the attendance is likely to be. The sports product is *non-durable.* Once played, a game or a match is over. It cannot be stored for future consumption (except as a DVD or video but the result is known and the excitement dissipated). The key point here is that an appropriate time slot needs to be found in which the event will take place if attendances are to be maximized. You cannot have the home fans watching at 2 o'clock and then the away supporters watching at 6.30. Sports events are one-offs. Hence, the late nineteenth-century importance of the free Saturday afternoon and, earlier, the time available for the annual race meeting. Sport is often a *complementary product* that is rarely sold to the consumer without being in a package with other consumer goods and services. Going to the event can also involve the travel product, the betting product, the catering product and the alcohol product: indeed it could be argued that these other products preceded gate-money sport.

Despite the substantial work that has been done by sports economists and economic historians – myself included – on the peculiar economics of sport, perhaps to the detriment of analysis on the sports product itself historically, it must be emphasized that much of the business activity both in and associated with sport can be classified as conventional economic behaviour. Ground staff in cricket clubs and craftsmen producing equipment as well as the less sports-specific occupations of clerks, receptionists and salespersons, all of which are needed to get the game under way, function no differently from workers in non-sport organizations. Equipment manufacturers and landlords who put on sports fixtures to attract a drinking clientele are seeking revenue like many other entrepreneurs.

The attempts of promoters and others in the sports sector to raise further revenue can be categorized in four ways. *Commercial widening* occurred when more revenue was sought from traditional gate revenue sources: in effect a business strategy of more of the same. In football, for example, the move from friendly fixtures to cup and later league competitions made games more meaningful to the paying spectator; expansion of leagues meant that more competitive games could be played; and, when there was an excess demand for the product, stadiums were reconstructed to accommodate more customers. In contrast, *commercial deepening* inferred looking for new revenue sources such as sponsorship, merchandizing, advertising and media rights, though, apart from signage on stadium roofs, this was not of significance before 1914. Then, there was *product improvement* which involved modifying the original sporting competition so as to attract larger audiences, either for one event or over a season. Such changes include the establishment of new competitions within the sport (as with establishment of county championship in cricket), or the introduction of play-offs for promotion from one division to another (as operated in the Football League for six seasons in 1890s). These add more events to the sporting calendar but do not change the essence of the traditional game. *Product development*, on the other hand, can drastically change the nature of a sport and the way in which it is played. In horse racing, long-distance heats gave way to sprints for two-year-old horses (where the result was much more uncertain) and in boxing bare-knuckled prize-fighting to exhaustion was superseded by gloved, time-limited contests (more attractive to spectators who had other demands on their time).

All this is conventional economic behaviour so what are the exceptions on which so much attention, perhaps disproportionately so, has been lavished? Competing firms in the normal economy do not need to collaborate to make a product, but as was remarked many years ago by a pioneering sports economist 'it's little economic use being world boxing champion if there is no-one to fight' (Neale 1964, 2). A dominant idea has been that team owners might not be seeking to maximize their income/profits and instead be looking to maximize what is labelled utility. In essence, they sought to win as many games and trophies as they could rather than concentrating on making profits. Within the parameters of not going bankrupt, utility maximizers will spend to create a winning team. Although this might attract more spectators and increase revenues, profit maximizers, however, are well aware that profit is not determined by revenue but by revenue minus costs. Conventional businesses might be concerned with controlling the margin between outlay and revenue, whereas the utility seeker might be willing to spend – sometimes at the risk of insolvency – to try to produce a winning team. In conventional businesses, cartels are frowned upon by the authorities, whereas in some sports, they are seen as necessary for survival. Although on-field competition is the lifeblood of elite sport, unrestrained competition off it is seen as detrimental. If the richest clubs can afford the best players, they will dominate the tournaments and results will become more predictable. If the 'uncertainty' hypothesis holds, then overall demand, i.e. attendances for the tournament's output will decline. This can only be offset by collaborative preventative measures. Hence, the league or other organization will operate as a cartel (a monopoly supplier of output) to restrict competition between clubs. This can involve centrally enforced agreements on such matters as the distribution of revenue (gate receipts were pooled in the early years of Football League); restricting the costs of inputs (such as introducing the maximum wage in English football 1900); and restraining the free flow of inputs by placing restrictions on player mobility (as with residential qualifications in county cricket and transfer payments in football) (Vamplew 2004, 112–153).

One major service ancillary to the game form was the print media which had a symbiotic relationship with sport, helping the latter publicize its product whilst gaining a readership from those interested in sport. In Britain, the abandonment of punitive taxes on newspapers, the emergence of a reading public in commercial proportions, and advances in transport, telegraph and printing technology all contributed to the development of a media industry with which sport could have a symbiotic relationship. Specialized sporting magazines existed in Britain from the late eighteenth-century but they were expensive, catered for a select market and were London based. They were joined in the 1860s by a cheaper product, also produced in the capital but aimed at a clerical and artisan market, with an emphasis on horse racing news. New titles were promoted in the provinces in the 1870s which concentrated on football, rugby, cricket, athletics and cycling. The next decade saw the publication of Saturday-night football special editions giving the afternoon's results. All this was in addition to the gradual intrusion of sport into the daily press (Mason 1986; Tate 2005).

Mass viewing of sport necessitated special spectator facilities. Grandstands had featured at racecourses and cricket grounds for those willing to pay an extra fee but regular large crowds justified the erection of stadia in which to hold events. Most academic literature on stadia has focussed on football in the post-Taylor Report period when anti-hooligan legislation forced changes in stadium design and, in some cases, actual relocation. Perhaps the best work covering pre-1914 stadia, though not academically referenced, is Inglis's (2005) study of the stadium designer/engineer Archibald Leitch. Sports geographer Bale, who introduced the concept of topophilia – love of place – into sport history has written on early football stadia and Paramio and his colleagues have summarized work on the first generation of football stadia, generally acknowledged to have been a British development (Bale 1993a, 124–125; Bale 1993b, 17–22; Paramio, Buraimo, and Campos 2008, 519–523). Clearly, there is a research gap for work on other sports.

Equipment manufacturers, the subject of Hardy's third category, were more concerned with the participant market than the spectator one. This market obtained a national dimension earlier than the spectator sports market which remained essentially a local or regional one. By 1914, there were in Britain alone some 350,000 golf club members and between

300,000 and 500,000 amateur soccer players, all requiring equipment of various kinds. The extent of the ancillary industry that this generated can be seen in the advertisements in the various golf and football annuals of the time. Tranter (1998, 75–77) has outlined some successes and failures among sports goods manufacturers in Victorian and Edwardian Britain including those producing cricket and golf balls, cycles, fishing tackle and guns as well as lawn and table tennis equipment. Supplying equipment was a 'profitable experience for many companies' though many small enterprises went to the wall as mass-production technology undermined the craftsman (Tranter 1998, 77). Selling such sports goods led to the emergence of specialist retailers epitomized by the rise of Gamage's to the self-titled 'world's largest sport and athletic outfitters' (Biddle-Perry 2014).[5]

One aspect of sport as an industry is that of employment, a neglected area of research. A fair amount is known about professional sportsmen; much less on the semi-professionals and very little on those that worked rather than played: the umpires and referees, the craftsmen who made the equipment or the groundsmen who sorted out the playing surfaces. Huggins (1991) has written on trainers in horseracing; Carter (2010) on football trainers; and Vamplew (2008b) on golf caddies.

What must not be forgotten in all this talk of economic factors, commercialization, investment, human capital formation, etc. is the role of agency in the promotion of sport both for spectators and participants. Several categories of investor/entrepreneur can be identified.

First, there were the conventional businessmen seeking profits. Football stadia and enclosed racecourses might be irrational economic projects in being vastly underutilized, but the people who built and designed them were conventional businessmen. A prime example would be football ground designer Archibald Leitch who was the architect and engineer responsible for at least 46 individual stands and pavilions in Britain between 1899 and 1939 (Inglis 2005). On a smaller scale were the golf professionals who ran their 'shop' at the golf club by whom they were retained and sought to earn money from making, repairing and selling golf equipment (Vamplew 2008a).

Others sought profits more indirectly. As well as the businessmen who patronized works teams as part of their industrial welfare policies, there were the penny capitalists and wealthier organizers of illegal off-course betting, cycle manufacturers who regarded the sponsoring of meetings and riders as a form of advertising, and those builders, caterers and sports outfitters who took shares in football clubs in the expectation of contracts (Tischler 1981; Huggins 2000; Huggins 2004). Another major group of football shareholders who looked to benefit indirectly was the drink and hospitality trade who hoped that fans would celebrate their victories or drown their sorrows in public houses and eateries owned by men who supported their club financially (Dixon, Garnham, and Jackson 2004, 517). Brewers William Younger bought Heart of Midlothian shares because of 'the benefit to the trade of customers in the neighbourhood' (William Younger Directors' Minute Books, 25 April 1905). Transport enterprises expected to benefit from sports passenger traffic and hence extended facilities to football grounds and race-tracks, occasionally also sponsoring races at the latter (Tolson and Vamplew 2003).

Second, there were those promoting sport hoping perhaps to cover their costs, sometimes utilizing profits rather than trying to maximize them. There were rentiers satisfied with the safe return rather than the high-risk, high-yield investment: such a group would include the shareholders who financed the Edgbaston cricket ground and felt that they were entitled to a fair return though their main objective was 'not to make dividends but to advance the interests and position of the county club' (Duckworth 1974, 19). Yet others were prepared to subsidize their local or county cricket team for reasons of civic pride, county allegiance or national jingoism with no thought of the sport being a commodity in the market place. Here, the founders of the Football League in England and the boards of the constituent clubs can be considered. In a way these can be compared to the early gamblers who promoted sport as a means to other ends. The new men, however, were looking for psychic income rather than economic rewards from gate revenue or gambling; they invested for civic pride rather than pocketbook (Collins 2007). Such non-profit maximizing behaviour can be found in other sports: county cricket clubs were dependent on the distribution of revenue from matches involving the national team to keep themselves afloat and horse racing existed only because owners were prepared to treat it as a hobby rather than a business (Sandiford and Vamplew 1986; Vamplew 2006). Some upper-class and middle-class expenditure can be viewed as consumption, sometimes of the conspicuous variety despite its apparent invest-ment nature. The net cost per kilogram of some game birds must have been high considering the establishment, maintenance and killing expenses (Durie 2008). Clearly, as in racehorse ownership, there was a strong social status element to the heavy expenditure involved. Other members of the middle class laid out substantial sums to purchase social exclusivity in their capital-intensive and land-extensive golf clubs (Vamplew 2012).

Finally, there were political promoters of sport. In Britain, in the late nineteenth century, the development of golf courses and recreational parks by local authorities were part of a wider movement in which the health and welfare of their electorates were served by the provision of municipally owned transport and utility companies (Vamplew 2008c, 1–2; Vamplew 2010, 370–371).

What apparently disappears is the promotion of sport by the professionals themselves. In the 1840s, various cricketing elevens toured Britain playing matches for a share of the gate which was distributed, not always equally, between the players. By the late nineteenth century, this could be seen only in such exhibitions as the footballing 'Zulus' and the like for charity matches (Curry 2004, 345–346). By the turn of the century, the authorities of the various sports were in full control and self-help professionalism was frowned upon. There was one major exception. The Professional Golfers' Association (formed in 1902) had by 1913 played a major role in establishing an incipient tour by organizing tournaments at national, regional and local level and actively seeking sponsorship for them (Holt, Lewis, and Vamplew 2002).

Industrial sport

Industrial sport is defined here as work-associated sport of which there are three main strands: work as sport, sport as work and workplace sport. The first is related to the demon-stration of work skills as in many traditional rural sports where participants were seeking employment or local kudos; the second, particularly professionalism in elite sport, has been the focus of most academic study; and the third, on which this section concentrates, has gen-erated relatively little interest from either sports or economic historians. The limited number of studies so far for pre-1914 cover selected industries (brewing: Collins and Vamplew 2002, 41–44), geographical areas (London, East Anglia and the West of Scotland: Munting 2003; Fitzgerald 2006; Heller 2008; McDowell 2012), occupations (clerks, dockworkers, gas workers: Fitzgerald 2006; Heller 2008), sports (tennis: Kay 2012), specific companies (Lever Brothers, Boots, Bryant and May, Cadbury, and Rowntree: Griffiths 1995; Parratt

1996; Bromhead 2000; Phillips 2004; Fitzgerald 2006) and a pan-Atlantic comparison of model factory landscapes (Chance 2012). Some of these are detailed studies of industrial recreation; others look at industrial welfare more generally but with some reference to sport and recreation.[6]

Nevertheless sufficient material has been published to allow some provisional hypotheses to be advanced. First, it was industrial in origin, but this was to be expected as agricultural enterprises rarely employed large numbers of workers,[7] and later developed in the service sector. In nineteenth-century Britain, several philanthropic employers, including choc-olate-makers, Cadbury and Rowntree, the chemist Boot and soap-manufacturer Lever, provided sports facilities for their workers and this seems to have spread across a range of industries by the early twentieth-century. In London, by the 1890s, many of the banks, railway companies, insurance firms and utility providers were offering sporting facilities to their employees including grounds, clubhouses, boating houses and rifle ranges (Heller 2008, 582). Regionally, in the north of England from the 1880s, there was a Manchester Business Houses Cross-Country Championships and pre-1914 cricket in the south encom-passed hospital teams and leagues for the music trades, newspapers and postal workers (Wigglesworth 1996, 108; Stone 2012, 198). Although most angling clubs grew out of pubs, some were sponsored by employers such as the railway companies in London and the steel firms in Sheffield, the two major centres of the sport (Lowerson 1988, 109). Kay's work on tennis mainly concerns the post-First World War period but she shows that even before that date, a few firms had introduced the sport: Lever Brothers' Port Sunlight works in Cheshire as well as Cadburys' Bournville factory had constructed tennis courts as early as 1897 and 1904 and several companies in the Norwich area offered the sport before 1914 (Lever Brothers Archive, *Progress* 1900, 382–383; Bournville Athletic Club 1946, 7; Munting 2003; Kay 2012).

Second, it can be suggested that company provision of sport can be categorized chrono-logically into a set of eras, each with persuasive driving forces. Two of these fall before the First World War.[8] The first is that of the philanthropic, often authoritarian, paternalistic family firm. Here, the provision of sport was often independent of other benefits. The start date of this phase is being pushed further back in time. When I worked on my book *Pay Up and Play the Game* back in the 1980s, the earliest reference to company sport that I found was Pilkingtons in the 1860s. Now Swain (2013, 153) has uncovered the provision of a bowling green and cricket field for the employees of Chadwick's Eagley Mills in Bolton in the 1830s. Another early example, again from Lancashire, was the opening of a gymnasium for workers at the Brookhouse Mills, Blackburn in 1841 for activities such as quoiting and skittles (*Preston Chronicle* August 28, 1841, quoting the *Blackburn Standard*. Information provided by Peter Swain). In Scotland, there was a shinty match in February 1852 between two calico works owned by the brothers Alexander and John Orr-Ewing (McDowell 2014, 548).

Fitzgerald (2006, 50) dates the termination of this phase, perhaps too precisely at 1880, but certainly from around that time joint stock company formation, more complex man-agerial structures, and increased labour militancy including the rise of 'New Unionism' paved the way for a switch from family firm 'caring paternalism' to formal company wel-fare provision, offered to workers as part of 'long-term managerial policies towards work-forces beyond that of the market relationship of the wage contract'. The demarcation line between the two phases is not hard and fast – no doubt there were still small firm 'caring paternalists' in the 1890s – but corporate welfare was becoming the more significant form of welfare provision. As firms became bigger and organization of production more complex, the workplace face-to-face contact between employer and worker was severed, and, although conscientious management might offset this loss of direct contact, generally the relationship between managers and staff became more impersonal. Loyalty to the enterprise became of increased importance as new technology led to interdependent continuous production processes in which stoppages and strikes in one department could close down a whole factory: Indeed 'loyalty' became the overarching ideology at Lever Brothers (Griffiths 1995, 33). And there was a danger of strikes as labour became more militant. Although the extent of 'New Unionism' among the unskilled and semi-skilled workers should not be exaggerated, there is no doubt that a strike by their matchmakers in 1888 forced Bryant and May towards a welfare policy which included sporting clubs (Fitzgerald 2006, 56). Whether developments further to this response were a cause of the winding up of the Matchmakers Union in 1903 is conjectural (Fitzgerald 2006, 58). Other firms, such as the London gas suppliers, the Gas Light and Coke Company and the South Metropolitan Gas Company, too moved into welfare provision to offset the growing influence of the unions (Melling 1979, 168–171; Fitzgerald 2006, 53). The Thames Ironworks F.C. (later West Ham United) was started by the foundry owner shortly after a major strike and was part of a programme to improve 'co-operation between workers and management' (Korr 1978). Certainly, despite their humanitarianism, even Levers saw welfare provision as a weapon in their 'desire to defeat unionism' (Griffiths 1995, 35). In phase two, sport often came as part of a strategic welfare package along with pension schemes, savings banks and other economic benefits. By this time of course, many businessmen accepted that sport was respectable, having shed its earlier association with violence and animal brutality.

The timing of particular firms opting to provide welfare and recreation facilities would be influenced by the circumstances of the industrial sector of which they were part and also by the ideologies of the company leadership. Munting cautions against generalizing from the experience of Cadburys and Rowntree, even for Quaker entrepreneurs and it is apposite to note Child's comment that 'devoutness was no guarantee of philanthropy' (Munting 2003, 56; Child cited in Fitzgerald 2006, 62). Certainly, the Quakers who ran Bryant and May were not philosophically inclined to be humane employers. It took labour militancy for them to offer welfare provision: it was a concession rather than an initiative. Dunbartonshire calico producer, Alexander Wylie saw workers' sport as a means of self-improvement maintaining that 'recreation of the proper sort, following moderate work, helps to make a man in as much as it brings into play, and develops those faculties that would otherwise remain dormant ...'. He advocated muscular Christianity and the 'encouragement of that manly, brave, thoroughly fair and gentlemanly demeanour in games which has characterised the youth of so many of our public schools'. Similarly Scottish shipbuilder William Denny, another supporter of muscular Christianity, saw sport promoting 'manliness' which he defined as 'a readiness to meet any emergency frankly and courageously' (McDowell 2014, 552–553). William Lever, founder of company town Port Sunlight, was, according to his son, a 'humanitarian coupled with enlightened self-interest' who believed that a healthier and more educated labour force would also be a more productive one (Griffiths 1995, 26). George Cadbury and his brother Richard were both keen sportsmen themselves and sometimes played cricket or football with men from their chocolate factory for the sheer enjoyment, but, additionally, they felt that a healthy workforce was a better workforce and hence made available facilities for sporting activity for both male and female workers (Bromhead 2000, 98–107).

It can of course never be established whether all this was just rhetoric. Nor can we ever be sure whether the workers accepted the views of the employers or simply accepted the facilities and other support whilst ignoring the moral improvement aspects of patronage. It should be stressed that, unlike agricultural work and early factories distant from towns, most patrons could not control the lives of their workers and insist on church attendance and other obligations. Even playing sport was a voluntary activity. A third unknown is where the initiative came from. The prevailing view among business historians is that the provision was a management strategy designed to encourage loyalty to the firm but, in his review of some works-based sport after 1918, Crewe argues that it was often the workers who initiated, organized and sustained clubs, albeit with financial and logistical support from their employers (Crewe 2014, 544).

A third hypothesis is that there is no single all-encompassing model of workplace sport. The following typology of provision is suggested as a guide for analysis.

(1) Provision of facilities and control of affairs.
(2) Provision but non-managerial patronage. McDowell argues that the paternalistic employers in the coalfields and industrial areas of the West of Scotland typically operated in association with the clubs and teams that they financed rather than in a controlling management capacity (McDowell 2012). Here too, there might be a limit to the employer's generosity, as at Rowntrees in York where playing fields and changing facilities were provided but, apart from occasional donations, the financial responsibility for the sports clubs was left to the members as the firm did not want the labour force to become overly dependent on their employers (Parratt 1996, 63).
(3) Provision of multi-sport facilities. This came late with breweries but Boots, Cadbury and Levers all had such facilities by the turn of the century. The latter as attachments to the almost self-contained communities which they had established at Port Sunlight and Bourneville, respectively (Bromhead 2000; Phillips 2004, 110).
(4) Sponsorship solely of a works team. This as was common in the breweries before the First World War (Collins and Vamplew 2002, 41–44).
(5) Provision of facilities for community use. Some employers did not go so far as to establish workplace sport but still felt physical recreation could be beneficial for their workers. In Dunbartonshire, the calico producers, Alexander Wylie and brothers Alexander and John Orr-Ewing, provided grounds for local football teams to use as 'a gift to their communities' (McDowell 2014, 550). As dominant employers in the relevant local communities, it is more than likely that their workers played in teams using those facilities. This raises the question of why they did not go one step further and organize works teams as such. One possibility is that, despite their sense of duty to the community, they felt that they might not be able to exert sufficient control over a works club. Certainly in the case of the Dunbartonshire manufacturers, they did raise works-based Volunteer Forces in which they became commanding officers and their managers became officers; thus, they were able to exercise more influence over the leisure activities of their employees (McDowell 2014, 553).
(6) Provision of playing facilities in return for services rendered as exemplified by some artisan golf clubs. The rapid expansion of golf clubs from 1880 led to a labour shortage in some areas where clubs established artisans' clubs as part of a socio-economic transaction between the parent club and local workmen in which the latter gained playing rights, at greatly reduced fees and under strict conditions, in exchange for undertaking maintenance tasks around the course (Lowerson 1995, 143; Vamplew 2010, 368–369).
(7) Provision of annual events such as factory sports days for workers and golf competitions organized by golf clubs for their caddies. The former served to establish a company

tradition and indeed became almost ritualized in their organization, incorporating events for family members as well as the workforce (Phillips 2004, 112–113).

The extent of workplace sport before 1914 can only be speculated on. The few figures that have come to light for the pre-1914 period are indicative of workplace sport not yet being a significant element of aggregate adult sport. Of the cricket and football teams mentioned in the Birmingham press between 1876 and 1884, only 11.7 and 9.2%, respectively, had workplace names (Holt 1988, 74). A similar press trawl for eight northern towns revealed proportions of 5.0 and 5.7% for cricket and football in 1900 and 6.1 and 5.9% in 1914 (Williams 1996, 123–124). The highest figure was 20% for Burnley football teams in 1900 but we are talking only of 4 clubs in total. Only five of the other 31 measures topped 10%.[9] The real era of workplace sport is probably the interwar years, perhaps extending up to the 1970s. Nevertheless, the pre-1914 teams can be seen as a precursor of what was to come when neighbourhood and workplace became increasingly separated.

I am beginning to work in this area by using the extant literature to create a typology as a mechanism for evaluating of the workplace as a stimulus to sporting activity. It will suggest that key variables to be considered will include the type and size of business, whether the initiative – and later the ongoing management and organization – came from the employer or the workforce, what sports were offered and what facilities were provided, whether the sports were open to the wider community, the motivation for development and participation, and, as I am a historian, the chronology of the development.

Work-based sport is an unrewarding topic to research as each case study is just another brick in the wall. What is really needed is a collective research project where the wall gets constructed more quickly. It ought to be done as such sport, especially in the days when there was no sports provision in state schools, might have been the way in which many young adults were introduced to formal, organized sport. Company sport provision could have been important for a sizeable section of the population as it offered opportunities to lower income households to take part in activities that otherwise might have been beyond their means. Workplace sport also had gender implications in that it often offered facilities to both men and women. Admittedly, the range of sports offered was less than for the men but nevertheless there was opportunity for females to play sport.[10] This may be an avenue that has not been appreciated by those writers declaiming the obstacles to female participation in sport in late Victorian and Edwardian Britain. It may turn out that there was more female sports participation than had previously been believed. Perhaps Hill (2002, 5) was too quick to dismiss company sport as 'relatively peripheral'.

Notes

1. For a fuller discussion of pre-industrial work patterns, see Vamplew (2004, 21–24.
2. See concluding section.
3. It should be noted that participant and spectatorship may have required different environments for their development.
4. Where Harvey might be on stronger ground is in his assertion that there was a major expansion in sporting activity in Manchester, the cotton capital of Britain. Without urbanization and the associated concentration of population, there could be no mass market for regular spectator sport. The vast population of London had long stimulated commercialized leisure (including sport) for a mass market (Brailsford 1969, 215–217).
5. See also Williams (2015).

6. What might also be counted as workplace sport is that provided by the army though this will not be discussed here. See Mason and Riedi (2010) and Vamplew (2014).
7. Some eighteenth-century, cricket-loving aristocrats employed gardeners and other servants for their talents as cricketers but there is no evidence that any teams raised were full of workers from their estate (Underdown 2000, 69).
8. Work is still in progress to determine the other periods. These will be presented at the International Economic History Conference in Kyoto, August 2015.
9. Within the factories and plants, there is also a lack of detail on membership figures. Even in the well-documented archives of Boots, there is a 'lack of quantitative ... material detailing membership for the many clubs and societies' (Phillips 2004, 116). However, we do know that membership of the Bourneville Athletic Club was 1248 in 1913/14 (Cadbury Archive, *1896 and All That*, 10).
10. For a detailed study of recreation for women at one factory and the motivation behind its introduction see Parratt (1996).

Disclosure statement

No potential conflict of interest was reported by the author.

References

Bale, J. 1993a. "The Spatial Development of the Modern Stadium." *International Review for the Sociology of Sport* 28 (2–3): 121–133.
Bale, J. 1993b. *Sport, Space and the City*. London: Routledge.
Biddle-Perry, G. 2014. "The Rise of 'The World's Largest Sport and Athletic Outfitter': A Study of Gamage's of Holborn, 1878–1913." *Sport in History* 34 (2): 295–317.
Bourg, J.-F., and J.-J. Gouguet. 2005. *Economie du Sport*. La Découverte. Translated and cited in Szymanski, 'A Theory of the Evolution of Modern Sport'. Paris.
Bourneville Athletic Club. 1946. *1896 and All That: 50 Years of the Bourneville Athletic Club, 1896–1946*. Birmingham: Bourneville Athletic Club.
Brailsford, D. 1969. *Sport and Society: Elizabeth to Anne*. London: Routledge and Kegan Paul.
Brailsford, D. 1991. *Sport, Time and Society*. London: Routledge.
Bromhead, J. 2000. "George Cadbury's Contribution to Sport." *The Sports Historian* 20: 97–117.
Carter, N. 2010. "The Rise and Fall of the Magic Sponge: Medicine and the Transformation of the Football Trainer." *Social History of Medicine* 23 (2): 261–279.
Chance, H. 2012. "Mobilising the Modern Industrial Landscape for Sports and Leisure in the Early Twentieth Century." *The International Journal of the History of Sport* 29 (11): 1600–1625.
Collins, T. 2007. "Review Article: Work, Rest and Play: Recent Trends in the History of Sport and Leisure." *Journal of Contemporary History* 42: 397–410.
Collins, T., J. Martin, and W. Vamplew, eds. 2005. *Encyclopedia of British Traditional Rural Sports*. Abingdon: Routledge.
Collins, T., and W. Vamplew. 2002. *Mud, Sweat and Beers: A Cultural History of Sport and Alcohol*. Oxford: Berg.
Crewe, S. 2014. "What About the Workers? Works-based Sport and Recreation in England c.1918–c.1970." *Sport in History* 34 (4): 544–568.
Cronin, M. 2014. *Sport: A Very Short Introduction*. Oxford: Oxford University Press.
Cunningham, H. 1980. *Leisure in the Industrial Revolution*. London: Croom Helm.
Curry, G. 2004. "Playing for Money: James J. Lang and Emergent Soccer Professionals in Sheffield." *Soccer and Society* 5 (3): 336–355.
Dixon, P., N. Garnham, and A. Jackson. 2004. "Shareholders and Shareholding: The Case of the Football Company in Late Victorian England." *Business History* 46 (4): 503–524.
Duckworth, L. 1974. *The Story of Warwickshire Cricket*. London: Stanley Paul.
Durie, A. J. 2008. "Game Shooting: An Elite Sport c .1870–1980." *Sport in History* 28 (3): 431–449.
Fitzgerald, R. 2006. "Employers' Labour Strategies, Industrial Welfare, and the Response to New Unionism at Bryant and May, 1888–1930." *Business History* 31 (2): 48–65.

Griffiths, J. 1995. "'Give my Regards to Uncle Billy...': The Rites and Rituals of Company Life at Lever Brothers, c.1900-c.1990[1]." *Business History* 37 (4): 25-45.

Guttmann, A. 2004. *From Ritual to Record: The Nature of Modern Sports*. New York: Columbia University Press.

Hardy, S. 1986. "Entrepreneurs, Organizations and the Sport Marketplace: Subjects in Search of Historians." *Journal of Sport History* 13 (1): 14-33.

Harvey, A. 2004. *The Beginnings of a Commercial Sporting Culture in Britain, 1793-1850*. Aldershot: Ashgate.

Heller, M. 2008. "Sport, Bureaucracies and London Clerks 1880-1939." *The International Journal of the History of Sport* 25 (5): 579-614.

Hill, J. 2002. *Sport, Leisure and Culture in Twentieth-Century Britain*. Basingstoke: Palgrave.

Holt, R. J. 1988. "Football and the Urban Way of Life in Nineteenth-Century Britain." In *Pleasure, Profit, Proselytism: British Culture and Sport at Home and Abroad 1700-1914*, edited by J. A. Mangan, 67-85. London: Cass.

Holt, R., P. N. Lewis, and W. Vamplew. 2002. *The Professional Golfers Association 1901-2001*. Worcestershire: Grant.

Huggins, M. 1991. "Kings of the Moor; Yorkshire Racehorse Trainers 1760-1900." Teesside University Papers in North Eastern History.

Huggins, M. 2000. "The First Generation of Street Bookmakers in Victorian England: Demonic Fiends or 'Decent Fellers'?" *Northern History* 36: 129-145.

Huggins, M. 2004. *The Victorians and Sport*. London: Hambledon and London.

Inglis, S. 2005. *Engineering Archie*. Swindon: English Heritage.

Kay, J. 2012. "Grass Roots: The Development of Tennis in Britain, 1918-1978." *The International Journal of the History of Sport* 29 (18): 2532-2550.

Korr, C. P. 1978. "West Ham United Football Club and the Beginnings of Professional Football in East London, 1895-1914." *Journal of Contemporary History* 13: 211-232.

Lowerson, J. 1995. *Sport and the English Middle Classes 1870-1914*. Manchester, NH: Manchester University Press.

Lowerson, J. 1988. "Brothers of the Angle: Coarse Fishing and English Working-Class Culture, 1850-1914." In *Pleasure, Profit, Proselytism: British Culture and Sport at Home and Abroad 1700-1914*, edited by J. A. Mangan, 105-127. London: Cass.

McDowell, M. L. 2012. "Football, Migration and Industrial Patronage in the West of Scotland, c.1870-1900." *Sport in History* 32 (3): 405-425.

McDowell, M. L. 2014. "'Social Physical Exercise?' Football, Industrial Paternalism, and Professionalism in West Dunbartonshire, Scotland, c.1870-1900." *Labor History* 55 (5): 547-562.

Malcolmson, R. 1975. *Popular Recreations in English Society 1770-1850*. Cambridge: Cambridge University Press.

Mason, T. 1986. "Sporting News, 1860-1914." In *The Press in English Society from the Seventeenth to Nineteenth Centuries*, edited by M. Harris and A. J. Lee, 168-186. Cranbury, NJ: Associated University Presses.

Mason, T., and E. Riedi. 2010. *Sport and the Military*. Cambridge: Cambridge University Press.

Melling, J. 1979. "Industrial Strife and Business Welfare Philosophy: The Case of the South Metropolitan Gas Company from the 1880s to the War." *Business History* 21 (2): 163-179.

Munting, R. 2003. "The Games Ethic and Industrial Capitalism Before 1914: The Provision of Company Sports." *Sport in History* 23: 45-63.

Neale, W. C. 1964. "The Peculiar Economics of Professional Sports: A Contribution to the Theory of the Firm in Sporting Competition and in Market Competition." *The Quarterly Journal of Economics* 78: 1-14.

Paramio, J. L., B. Buraimo and C. Campos. 2008. "From Modern to Postmodern: The Development of Football Stadia in Europe." *Sport in Society* 11 (5): 517-534.

Parratt, C. M. 1996. "'The Making of the Healthy and the Happy Home' Recreation, Education, and the Production of Working-Class Womanhood at the Rowntree Cocoa Works, York, c.1898-1914". In *Sport and Identity in the North of England*, edited by J. Hill and J. Williams, 53-84. Keele: Keele University Press.

Phillips, S. 2004. "'Fellowship in Recreation, Fellowship in Ideals': Sport, Leisure and Culture at Boots Pure Drug Company, Nottingham.1883–1945[1]." *Midland History* 29 (1): 107–123.

Sandiford, K., and W. Vamplew. 1986. "The Peculiar Economics of English Cricket before 1914." *The International Journal of the History of Sport* 3 (3): 311–326.

Stone, D. 2012. "'It's All Friendly Down There': The Cricket Club Conference, Amateurism and the Cultural Meaning of Cricket in the South of England." *Sport and Society* 15 (2): 194–208.

Swain, P. 2013. "'Bolton Against All England for a Cool Hundred': Crown Green Bowls in South Lancashire, 1787–1914." *Sport in History* 33 (2): 146–168.

Szymanski, S. 2008. "A Theory of the Evolution of Modern Sport." *Journal of Sport History* 35 (1): 1–32.

Tate, S. 2005. "James Catton, 'Tityrus' of The Athletic News (1860 to 1936): A Biographical Study." *Sport in History* 25 (1): 98–115.

Tischler, S. 1981. *Footballers and Businessmen*. New York: Holmes and Meier.

Tolson, J., and W. Vamplew. 2003. "Facilitation Not Revolution: Railways and British Flat Racing 1830–1914." *Sport in History* 23 (1): 89–106.

Tomlinson, A., and C. Young. 2011. "Towards a New History of European Sport." *European Review* 19: 487–507.

Tranter, N. 1998. *Sport, Economy and Society in Britain 1750–1914*. Cambridge: Cambridge University Press.

Underdown, D. 2000. *Start of Play: Cricket and Culture in Eighteenth-Century England*. London: Allen Lane.

Vamplew, W. 1988. "Sport and Industrialization: An Economic Interpretation of the Changes in Popular Sport in Nineteenth- Century England." In *Pleasure, Profit, Proselytism: British Culture and Sport at Home and Abroad 1700–1914*, edited by J. A. Mangan, 7–20. London: Cass.

Vamplew, W. 2004. *Pay Up and Play the Game*. Cambridge: Cambridge University Press.

Vamplew, W. 2006. "The Economics of British Horseracing." In *Handbook on the Economics of Sport*, edited by W. Andreff and S. Szymanski, 374–378. Cheltenham: Edward Elgar.

Vamplew, W. 2008a. "Successful Workers or Exploited Labour? Golf Professionals and Professional Golfers in Britain 1888–1914." *The Economic History Review* 61: 54–79.

Vamplew, W. 2008b. "Childwork or Child Labour? The Caddie Question in Edwardian Golf". www.idrottsforum.

Vamplew, W. 2008c. "'Remembering Us Year After Year': The Glasgow Charity Cup 1876–1966." *Recorde* 1 (2): 1–27.

Vamplew, W. 2010. "Sharing Space: Inclusion, Exclusion, and Accommodation at the British Golf Club Before 1914." *Journal of Sport & Social Issues* 34 (3): 359–375.

Vamplew, W. 2012. "Concepts of Capital: An Approach Shot to the History of the British Sports Club before 1914." *Journal of Sport History* 39 (2): 299–331.

Vamplew, W. 2014. "Exploding the Myths of Sport and the Great War: A First Salvo." *The International Journal of the History of Sport* 31 (18): 2297–2312.

Vamplew, W. Forthcoming. "Industrialization". In *The Oxford Handbook to Sports History*, edited by W. Wilson and R. Edelmann. New York: Oxford University Press.

Wigglesworth, N. 1996. *The Evolution of English Sport*. London: Cass.

Williams, J. 1996. "Churches, Sports and Identities in the North, 1900–1939." In *Sport and Identity in the North of England*, edited by J. Hill and J. Williams, 113–136. Keele: Keele University Press.

Williams, J. 2015. "Kit: Fashioning the Sporting Body – Introduction to the Special Edition." *Sport in History* 35 (1): 1–18.

Young, A. 1771. *Farmer's Tour Through the East of England*. No publisher IV, 391.

'It is pleasing to know that football can be devoted to charitable purposes': British football and charity 1870–1918

Wray Vamplew

ABSTRACT

Football charity matches and tournaments played a significant role in the development of the sport in Britain, overlapping the era of friendly games and the coming of competitive leagues. The football community prided itself on its contributions to charity, raising more money than any other sport before 1918, and stakeholders within the game – associations, clubs, players and patrons – gained kudos for this perceived altruism. However the amounts donated, though welcomed by the recipients, were relatively minor sources of revenue for both institutions and individuals. Moreover the charity match became less important to clubs in an era of growing professionalism and commercialisation.

Comment

Sport and charity are major British institutions with significant resources devoted to their activities but which in the main are not profit-driven. However, they are linked by more than their 'peculiar economics': charity makes use of sports stars and sports events to raise revenue and sport itself has over 150,000 charitable organisations within its ranks. Yet the connection between the two remains largely unexplored save for a growing academic literature on corporate social responsibility (CSR) in modern sport.[1]

However the relationship between sport and charity is a longstanding one. The 1840s and 1850s saw horseracing authorities establish the Bentinck and Rous Funds to offer aid to distressed jockeys. Aristocratic shoots often presented game to local hospitals and a Hunt Servants Benefit Society was set up in the 1870s: by the Edwardian era 'field sports ... (had developed) ... hand in hand with the charitable and the philanthropic' (Salt 1906, 490). Alongside traditional rural-based sports the late nineteenth century witnessed the rapid development of commercialised, urban-based, mass spectator sports and a consequent new relationship between sport and charity. Regular fixtures provided opportunities for frequent charitable collections and the increased number of sports professionals employed led to the emergence of yet more benevolent organisations to look after their interests such as the Professional Golfers' Association (from 1901) and the Association Football Players' Union (from 1907).

The antecedents to football's involvement in CSR can be traced to late nineteenth-century charity matches and tournaments by which clubs and associations raised money for hospitals, homes and other 'good causes'. They began as a symbiotic relationship in which charities obtained funds and the clubs gained meaningful competitive games at a time when fixture lists were dominated by friendly matches. However, even when leagues, at both the elite and local level, developed such competitions continued. By 1914 there were over 100 regular charity tournaments in Britain including the Glasgow Charity Cup (which from 1874 to its demise in 1966) raised the present day equivalent of over £12 million) and the Charity Shield (founded in 1908, now significantly renamed the Community Shield).[2] Additionally throughout the period to 1914 one-off matches were often staged in the aftermath of tragedies such as mining disasters, railway crashes, and the sinking of the *Titanic*.

This is a revised and expanded version of an article authored by Joyce Kay and myself titled 'Beyond altruism: British football and charity 1877–1914' originally published in *Soccer and Society*, vol. 11, no. 10 (2010), 181–197. I applied for grants to pursue this topic further but was unsuccessful. Perhaps it was not an appealing topic, though I hazard a guess that my criticism of 'charitable' trusts did not go down well with some awarding bodies, themselves holding that status. Thanks go the Nuffield Foundation and the Professional Footballers' Association for financial assistance towards the research costs of this paper and the staff of the National Football Museum, Preston and the Scottish Football Museum, Glasgow for access to research materials.

Introduction

Ten minutes into the 1902 football international between Scotland and England at Ibrox Park, Glasgow, a wooden stand collapsed plunging spectators 40 feet through the broken boards. Twenty-six of them were killed and over 500 injured (Sheils 1997). It was Britain's first football disaster. In Scotland the Scottish Football Association (SFA) immediately subscribed £3000 to the Lord Provost's relief fund and, via the Glasgow Charity Cup Committee, broadened that end-of-season tournament 'under the exceptional circumstances' to increase the number of games and include teams from Edinburgh in an attempt to secure more funds for the relief of victims and their families (*Annual Reports of SFA*, 1901/02; Minutes of GCCC, April 17, 1902). In England the Football Association (FA) opened a relief fund with a donation of £500; requested clubs to play games to supplement that money; and arranged a special international match against Scotland with the gross proceeds going to the fund. In all £3000 was raised (Minutes of FA Council, April 18, 1902, August 8, 1902).

In providing aid to those killed and injured at a football match both Associations were doing what might have been expected, but there were occasions when their generosity went beyond the boundaries of the game. On its maiden voyage in April 1912 the British passenger liner *Titanic* struck an iceberg and sank off Newfoundland with the loss of over 1500 lives. The immediate reaction of the FA was to donate 200 guineas to the relief fund organised by the Lord Mayor of London; promise to add the gross receipts of its Charity Shield match; and appeal to all affiliated clubs and associations to hold collections or arrange special matches. In total £2235 was raised (Minutes of FA Council, April 19, 1912, June 3, 1912). Such generosity to the unfortunate outside football was not unprecedented. In 1897 the FA had given £157, the whole proceeds of an international trial match, to the Mansion House Indian Famine Relief Fund and two years later it subscribed 100 guineas for the benefit of those widowed, orphaned or wounded as a result of the South African War as well as declaring a 'Football Saturday' on which it 'invited' all affiliated clubs and associations to donate a minimum 10% of gate receipts from matches played on that day (Minutes of FA Council, March 1, 1897, December 18, 1899).

Throughout Britain regional associations and individual clubs often responded to local disasters and tragedies by playing matches or allowing collections to be made. The Lancashire FA organised matches to help the families of those killed in the county's major mining disasters at Altham (1883), Maypole (1908) and Pretoria (1910); the victims of the latter were also assisted by Chelsea, West Ham, Leicester Fosse and the Football League itself which raised £1200 (Minutes of FA Consultative Committee, January 16, 1911; Bentley 1912, 390; Sutcliffe and Hargreaves 1992, 278). Three years later the gross receipts of £391 from the FA Charity Shield match was given to the sufferers of the Senghennydd colliery explosion in Wales in which 439 miners were killed (Minutes of FA Consultative Committee, February 21, 1910; Minutes of FA Council, November 3, 1913). In 1883 Dumbarton played Rangers to raise funds for the victims of the Daphne tragedy in which almost 200 workers perished in the hull of a ship that capsized on launch at its Glasgow shipyard (Goldblatt 2006, 70). Everton played a game in 1910 for the relief of the families of those lost when the steam packet *Ellan Vannin* sank in Liverpool Bay and Exeter one the following year for the victims of the Brixham fishing fleet disaster (Minutes of FA Consultative Committee, January 17, 1910; January 16, 1911).

Disaster funds were only part of the connection between philanthropy and football. In an age of limited state intervention, Victorian social welfare was founded on private charitable enterprise: orphanages, hospitals and convalescent homes all relied on regular voluntary subscriptions and donations, while economic depression and unemployment were alleviated by privately-resourced soup kitchens and distress relief funds. Football contributed to all these. In May 1877 Glasgow Rangers played a match which raised £30 in aid of the unemployed in the weaving village of Newmilns (*Glasgow Evening Times*, May 21, 1877). In season 1878/79 a charity tournament was played under electric light, which, although the illumination was 'far from what was desired', raised £50 for the Glasgow Unemployed Fund (*SFA Annual*, 1879–80, 25). In 1893 Everton played a match to raise funds to help the destitute families of cotton trade operatives thrown out of work leading the *Athletic News* to comment 'it is pleasing to know that football can be devoted to charitable purposes' (*Athletic News*, February 6, 1891, 1). The following season Walsall played a match for the Mayor's Distress Fund (Minutes of FA Council, February 14, 1894). In 1908, when the West of Scotland faced its worst industrial slump since the 1870s with unemployment rising to over 20%, the Glasgow Charity Cup Committee (GCCC) gave £200 to the Glasgow Unemployed Distress Relief Fund, and £25 for the same cause in Govan and Partick, while the SFA donated £500 to similar funds throughout Scotland (Minutes of GCCC, May 13, 1908; Minutes of SFA, November 17, 1908). Distress was relieved by matches and collections at games for local soup kitchens in Fulham and Portsmouth; to aid the poor boys of Manchester (Minutes of FA Emergency Committee, September 5–30, 1895); to provide Christmas dinners for destitute children; and to house waifs and strays at Millwall (Minutes of FA Council, December 6, 1909; December 5, 1910; Minutes of FA Consultative Committee, January 17, 1910; February 21, 1910). Many matches were also played to raise money for local hospitals and it was these that provided the rationale for the emergence of regular tournaments rather than the one-off reactive event. At the end of the 1880s there were at least 23 Scottish charity competitions of note being played and on the eve of the First World War over 200 in England.[3]

The War itself offered further opportunities for charitable actions by those involved in football. The FA immediately donated £1000 to the National Relief Fund inaugurated by the Prince of Wales, recommended all associations, clubs, and competitions to make a grant, and authorised matches to be played during the forthcoming season to raise further money. An additional £250 was given to the Belgian Relief Fund. The body urged all those interested in the game to volunteer for the forces or to help 'in all possible ways' and 'to those who are unable to render personal assistance the Association would appeal for their generous support of the funds for the relief and assistance of the dependents of those who are engaged in serving their country.' North of the border the Scottish Football League subscribed £300 to the National Relief Fund (Minutes of FA Consultative Committee, August 31, 1914; Crampsey 1990, 57). As the war progressed associations such as the Hampshire FA set up wounded soldiers funds and the sectionalised Football League raised £4722 for war charities and the London Combination £840 (*Gamage's Football Annual*, 1919–20, 364; Pickford 1937, 83).

Stakeholders

Several groups had an interest in the football/charity relationship, not least the charities themselves who were concerned with obtaining funds to finance their activities. Football associations authorised, and sometimes organised, charity matches; clubs and their players participated in the games; patrons provided trophies and lent status; and fans paid to watch, thus funding the charities.

Associations

The pioneering association in organising regular charity competitions was the SFA which, three years after its foundation in 1873, was so confident that it had become 'a very prominent public institution' and that the matches held under its auspices had given considerable pleasure to thousands of spectators, felt that it would be 'a graceful as well as a rightful act … to close the season with a match for the benefit of some Charitable Institution.' A game was accordingly played in April 1876 between Glasgow and Dumbartonshire which raised £100 for the Glasgow Western Infirmary (*Scottish Football Association Annual*, 1876–77, 27, 45).[4] Around the same time a group of Glasgow merchants also organised a charity football contest, but by 1878 the two competitions had merged into one which was run by the GCCC, a joint board of merchants and SFA representatives. It was suggested by a contemporary sporting newspaper that this tournament acted as a catalyst for the wider development of charity matches as the fund-raising success of the Glasgow Charity Cup competition proved to have 'the power of a magnet … so that [by 1880] a season without its charity games would present the same spectacle as a man without his nose' (*Athletic News*, April 14, 1880, 3).

The Glasgow Association (founded 1884) did not sponsor a charity competition, although it gave its blessing to those hosted by local associations within its jurisdiction. It may have seen little point in competing with the one already established by the SFA (with whom it shared a secretary, several committee members, and office premises) given that the trophy was generally restricted to the leading Glasgow and West of Scotland clubs. In 1886 a Rangers' spokesman asked the SFA what steps could be taken by the Glasgow Association to get the Glasgow Charity Cup under its control. He was told that only the GCCC could consider the matter and nothing further eventuated (Minutes of SFA, March 9, 1886).

Several other leading regional associations followed the Glasgow Charity Cup example. When, in September 1878, Lord Wharncliffe offered a cup to the Sheffield Association (founded 1871) 'to serve the interests of Sheffield footballers' it was decided to accept the proposal of the secretary that it be for a competition in aid of medical charities 'on the custom in favour at Glasgow' (*Athletic News*, September 11, 1878, 6; Sparling 1926, 49). Similarly N.L. Jackson, a member of the FA Council, claimed that when he persuaded Sir Reginald Hanson, Lord Mayor of London and patron of the London FA (founded 1882), to present a charity trophy in 1886 for competition among the London clubs it was 'in imitation of Glasgow' with hopes of 'similar success' (Jackson 1900, 153). This tournament came under the management of the London FA (Jackson 1932, 99). It had already been noted by a Scottish critic that there were charity competitions in all the principal cities in England but that in London 'the idea has not been deemed worthy of adoption' (*Scottish Athletic News*, May 4, 1883, 4). Whether this barb was aimed at the London FA or the national organisation based in the city is not clear.

Of the other two major English associations, the Birmingham and District FA (founded 1875) began a charity competition in 1880 which became the Mayor of Birmingham's Charity Cup in 1882 and it is possible that it too was influenced by the Glasgow precedent, given the close relationship between itself and its Glasgow counterpart which included regular inter-association fixtures (Green 1953, 55). The Lancashire FA was established in 1878 but it was four constituent clubs that set up the major regional charity tournament, the East Lancashire Charity Cup in 1882 (Baron 1906, 22). Three of these clubs were known to have played matches in Glasgow.

In contrast to other major associations, the FA itself was late in instituting its own charity competition, the Charity Shield not being played for until 1908. However it did become involved with the holding of three Charity Football Festivals held annually at the Kennington Oval in London from 1886, the first of which, along with an associated smoking concert, raised £405. Unusually these featured both football and rugby matches (FA Balance Sheet, August 31, 1886; Wilson 1981, 12; Jackson 1900, 65). The FA had first become involved in charity donations in 1882 when an above-expected FA Cup semi-final gate in the match between Blackburn Rovers and Sheffield Wednesday led it to allocate £70 to the charities of the two towns, the money to be distributed by the respective mayors (Green 1953, 66). Three years later, on the recommendation of its Finance Committee donations of either £25 or £50 were sent for distribution to charities in towns where the largest receipts had been taken by the Association in matches (FA Balance Sheet, August 31, 1886). However from then on there were no specific donations cited in the balance sheets until one to the Indian Famine Relief Fund in 1897. In essence the FA adopted a policy of keeping football's charitable activities under control without becoming seriously involved in fund-raising itself until 1908, apart from the occasional foray to support victims of major disasters such as the Indian Famine and the Ibrox stand collapse.

The establishment of the FA Charity Shield stemmed from a major dispute with amateur clubs when several of them refused to accept an FA ruling that the associations to which they belonged must accept membership and responsibility for professional clubs in their area and in 1907 broke away to form the Amateur Football Association. The FA then ruled that any team that played against one of the renegades would itself be liable for disaffiliation. When the organisers of the Sheriff of London charity competition, begun in 1898, asked if they were still free to chose the teams to play for their trophy, traditionally a match between a professional and an amateur side, even if one of them was not affiliated to the FA, they were told that this would be against FA policy but that the Council was 'most anxious that the cause of charity should not suffer, and would be pleased to arrange with the Committee for a match between two teams of this association, either club teams or selected teams' (Minutes of FA Council, November 4, 1907). No more was heard from the Sheriff of London Committee till March 1908 when it asked for, and was given, consent for a match between Queen's Park from Glasgow and a professional club but the match never took place. In the meantime the FA had decided to run its own annual match, 'the object being that charity should benefit by receiving the gross receipts of the matches' (Minutes of FA Council, February 24; March 9, 1908). Accordingly it was arranged for the Football League champions Manchester United to play Queen's Park Rangers, its Southern League counterpart. This match had to be replayed before the northern side became the first holders of the FA Charity Shield. In total £1275 was raised for charity. Next season saw Newcastle United versus Northampton Town. Both teams received £45 for distribution to local charities and twelve London hospitals each received between £5 and £10 (Minutes of FA Benevolent Fund Committee, July 10, 1909). In total some £226 was given out, all but £12 going to medical charities. The Sheriff of London trophy remained in abeyance and the Charity Shield became the major charity match in England. Customarily it was the Southern League and Football League champions who played but in 1913 it involved a professional eleven versus an amateur one.

Clubs

Although clubs often loaned out their grounds for one-off charity matches – between groups as diverse as boxers versus jockeys, sweeps against bakers, or, more commonly, touring theatrical troupes and pantomime companies (FA Minutes *passim*; Minutes of Sheffield Wednesday FC, January 29, October 27, 1897, May 4, 1898, May 31, 1901; Curry 2004, 193; Huggins 2004, 138) – they often welcomed the opportunity to play in charity tournaments. In the 1870s and 1880s, prior to the development of leagues with regular matches scheduled, there was virtually a free market in fixtures. These were mainly friendly games which might be cast aside if one of the clubs progressed in a cup competition or obtained a better offer in terms of the quality of the opposition or expenses promised. Charity matches with a trophy attached meant that the clubs obtained meaningful fixtures, often with selected opponents rather than the random draw of cup competitions. This was as true of the village club as of the elite teams. Charity competitions if played at the end of the season, as many were, gave clubs a chance of redeeming a poor year by winning a cup, often at the expense of a local rival. This remained cogent even when the league system spread bringing with it a regularity of fixtures.[5] There could only be one league winner: the majority of teams were losers. It could be argued that over time friendly fixtures lost their gloss but league titles, challenge cup wins, and charity cup trophies (in that order) maintained their attraction for clubs.

It can be suggested that many clubs exhibited a sense of what is now termed CSR in which businesses see it as in their interest to foster good relations with relevant stakeholders which, in the case of football teams, includes fans and the local community. They organised charity matches at the time of local depressions and disasters and, as Huggins put it regarding the early years of organised football in the North East, charity 'cups helped to link soccer more firmly into the community, acting in support of local enterprises, often hospitals, but increasingly also for the benefit of individuals, widows and orphans' (Huggins 1989, 310).

Players

An editorial in a leading sports journal in 1880 argued that 'our football players, if only they had the inclination, have the power to enrich many of our needy institutions' (*Athletic News*, April 14, 1880, 4). Some at least were so disposed and in the early 1880s the SFA gave public thanks given to all the players who took part in the Glasgow Charity Cup 'for the ready and cheerful way in which they responded to the appeal made to them' (*SFA Annual*, 1882–83, 32). These of course were amateurs but, as was pointed out by 'an old player' in 1902 'it must not be forgotten that professional players have throughout been prominent in contributing to deserving charities' (An Old Player 1902, 77). Individuals such as Billy Meredith, later a stalwart of the Players' Union, helped out their fellow professionals by playing in their benefit games. He also helped organise a match to aid the poor of Manchester and in 1907, played for a George Robey XI at Stamford Bridge against Chelsea to raise money for charity (Harding 1985, 44).

Collectively players aided each other via the benevolent fund of their unions. The first semi-permanent union for professional footballers, the Association Footballers' Union (AFU) set up a benevolent fund, financed partly by contributions from players but also via other fund-raising activities including a benefit match, English versus Scottish players, at Ibrox in April 1898, for which it received permission from the FA and SFA (Minutes of FA Emergency Committee, January 4–27, 1899). Although this was poorly attended, nevertheless subscriptions from over 400 members enabled the organisation to send money to relatives of deceased players. During the next two years several matches were played to raise funds to assist individual players and their families. Such matches of course required permission of the FA or its affiliated associations (Harding 1991, 13, 25). Within a few months of being established, its successor, the Association Football Players Union (AFPU), was arranging money for families of men who had died leaving inadequate provision. When Frank Levich of Sheffield United died the Union sent his mother £20 and wrote to the Sheffield club to ask that the amount equal to his wages for rest of season be paid. It also wrote to FA asking for a grant from its Benevolent Fund (Minutes of AFPU, April 1, 1908). In 1908 the first AGM of the Union agreed that in the case of the death of a member a shilling levy would be made on each member to be paid to his nearest relative without any deduction (Minutes of AFPU, December 15, 1908). Although the AFPU made little headway in its challenge to the issues of wage limitation and the retain and transfer system, day-to-day benevolent work was a 'solid achievement'. Between 1908 and 1914 hundreds of players and their families were assisted. Widows automatically received a £10 grant (raised by a levy on all members) and other small but crucial sums were paid towards funeral expenses, removal costs, furniture replacement, and hospital fees (Harding 1991, 108).

Patrons

Patronage came from various sources. Some charity competitions followed the pattern of patronage at association level where titled men and those from the professions and politics were dominant.[6] In London Sir Thomas Dewar, at the time Sheriff of London, had already donated a cup for London schoolboy football competition, when, in early 1898, he applied to the FA to organise a match between the best amateur and best professional team under the title Champion Charity Cup Competition. He would provide the trophy and the proceeds (after payment of the expenses of the match and one-third of the net receipts to the professional club) would be distributed to charities selected by a committee headed by himself. Consent was given, provided that the match was held after 21 March so as not to interfere with the home international matches, but the FA suggested that the title be changed to the Sheriff of London Charity Cup. Eventually a shield, an imposing six feet high, rather than a cup became the preferred trophy (Minutes of FA Consultative Committee, February 2, 1898). Most of the money raised went to London charities but some also to charities of the towns represented by the professional team (Creek 1933, 125).

In Burnley the local Medical Officer of Health, Dr Dean, donated a trophy with the funds raised from the associated matches to go to the new hospital (Wiseman 1973, 15). North of the border the Paisley Charity Cup was funded by subscriptions from local gentlemen, and, thanks to the generosity of several noblemen and MPs, together with the gentry and a large number of smaller subscribers, the Southern Counties Football Association purchased a cup which, 'for beauty of design, is not equalled in Scotland.' Eight clubs, including those from Moffat, Dumfries, Stranraer and Lockerbie, were invited to compete for the prize and raised £24 for charities in the south of Scotland (*SFA Annual*, 1884–85, 85). Over the water a 'number of leading merchants and gentlemen' subscribed for the Irish Football Association Charity Cup, placing the power to invite clubs to compete and to distribute the proceeds to 'certain charitable institutions' in a board of trustees (*SFA Annual*, 1885–86, 108).

Some patrons came from the commercial world. The press were prominent with the *Grimsby Mirror* Charity Association, the *Hull Times* Charity Cup and the Southern Combination Charity Cup established in 1900 'for and on behalf of southern charities' was organised by J.M. Dick, editor of the *Football News*, and the cup itself was donated by the [London] *Evening News* (Minutes of FA Council, February 28, 1894; Minutes of FA Consultative Committee, February 3, 1897; *Gamage's Association Football Annual*, 1914/15, 598–600). Others included the Glasgow merchants who purchased the Glasgow Charity Cup, the Bass brewing firm and the donors of the Sunderland Shipowners Charity Cup.

Fans

Most of the major charity competitions began before the creation of elite leagues which came in England in 1888 and Scotland two years later. Hence spectators had not become used to the idea of regular, competitive fixtures between high quality teams and were often willing to turn up in large numbers, thus providing revenue for the charities and status to those that provided the competition. There is no strong evidence that this spectator support for charity matches fell away as the elite leagues developed. Certainly Barnsley had its highest attendance to that date in the town's 1892 charity cup final and a Glasgow Charity Cup tie between Rangers and Celtic in 1897 produced a record week-night crowd of over 23,000 (*SFA Annual*, 1898–99, 50; Firth 1978, 10).

Charities

No evidence has been found that charities themselves instigated football matches as a means of raising funds. Some sent letters to the football authorities requesting contributions, usually unsuccessfully, though the GCCC finally rewarded Sister Aloysius for her persistence and added the St Vincent School for the Deaf to its list of recipients in 1913 (Letter book of J.K. MacDowell, May 16, 1913; Scottish Football Museum, Glasgow). They did, however, reject the applications of the Royal Normal College and the local cat and dog home in 1912. The FA Council turned down an application from St Thomas's Hospital in 1895 on the grounds that 'it was not within the province of the Council to deal with such matters, the Council having declined all such applications before' (Minutes of FA Council, July 12, 1895).

Not necessarily [just] altruism

Public image and psychic income

Football's contribution to charities led to psychic income, in terms of a favourable image and public acclaim, for those running the game, chairing the clubs or donating trophies. An editorial in the *Athletic News* claimed that once the 'thread of philanthropy was woven into its constitution … the [Scottish Football] Association was elevated into a position at once enviable and sacred' ("Sport and Charity." *Athletic News*, April 14, 1880, 4). Each year of competition reinforced the admiring view in some quarters of the football entrepreneur as a civic benefactor.

Patronage of charity football kept the name of Members of Parliament in front of the electorate; for mayors it provided a legacy of their term of office. Admittedly the initial outlay could be high but, once the trophy had been purchased, it was others who had to make the competition work. Yet it was the donor's name that continued to be associated with the event. Some patronage was commercially oriented. If newspapers and businessmen were totally disinterested in promoting themselves they could have donated cups anonymously. Instead their name became indelibly associated with the competitions that they sponsored, a relatively cheap form of advertising; even when the cup could cost over £100 it was a one-off payment that brought renewed publicity every year. For others, however, it was more a question of kudos and approbation. N.L. 'Pa' Jackson's charity matches for the funds of the Poplar Hospital brought him a life governorship of that institution (Jackson 1932, 51).[7]

Not everyone shared the fans' enthusiasm for the game and there were some trenchant critiques of association football, particularly of the professional and mass-spectator versions. Some critics felt that those who watched really should be playing; others believed that the passion for football distracted its followers from real world issues. There were warnings of the sport's relationship with the alcohol trade and the opportunities it provided for gambling and misbehaviour (Edwardes 1892, 622; Smith 1897, 571; Ensor 1898, 758; Thorne 1906, 196–198; Peatling 2005, 353–371). It could be speculated that football assisted charity to counter some of the criticism it received. But did those who ran football care about the views of those outside the game? Possibly not until the First World War when, stung by criticisms of the continuance of the game while men were dying at the front, the FA retaliated by pointing out that ' it [football] is producing more men for the Army and money for relief than all the other' sports (Minutes of FA Council, October 12, 1914).

Power relations

Charity fixtures provided an opportunity for the governors of football to exercise their authority. The Lancashire FA, for example, had a rule from its inauguration in 1878 that 'any club competing for a prize offered by an individual or individuals unless the net proceeds go to some football club or clubs or charity or charities, shall cease to be members of this Association' (Sutcliffe and Hargreaves 1992, 24). Simultaneously charity matches were encouraged and the threat of disaffiliation used to consolidate the position of the Association.

NUMBERS AND NARRATIVES

The FA itself had cemented its authority over English football in the 1870s and was effectively in charge of the game by the 1880s by which time its cup competition was recognised as *the* trophy to win. Hence any threat to disaffiliate a club or association was meaningful. Its Council was determined to keep charity football under [its] control and passed regulations as to when games could be played, who could participate, and what should happen to the proceeds and, of course, whether it was a final of a serious charity competition or a burlesque involving pantomime artists, no game was allowed unless it was played under FA match rules. Normal disciplinary procedures were expected to be upheld and no charity was shown to Manchester United player E.J. West who was not allowed to receive a Charity Shield medal because he was under suspension at the time of the final (Minutes of FA Consultative Committee, November 20, 1911).

By the early 1890s every meeting of the FA Council or Consultative Committee was dealing with at least half-a-dozen applications for charity or benefit matches, so many in fact that the approval decision was delegated to the regional associations. Nevertheless the FA was adamant that the hierarchy of control should be maintained. When the Rotherham Charity Cup Association applied for affiliation in 1892 it was turned down as it lay within the Sheffield Association's catchment area and eventually it was that association which approved the competition (Minutes of FA Council, December 12, 1892, August 7, 1893). In 1899 the FA had no objection to an application from the Norwood Junior Charity Cup Committee to expand the number of teams in its competition but refused to let it transfer supervision of the event from its local association to the Southern Suburban League, that organisation 'having been authorised for a certain competition should keep within its jurisdiction' (Minutes of FA Emergency Committee, 30 June–5 August 1899).

The FA's insistence that all charity matches must be officially approved was even used to sanction one of its own executive members, N.L. Jackson, when he arranged scratch matches for charity without first gaining approval (Minutes of FA Council, December 14, 1896; X.Y. 1897, 574–576; Jackson 1932, 174).[8] It also proved a major weapon in its confrontation with the Players' Union over the latter's non-benevolent activities. To meet the legal costs of a test case which challenged the retain and transfer system, the Union borrowed money from its benevolent fund leading to the consequent refusal of the FA to sanction the Union's annual fund-raising match (Minutes of AFPU, November 2, 1909).

When the SFA became involved in the Glasgow Charity Cup it had only been established for three years and was scarcely in control of the Scottish game though it was in charge of the nation's challenge cup competition. The charity competition gave it an opportunity to cement its position at the head of Scottish football with two major trophies held under its auspices. However the inauguration of the Scottish Football League (SFL) meant that the Glasgow Charity Cup became the site of a power struggle between the two bodies. They were already at odds as the SFA, who chose the national team, had set aside without consultation two Saturdays for international trial matches thus interfering with league games fixed for those days. When the GCCC [comprising local merchants and SFA representatives] then also scheduled its ties for Saturdays before the end of the league season the SFL instructed its member clubs, Celtic, Rangers and Third Lanark, not to play in the competition. Without these leading teams, the Charity Cup, consisting of Airdrieonians, Partick Thistle, and Queen's Park who played Northern in the final, raised only £150. Moreover the League flexed its muscles and organised its own charity competition which brought in £820 (Minutes of SFA, March 24, 1891, April 2, 1891; *Scottish Sport*, 5 April 1892, 4; Robinson

1920, 181–182). A lesson learned, the Committee gave way and next season switched its fixtures to dates after the League season ended, but the SFA Annual General Meeting also passed a rule saying that all matches including charities and friendlies had to have their permission (Minutes of SFA, May 12, 1891). In turn the League dropped its charity tournament and the official records encompass the revenue from both the 1891 charity cups, though labelling the League contribution as coming via a supplementary charity committee (*Athletic News Football Annual*, 1894, 109). It was, as a Scottish newspaper noted, 'certainly not too creditable to the boasted generosity of footballers that we should have the prospect of yearly disputes over the details of the Charity competition' (*Scottish Sport*, April 22, 1892, 30). Ironically, after the Charity Cup Committee faced reality and switched to more suitable dates for the League teams, Queen's Park, a stalwart of the Charity Cup but a club that refused to join the League for a decade, did not play in the 1893 tournament as it ended its season before League fixtures were complete and hence before the Charity Cup competition began (Minutes of GCCC, April 18, 1893).

The level of control by the football authorities could operate against the interests of charity, specifically in terms of the close season. For many years the FA refused to allow clubs to charge entrance fees or hold collections for charity at pre-season practice matches. After this decision was rescinded some 50 clubs took advantage of the situation in 1909 to raise money for charity, suggesting that an opportunity had been missed earlier (Minutes of FA Council, September 16, 1890; Minutes of FA Emergency Committee, June 11–August 19, 1897; Minutes of FA Consultative Committee, September 5, 1910). At the other end of the season the FA restricted matches to the pre-determined cut-off date 'except under very special circumstances' (Minutes of FA Council, July 10, 1909). In Scotland the SFA adopted a similar policy but decided that matches to aid victims of the Ibrox disaster could be allowed 'under the exceptional circumstances'. It had done the same in the mid 1890s when bad weather had led to a fixture backlog 'in the interests of the many institutions which depend so largely on football for a helping hand' (Minutes of GCCC, April 17, 1902; *Annual Report of SFA*, 1894/95, 6).

There was also power involved in the selection of teams to play in the various charity fixtures. In 1902 Aston Villa was not invited to defend the Sheriff of London Shield even though the team had again won the league; instead the committee in charge 'in considering the interests of charity' chose Tottenham, the FA Cup winners, to play against the Corinthians at White Hart Lane, their own ground (Creek 1933, 131). In contrast petty politics meant that Everton refused to participate in an annual charitable fixture between professional footballers and pantomime artistes in support of local hospitals because it was to be held at Anfield, home of their arch rivals Liverpool, leading to the scathing query in the local press as to whether 'Charity is to be ridden over for Jealousy's sake?' ([Liverpool] *Review*, December 17, 1892). The choice of teams to play in the Glasgow Charity Cup was at the discretion of the organising committee and no criteria were published. When SFA cup-winners Vale of Leven queried its non-selection in 1890 it was simply told that those chosen were 'the most suitable' (Minutes of SFA, March 28, 1890). Throughout the 1880s clubs used SFA meetings to make recommendations about the composition of the charity tournament, but the cup committee, with merchant representation in the majority and in the chair, remained of independent mind. In 1885, for example, there was a movement by a group of clubs to expand the competition to eight clubs. The SFA went so far as to select the eight from ten nominations, but when one of the omitted clubs protested to organisers, the committee refused to join the debate and opted again to have only four clubs (Minutes of SFA, March 10, 19, 1885). However, in later years, aware of the drawing power of the leading clubs, the Glasgow committee often capitulated to their demands, though usually after a show of resistance. Hence, at the instigation of the clubs, the committee approved neutral venues (1894), accepted that clubs could switch match dates by mutual agreement (1897) and allowed players SFA-cup tied for other clubs to play in the Charity Cup matches (1902) (Minutes of GCCC, March 1, 1894; April 22, 1897; June 6, 1902). Political machinations also contrasted with the overt aims of charity elsewhere in Scotland. In Dundee there were complaints that four established clubs – East End, Our Boys, Harp and Johnstone – set up a Charity Football Association which deliberately excluded clubs like Strathmore and Lochee United to prevent them from improving and the Southern Counties Football Association began the report on its charity tournament with the ominous statement, 'there must be considerable eliminations from the committee before harmonious working can be attained' with the vice-president explained that the some members of the outgoing committee had 'pretty much decided among themselves' which clubs were to play (*SFA Annual*, 1886–87, 101; *Scottish Sport*, January 5, 1892).

Another aspect of power was to decide who were the deserving poor. In most cases this involved only the selection of charitable organisations who were then left to distribute the money as they saw fit. In Glasgow this was done by the Charity Cup Committee though in Edinburgh it was 'subject to the approval of the Earl of Rosebery', the patron of the charity tournament (*SFA Annual*, 1884–85, 81). None of the GCCC Minute Books consulted give any indication as to how or why deserving causes were chosen by the various committees. Presumably a consensus had to be reached, though personal advocacy in favour of a pet project probably occurred: it is notable that no Catholic charities were funded until a representative from Celtic joined the GCCC in 1894. Perhaps the most powerful voices also held sway in the selection of even more controversial recipients such as the Lock Hospitals for female venereal disease patients and Magdalene Asylums that dealt with 'females who have strayed from the paths of virtue' (Aird 1894, *passim*; Checkland 1980, 180). In times of economic crisis or local tragedy the choice of beneficiaries may have been more straightforward. Although the London FA Council selected the teams to play in its charity cup, the subcommittee comprising three LFA delegates and three co-opted members determined the grounds and dates, took all the receipts, paid all the expenses and had 'absolute control' over the distribution of funds (*London Football Association Annual*, 1905–06, 62–63).

With benevolent societies each application was considered on its merits. After the death of George Smith the secretary of AFPU was instructed that 'if the case is a deserving one, to consider what grant shall be given to the wife at the next meeting' (Minutes of AFPU, August 27, 1908). After a satisfactory report she was granted £10 as was Norwich City's F. Thompson who was in destitute circumstances'. However W. Hall of Bolton Wanderers was to get only up to £5 'if married and in absolute need' but nothing if unmarried 'unless it is a very exceptional case' (Minutes of AFPU, November 16, 1908). By the end of 1910 the standard assistance given was £5 but it was always checked that the case was a 'deserving one' (Minutes of AFPU, December 5, 1910).

Did charity begin at home?

Football was a physical contact sport with socially-sanctioned violence which produced its share of injuries, some of them serious enough to affect the amateur player's ability to follow his everyday job or even career-threatening for the professional player. Although some clubs – Aston Villa as early as 1879 – gave gratuities to injured amateur players and others took out insurance policies on their professionals, for most of the period to 1914 many distressed players relied on charity for assistance (Minutes of Sheffield FC, July 23, 1907; Carter 2007, 57).[9] It was thus in the players collective interest to participate in charity matches as charity associations used some of the money raised to endow hospital beds and pay subscription lines which allowed them to nominate patients to receive treatment or undergo convalescence which, of course, could include footballers (Letters to Sir John Primrose, June 12, 1913 and to Mr Anderson, June 12, 1913. Letter Book of J.K. McDowall). In 1882 the GCCC sent a letter to the Western Infirmary asking what they intended to do in the future as several persons sent by the SFA had not been admitted. Whether these were players is not stated, but, thirty years later, the GCCC lambasted the Victoria Infirmary after two players had to wait several weeks for admission despite their injuries (Minutes of SFA, May 5, 1882; Minutes of GCCC, May 29, 1913). The incident led to a letter being sent to all three major infirmaries asking 'if you are prepared to facilitate the entrance of an injured football player to your institution' (Letter Book of J.K. McDowell, March 12, 1913).

Many matches were authorised to assist players who had to give up the game because of broken legs and other severe injuries as well as those who retired through ill health. Such matches were dependent upon the goodwill of both the relevant clubs and football authorities. More certain help could come from benevolent funds set up specifically to assist distressed players and their families. These were either subscription-based, as was the major one run by the AFPU, or, as with the Sheffield Football Players Accident Society in the 1870s, relied on donations, collections at football grounds and a variety of charity fundraisers such as smoking concerts or theatrical performances (Anon. 1983, 42). The GCCC considered establishing a separate benefit fund for football players but instead decided to deal with each case on its merits at the time of allocating its funds: in 1900 two ex-players received £10 and £2, respectively and another £10 went to a player's widow (Minutes of GCCC, April 18, 1900).

In 1899, however, the FA set up its own benevolent fund with an annual transfer of funds from its accounts of £400 'for distribution among necessitous players and others who have rendered service to the game' (Green 1953, 167). In 1913, in celebration of the Jubilee of the FA, a Charity Fund was established using £5000 from the Association's investment fund with the 'income to be devoted to the benefit of members who have worked for the good of the sport' (Minutes of FA Council, April 4, 1913). In 1918 the football authorities established the Football National War Fund 'to aid players and others who have rendered assistance to the game, and their dependents, who are in need of assistance arising from the War and other causes' (*Gammage's Association Football Annual*, 1919–1920, 20).

As these clauses suggest it was not just players who could benefit from inhouse charity. In 1907 the widow of Charles Alcock, long-serving secretary of the FA, received £100 from the Association's benevolent fund and continued to get an annual £24 (Minutes of Benevolent Fund Committee, July 6, 1907). Earlier when the committee of the Glasgow Football Association noted that the treasurer of the Cowlairs club had been advised by his doctor to go abroad for reasons of ill-health but could not afford to do so, it helped arrange a match between two clubs from the Association to raise enough money to send him to Australia (*SFA Annual*, 1887/88, 73). Even earlier the premature death of the SFA secretary led that association to hold a match between the holders of the SFA and FA cups to aid his widowed mother (*Athletic News*, May 12, 1880).

Some players were indirect beneficiaries of football's charitable work during the First World War. These were female players, particularly those drafted into war work in the munitions factories, who organised teams partly for their own entertainment but also to raise funds for war charities (Newsham 1997; Jacobs 2004; Brennan 2007). Previously the FA had declared football unsuitable for women, even warning member clubs in 1902 not to involve themselves in charitable matches with 'ladies teams' (MacBeth 2002, 152). Now women's football teams received grudging official blessing and were allowed to play on Football League grounds.

Fingers in the pie?

There was often concern that not enough of charity match proceeds went for charitable purposes. Although the competition was intended to raise money for charity, the ornate East Lancashire Charity Cup was part purchased from the gate-money of the first tournament (Baron 1906, 23). In 1883 a Scottish newspaper criticised various charity match organisers for 'allowing large numbers to sit down for tea', sometimes as many as 70. They were reminded that 'charity funds are not association funds' (*Scottish Athletic Journal*, April 27, 1883, 6). Three years later there were press allegations of financial irregularity when the Victoria Hospital in Burnley received only £62 from gate receipts of £215 from the final of the Hospital Cup and in 1892 a writer in *Scottish Sport* deplored the fact that 'expenses in charitable undertakings too often reach a high figure and run away with too big a proportion of the drawings' (*Scottish Sport*, April 15, 1892, 8; Wiseman 1973, 22).

An official eyebrow was occasionally raised in the late 1880s but increasingly over the next decade various charity football associations and charity match owners receiving warnings. Coalville Charity FA was made subject to an investigation by the Leicestershire FA as 'the amount given to charity was very small and the expenses very high'; Ashton-under-Lyne Charity Competition Committee was asked for an explanation as to 'certain items on the balance sheet' and informed that 'the amount given to charitable institutions was small by comparison with the amount paid to the competing clubs, and that it was contrary to the ruling of the FA that a payment should be given to a secretary of a charity competition' (Minutes of FA Emergency Committee, September 7–14, 1896, May 29–July 10, 1896).

Finally at the end of the 1890s the FA set up a commission to formulate a set of regulations under which to sanction charity competitions and matches. These were formally adopted in April 1898, just prior to the annual surge in requests for end-of-season charity fixtures. In those competitions conducted on a league principle not less than 10% of the gross gate of each fixture had to be given to charity and the ground expenses specifically excluded the expenses of the teams involved. Where competitions were conducted as a challenge cup, at least one-tenth of the gross receipts had to go to charity in the preliminary rounds and at least one-third in the semi-finals and finals. One-off matches would be dealt with on their merits but, after the deduction of reasonable expenses, the whole of the net gate had to go to charity. No salary or honorarium was to be given to any official of any charity competition. It was stressed that the recommended level of donations was a minimum and it was hoped that more would be given where possible and that existing competitions already giving more would continue to do so (Minutes of FA Council, April 1898). Not all secretaries appeared to have read the rules and in early 1899 the Apsley and District Charity

Competition were told that net gate receipts of just £4:18s were 'not sufficient justification for the existence of a competition described as a Football Charity Competition'. Further investigation revealed that actually less than a pound was passed on to charity mainly because the two clubs involved, Burton Swifts and Luton Town had been guaranteed £40 to play (Minutes of FA Emergency Committee, January 4–27, 1899, February 9–24, 1899). A decade later the Norfolk and Norwich Hospital Charity Cup Committee was informed that, as it had already expended £76 of the £194 raised, permission would not be granted for more to be spent on medals. It was reminded that 'the money was raised in the name of charity' (Minutes of FA Leagues Sanctions Committee, July 30, 1909).

Little is known about actual donations by clubs to charity. The *Athletic News* in 1880 was 'well aware that many clubs both in Lancashire and Yorkshire lay part of their earnings on the altar of charity', though it is not clear whether this refers to actual donations or revenue from charity matches (*Athletic News*, April 14, 1880, 4). Given the precarious state of early football finance, particular for lesser amateur clubs many of which went under, it may be that donating their time and ground for charity matches was an easier and more convenient way for clubs to give to charity. They were able to combine playing football, doing their civic duty, and raising money for local good causes. Moreover if expenses could be claimed then, depending on how flexible a definition they were given, a contribution could be obtained towards the running costs of the club. Rangers, for one, had received adverse publicity following a charity match where its opponent had provided its services free, but the Rangers' president took £10 for his club's expenses (Goldblatt 2006, 70).

In Scotland actual donations from the clubs to Glasgow Charity Cup funds were rare till the twentieth century. In 1899 Celtic donated £15 from its match expenses though no other professional club followed suit till 1906 when most rebated part of their expenses. In 1909 the clubs agreed only to take expenses for games played on Saturdays [when attendances were larger] and by 1910 giving back at least 10% of the expenses had become standard practice (Minutes of GCCC, May 26, 1909). Two years later the Secretary of the Charity Cup Committee wrote to all participating clubs requesting them 'to consider a reduction in your expenses for this season's competition'. Whether this embarrassed the clubs is a matter of conjecture but in 1914, when unfavourable weather affected the money raised, neither Rangers nor Celtic charged expenses and the other professional clubs reduced their charges.

One other development in football that had an impact on the fund-raising activities of charity competitions was the authorisation of professionalism in 1885 in England and eight years later in Scotland. Although in 1891 the FA resolved that no player could be paid in charity matches held in May, it specifically excluded 'old-established charity competitions' and specifically included May, a month outside the conventional season (Minutes of FA Council, April 27, May 3, 1891). When the Sheriff of London Shield was established in 1898 the FA agreed that the professional club involved could receive travel and hotel expenses plus a share of the net gate receipts not exceeding £100 (Minutes of FA Consultative Committee, February 2, 1898). Unless it was offset by larger gates once teams incurred extra costs there would be less surplus available for charity. Sheffield Wednesday offered their players an extra ten shillings should they win the 1888 Wharncliffe Charity Cup 'as some compensation for loss of time in preparing for the match' (Minutes of Sheffield Wednesday FC, February 27, 1888). In Scotland all the competing clubs in the Glasgow Charity Cup – except for Queen's Park who remained staunchly amateur – immediately began to claim for their players' wages. Initially the Charity Cup Committee insisted that it only pay 'an allowance towards expenses', so Rangers' claim for £49 was reduced to £34, Celtic's £38–£25 though Third Lanark was granted its full £15. However by 1896 contributions towards wages were clearly acknowledged. At times they were a significant proportion of the gate-money as in 1903 when wages of £242 took 29% of the £840 gate (Cashbook of GCCC). In 1914 Alex Wylie, a long-standing trustee of the GCCC, complained that players were absorbing too much money from charity gatemoney (Minutes of GCCC, June 10, 1914). This was in marked contrast to 1879 when a local councillor purchased gold medals for the winning team and was forcibly told that this would 'be not paid out of the funds collected for the unemployed' (Minutes of SFA, June 3, 1879).

Whether any of the money taken by the clubs actually reached the players is unclear. There was no maximum wage legislation in Scotland so players there could be paid, but, in England, from 1901 there was a stipulated maximum wage of £4 a week. However, it is quite conceivable that, at a time when employers and players colluded to circumvent the maximum wage for league matches, players were given some monetary consideration rather than have compulsory 'voluntary' work forced upon them (Taylor 2005, 111–112).

One group of players who took advantage of charity matches to earn money was the 'Zulus', established in Sheffield in 1879, ostensibly, at least initially, to raise funds for the dependents of soldiers killed in the Zulu Wars. However, they soon began to charge fees for their appearances, eventually leading the Sheffield Association in 1882 debarring from any Association contest players taking part in a Zulu match or in any way receiving remuneration for playing (Sparling 1926, 45; Curry 2004, 345–346). Others who apparently gained from playing in charity games were the women of Dick, Kerr's Ladies who during the war received ten shillings for each match, supposedly in lieu of lost wages and expenses though many matches were on Saturday afternoons when they were free of work and at local grounds which involved little travel. In its first season the club's revenue from charity matches was around £800 of which £554 went to charity, on a par with the least generous of the Glasgow Cup seasons. Indeed in 1921 allegations of misappropriation of charity funds were used by the FA as a pretext to ban women's football from all grounds under its jurisdiction (MacBeth 2002, 155–6; Jacobs 2004, 47–48). Those amateurs who turned out from theatrical companies and the music halls also gained by obtaining free publicity which helped drum up business for their shows (Huggins 2004, 138).

Then there are the Corinthians. In 1882, while Honorary Assistant Secretary of the FA, N.L. Jackson had founded the Corinthians, ostensibly to improve the standard of the English international team, and, under his management for 22 years, they played all over Britain and indeed throughout the football world often raising money for charity (Jackson 1932, 66). They featured in two of the first three London Football Festivals, played in all the Sheriff of London Shield matches except that of 1899 when the amateurs were represented by Queen's Park from Glasgow, and in the 1912 Charity Shield. In the early 1890s they had offered to meet 'any other Association club at football, cricket and athletic sports, the proceeds to be given to charity' and in 1915 those members who had volunteered for the forces played charity matches as a Corinthians-under-Arms XI (Creek 1933, 25, 43). However, the club also played 'friendlies' for a share of the gate 'which enabled them to pay all expenses without profit' (Robinson 1920, 236). Of course middle-class expenses could be high, justified in some quarters as simply the maintenance of an accustomed life style (Creston 1894, 30). Jackson maintained that the players in his scratch sides that played for charity paid all their own expenses but it is not so clear where the Corinthians were concerned

(Jackson 1932, 174). There is a suspicion that not everything was above board. Jackson promoted the interests of amateur football but arguably was a professional entrepreneur. At the AGM of the Lancashire RFU, A.N. Hornby, the Lancashire cricket captain, stated that 'the Corinthians went on tour, received big gates which more than covered their expenses, and nobody ever heard of the rest' (*Yorkshire Post*, October 4, 1893). Although an ensuing Commission of Enquiry instigated by Jackson himself found 'no payment has been made to members of the club, except for travelling and out of pocket expenses' (*Yorkshire Post*, December 13, 1893), it has to be queried why a nomadic club with no ground to maintain needed to raise its demand for the regular fixture with Queen's Park from half the net gate with a guarantee of £50 in 1887 to a £75 guarantee and half of all net gate money over £150 in 1897. A historian of Queen's Park summed up Jackson as being 'too good a financier' (Robinson 1920, 238–239).

Charity football – who benefited?

Those involved in running the game boasted of the sport's charitable work. On the inauguration of the Glasgow Charity Cup, the SFA thought it 'a matter of great congratulation' that it was the first Association of the kind that has linked itself with important public and benevolent purposes' (*SFA Annual*, 1878/79, 22). By 1880/81, when 129 clubs were listed as members of the SFA, it was announced that 'there is not a club in 'the Annual' that is not ready to play a 'Charity Match' and far more has been given to the funds of charitable institutions by the actions of Association football clubs than all the other games put together' (*SFA Annual*, 1880/81, 16). Four decades later, an ex-president of the Football League declared that 'no sport subscribes more to charity than does football' and at the outbreak of the First World War, the Chairman of the Football Association noted that 'the support which the FA in the past has given to the relief of suffering gives good guarantee that it will not now fail in its duty' (Bentley 1912, 390; Minutes of FA Consultative Committee, August 31, 1914).

Yet it can be queried whether this self congratulation was fully justified. Even at the end of the 1880s, a decade when 'football had seized upon charity', one critic complained that clubs did 'good only occasionally' (Guthrie 1889, 33–37). There are indications that in some parts of Scotland the universal support for charity matches, alluded to in the *SFA Annual* for 1880/81, could no longer be relied upon. Kilmarnock won that town's charity cup in 1886 but did not enter the Ayr competition, the other local tournament, leading the Ayrshire Football Association to 'hope that all clubs invited to take part in charity matches during the present season will be able to do so at once, and not in the half-hearted way that is so detrimental to the interests at stake' (*SFA Annual*, 1876–77, 90). Cambuslang were willing to participate in the Airdrie Charity Cup but only 'under conditions which the committee considered unreasonable' (*SFA Annual*, 1886–87, 84).

A combination of over expansion of charity tournaments and the establishment of leagues with their regular fixtures forced clubs into rethinking their participation in charity events. As charity tournaments proliferated, a hierarchy amongst the competitions developed and clubs began to select which competitions to enter. Having won the Wharncliffe Charity Cup for the fourth time in 1888, Sheffield Wednesday opted henceforth to enter its reserve team. More useful to the club were the early season matches against city rivals Sheffield United which began in 1903 and served as tests for the coming campaign, offered fans a derby competition for local bragging rights, while also raising money for charity (Sparling 1926, 266). Six years later the directors of Barnsley FC decided that, in fairness to other teams, they would do the same, leaving the senior side to compete in the more prestigious Wharncliffe Charity League (Firth 1978, 17). Similarly, although it had initially been regarded as a major tournament in the 1880s, by the 1890s the participating clubs in the East Lancashire Charity Cup often put in their reserve teams (Baron 1906, 73). In Birmingham it became increasingly difficult to get the Football League clubs to play in the knockout stages of the Mayor's Charity Cup and from 1906 it became a match between two invited teams (Clives 1975, 45). In fact in the Birmingham area generally by 1900 the growth of league competitions was adversely affecting the old charity associations (Clives 1975, 45). In Scotland the results noted in the *Scottish Football Annual* suggest that there may have been a decline in charity competitions as early as the 1890s.

For some clubs, as commercial considerations came to the fore, charity ambitions may have fallen away. Celtic is the prime example. Although founded in 1888 to support local Catholic charities, within a decade it had become a limited company, was declaring dividends of 10%, and had virtually ceased to donate to charity. In fact the decline in the club's charitable donations dates from 1893 to 1894, coincident with the formal adoption of professionalism in Scottish football (Handley 1960, *passim*; Vamplew 1988, 86). Nevertheless Celtic did continue to play in the Glasgow Charity Cup and used its influence to ensure that Catholic charities received their fair share of the proceeds. Of 37 profit and loss accounts that have been found covering twelve clubs in Scotland, only six clubs made charitable donations with contributions averaging less than 1% of net profits (Vamplew 1982, 558).

More generally clubs donated time and access rather than money. On several occasions Sheffield Wednesday declined to donate to particular charities though it was willing for them to make a collection at a match (Minutes of Sheffield Wednesday FC, April 16, 1902 (Ibrox), December 10, 1902 (Poor Children's Fund) and September 16, 1903 (Lifeboat Saturday Fund)). Hence the fans contributed but not the club itself. It did give over £180 to various local hospitals in both 1904 and 1905 but this was from practice matches the proceeds of which the FA had ruled must go to charity (Minutes of Sheffield Wednesday FC, August 18, 1904; August 10, 1905). That said, not all clubs were reluctant to use their funds to give a helping hand. During the 1894/95 football season Everton set up soup kitchens that provided at least 12,000 meals to the poor of the neighbourhood (Young 1964, 56).

Ultimately it was the fans who made the charitable donations with their payments at the turnstiles and their coins in the collecting cans and blankets. Many of those who paid to watch the games may have belonged to that half of working-class and artisan families who gave regularly to charity in the 1890s but, as well as helping others, they were also consumers purchasing the football product (Prochaska 1993, 358). For their money they received not just the feel good factor from helping others, but also entertainment and a reinforcement of social identity at the local level.

As football developed from an entertaining pastime to a commercial pursuit, initial benevolence towards charity was tempered by issues of control and rivalry. The charity football match was still employed in the service of the local community and the public good but the burgeoning sport was too important for the principal stakeholders to sanction its unregulated growth. Furthermore, they soon recognized its business potential; from the 1890s the football cash cow was increasingly milked for commercial gain as well as contributing to charitable coffers. The level of expenses or financial guarantees to clubs to persuade them to take part in charity contests appears to indicate that the era of unconditional philanthropy was a thing of the past: yet authorities and patrons continued to congratulate themselves on football's charitable achievements.

Although the FA subjected it to increasing scrutiny and regulation, the extent of charity football can only be estimated. Beyond a list of 275 FA-sanctioned charity competitions in 1913–14, all that can be quantified is the revenue generated by a few major charity competitions. In the 1880s the Wharncliffe Cup of 1880 produced £140; the first Football Festival of 1885/86 raised £405; the East Lancashire Charity Cup generated an average of £170 for charity in the six seasons for which data is available; and the Glasgow Charity tournament averaged £752 a year in donations The largesse of 'Generous Glasgow' continued through the 1890s with average donations of £999; these had increased to £1540 by the First World War. The Sheriff of London Shield produced £300 a year from 1898–99 to 1907–08 and the Southern Combination Charity Cup averaged £242 a year in the nine seasons from 1901 to 1902. After the novelty of the first match the FA Charity Shield gate receipts fell away markedly and the aggregate donation to charity in the next five seasons was only £14 more than was raised in its inaugural year, an average of £427 over the period.[10]

Clearly the Glasgow Charity Cup stands out, thanks partly to the concentration of elite clubs within the Scottish conurbation which made many games local derbies. The Glasgow figures can be put into a football perspective by comparing the gross receipts with those of the Scottish FA Cup final, and crowd sizes with average league attendances and, specifically, with the home gates of Rangers and Celtic, the two major crowd-drawing Scottish teams. These are shown in Table 1 and suggest that this charity tournament was a serious attraction to football fans. In contrast attendances at Charity Shield matches fared less well in relation to Football League games. Average crowds at the Charity Shield were around 14,650 but for the two seasons for which data is readily available (1908–09 and 1913–14) the Football League was attracting 19,450 per match (Minutes of Football Association; Vamplew 1988, 63). As shown in Table 2, the receipts generated fell far short of the FA Cup Final and were on a par with those of the Amateur Cup Final, a much less prestigious competition.

How much money in aggregate football raised for charity is conjectural. Writing in 1912, Bentley maintained that in England 'donations and subscriptions exceed £10,000 per year (Bentley 1912, 390). How he obtained this estimate is unknown but it is implicit in Bentley's article that it came from FA figures. Included in his figures must have been the pre-season matches that once they were once legalised as vehicles for charity brought in an average of £4122 between 1909/10 and 1913/14.[11]

Table 1. Comparative crowd receipts and match attendances in Scottish Football.

	Receipts £			Average match attendance		
Period	Glasgow GC	Scottish Cup final	Period	Glasgow CC	SFL	SFL Rangers Celtic
1892/93–1898/99	1010	769	1892/93–1893/94	8168	3823	7078
1899/00–1906/07	1035	978	1905/06–1913/14	12,615	6957	14,814
1907/08–1913/14	1764	1701	1914/15–1917/18	14,950	6096	13,398

Note: Cup final figures omit replays.
Sources: (a) and (c) Minutes of GCCC.
(b) Minutes of SFA.
(e) and (f) Ross (2005).

NUMBERS AND NARRATIVES

Table 2. Comparative crowd receipts in English Football (£).

Season	Charity shield	FA Cup final	FA Amateur Cup final
1908/09	1035 240 (replay)	3889	315
1909/10	226	4465 4149 replay	225
1910/11	354	4205 4478 replay	96
1911/12	230	3768 2612 replay	705 403 replay
1912/13	266	6134	177 235 replay
1913/14	391	4324	157

Source: Balance Sheets of FA.

Even less clear is the extent to which this money benefited charity. Certainly the amounts collected for disaster funds represented a tiny fraction of the totals. A total of £2235 was raised by the FA for the Titanic Relief Fund, but this amounted to less than 1% of the £250,000 donated overall (Bryceson 1997, 219). Calculations based on donations from the Glasgow Charity Cup, the major British fund-raising football tournament, and the annual incomes of several local charities – the Central Dispensary, the Glasgow Medical Mission and the Samaritan Hospital for Women – also suggest that football contributed only 1–2% of their total revenues.[12] Donations from the Glasgow Charity Cup to the Victoria Infirmary averaged £100 per annum in the period 1892–96: total income of that institution from legacies, subscriptions and gifts was £35,000 in 1889 (Slater and Dow 1990, 21).

Conclusion

Football changed extensively in the period under review. The early charity fixtures could be viewed as a stage in the growth of football, overlapping the era of friendly games and the coming of competitive leagues. However by the twentieth century, and possibly earlier, clubs were less keen to play for charity as league systems began to dominate and determine fixture lists, professionalism became accepted, and elite clubs invested heavily in grounds and facilities. Yet throughout there was a thread of charitable activity at all levels of the sport. The popularity of football made it an ideal vehicle for charity fund-raising and at the elite level it could bring together large masses of people, far more than could be accommodated in a theatre or music hall.

Football probably raised more money for charity than any other sport but no charity, except the benevolent funds of the football players and associations themselves, was dependent upon the game for more than a small proportion of its income. Football provided regular, but relatively minor, revenue to some hospitals and homes, and one-off contributions, again relatively small, to victims of tragedies and economic depression. Yet this overt giving of assistance was sufficient to gain associations, clubs and patrons psychic income, often at little direct cost to themselves: ultimately football was a vehicle for charity in which fans funded the donations.

Disclosure statement

No potential conflict of interest was reported by the author.

NUMBERS AND NARRATIVES

Notes

1. See, for example, Walters and Chadwick (2009); Sheth and Babiak (2010); Paramio-Salcines, Babiak and Walters (2013).
2. For more detailed information on the Glasgow competition see Vamplew (2008) and Kay (2009).
3. Calculated from *SFA Annuals* and list of FA-approved competitions in Minutes of FA. These figures are not comprehensive as in case of Scotland they were dependent on relevant secretaries forwarding the information to the SFA for publication in the journal and there were obvious gaps in the English data such as apparently no approved charity tournaments in Lancashire.
4. The SFA stated that £200 was handed over to charity and this appears in the [retrospective] official records of the Charity Cup. Where the other £100 came from is unknown.
5. Whether attractive gates against chosen opponents at charity fixtures encouraged the development of leagues is a moot point.
6. Based on a count of those associations cited in *Gamage's Association Football Annual* 1912/13.
7. At a smoking concert held in connection with the Mayor of London trophy he was also presented with 'a very handsome testimonial, including a valuable diamond ring and a cheque' (Jackson 1932, 107).
8. Nicholas 'Pa' Jackson, sports journalist and publisher, had a significant position in the history of charity football. He claims to have persuaded both Reginald Hanson and Thomas Dewar respectively to donate the Mayor of London Charity Cup (run by the London FA which he founded) and the Sheriff of London Charity Shield. He was involved in the development of the London Football Festivals in the late 1880s and for many years raised money for charity, especially the Poplar Hospital, by arranging scratch matches, the issue that brought trouble with the FA (Jackson 1900, 65, 153–154, 1932, 61).
9. In 1907, following the Workmen's Compensation Act of 1906, representatives of the Football League, the Southern League and the Scottish Football League established the Football Mutual Insurance Federation, but this comprehensive, self-funded scheme was voluntary and a minority of clubs did not join. In 1912, after national insurance legislation in 1911, a new compulsory scheme was set up but it applied only to Football League clubs (Taylor 2005, 148–150).
10. Figures calculated from data in FA Balance Sheets; Baron (1906); Wilson (1981, 11); *Gamage's Association Football Annual* (1910/11); Minutes of GCCC; *Athletic News*, September 22, 1880.
11. Calculated from data in Minutes of FA Benevolent Committee.
12. Calculated from figures in Checkland (1980).

References

Aird, A. 1894. *Glimpses of Old Glasgow*. Glasgow: Aird and Coghill.
Anon. 1983. *The Early Years 1863–78*. Basildon: Association of Football Statisticians.
Baron, J. 1906. *History of the Blackburn Rovers*. Blackburn: Weekly Telegraph.
Bentley, J. J. 1912. "Is Football a Business?" *World Today*, 383–393.
Brennan, P. 2007. *The Munitionettes*. Donmouth: Rowlands Gill.
Bryceson, D. 1997. *The Titanic Disaster*. Yeovil: Patrick Stephens.
Carter, N. 2007. "Metatarsals and Magic Sponges: English Football and the Development of Sports Medicine." *Journal of Sport History* 34 (1): 53–73.
Checkland, O. 1980. *Philanthropy in Victorian Scotland: Social Welfare and the Voluntary Principle*. Edinburgh: John Donald.
Clives, S. W. 1975. *Centenary Book of the Birmingham County FA 1875–1975*. Birmingham: Birmingham FA.
Crampsey, R. 1990. *The Scottish Football League: The First 100 Years*: Glasgow: SFL.
Creek, F. N. S. 1933. *A History of the Corinthian Football Club*. London: Longmans.
Creston, 1894. "Football." *Fortnightly Review* LV: 25–38.
Curry, G. 2004. "Playing For Money: James J. Lang and Emergent Soccer Professionals in Sheffield." *Soccer and Society* 5 (3): 336–355.
Edwardes, C. 1892. "The New Football Mania." *Nineteenth Century* 32: 622–631.
Ensor, E. 1898. "The Football Madness." *Contemporary Review* 74: 751–760.
Firth, G. 1978. *Oakwell*. Sheffield: Firth.

Goldblatt, D. 2006. *The Ball is Round: A Global History of Football*. London: Viking.

Green, G. 1953. *The History of the Football Association*. London: Naldrett.

Guthrie, G. 1889–90. "What's the Good of Football?" *SFA Annual* 33–37.

Handley, J. E. 1960. *The Celtic Story*. London: Stanley Paul.

Harding, J. 1985. *Football Wizard: The Story of Billy Meredith*. Derby: Breedon.

Harding, J. 1991. *For the Good of the Game: The Official History of the Professional Footballers' Association*. London: Robson.

Huggins, M. 1989. "The Spread of Association Football in North East England 1876–90: The Pattern of Diffusion." *International Journal of the History of Sport* 6 (3): 299–318.

Huggins, M. 2004. *Victorians and Sport*. London: Hambledon.

Jackson, N. L. 1900. *Association Football*. London: Newnes.

Jackson, N. L. 1932. *Sporting Days and Sporting Ways*. London: Hurst and Blackett.

Jacobs, B. 2004. *The Dick, Kerr's Ladies*. London: Robinson.

Kay, J. 2009. "The Archive, the Press and Victorian Football: The Case of the Glasgow Charity Cup." *Sport in History* 29 (4): 577–600.

MacBeth, J. 2002. "The Development of Women's Football in Scotland." *Sport in History* 22 (2): 149–163.

Newsham, G. J. 1997. *In a League of Their Own: The Dick, Kerr Ladies Football Club*. London: Scarlet Press.

An Old Player. 1902. "Football: The Game and Its Business." *World Today*, December, 70–90.

Paramio-Salcines, J. L., K. Babiak, and G. Walters, eds. 2013. *Routledge Handbook of Sport and Corporate Social Responsibility*. Abingdon: Routledge.

Peatling, G. K. 2005. "Rethinking the History of Criticism of Organised Sport." *Cultural and Social History* 2: 353–371.

Pickford, W. 1937. *Hampshire FA Golden Jubilee Book 1887–1937*. Southampton: Hampshire FA.

Prochaska, F. K. 1993. "Philanthropy." In *Cambridge Social History of Britain 1750–1950*, edited by F. M. L. Thompson, 357–394. Cambridge: Cambridge University Press.

Robinson, R. 1920. *History of Queen's Park F.C. 1867–1917*. Glasgow: Hay Nisbet.

Ross, D. 2005. *The Roar of the Crowd: Following Scottish Football Down the Years*. Argyll: Glendaruel.

Salt, H. S. 1906. "The Sportsman at Bay." *International Journal of Ethics* 16 (4): 487–497.

Sheils, R. S. 1997. "The Ibrox Disaster of 1902." *Judicial Review* 4: 230–240.

Sheth, H., and K. M. Babiak. 2010. "Beyond the Game: Perceptions and Practices of Corporate Social Responsibility in the Professional Sports Industry." *Journal of Business Ethics* 91 (3): 433–450.

Slater, S., and D. Dow, eds. 1990. *The Victoria Infirmary of Glasgow: 1890–1990*. Glasgow: Victoria Infirmary Centenary Committee.

Smith, G.O. 1897. "Football." *Pall Mall Magazine* 13: 370–371.

Sparling, R. A. 1926. *The Romance of the Wednesday 1867–1926*. Sheffield: Leng.

Sutcliffe, B. G., and F. Hargreaves. 1992. *History of the Lancashire Football Association 1878–1928*. Harefield: Yore.

Taylor, M. 2005. *The Leaguers: The Making of Professional Football in England 1900–1939*. Liverpool: Liverpool University Press.

Thorne, G. 1906. "Sport and Drink." *C.B. Fry's Magazine* 5 (27): 196–198.

Vamplew, W. 1982. "The Economics of a Sports Industry: Scottish Gate-Money Football, 1890–1914." *Economic History Review* XXXV (4): 549–567.

Vamplew, W. 1988. *Pay Up and Play the Game*. Cambridge: Cambridge University Press.

Vamplew, W. 2008. "'Remembering Us Year After Year': The Glasgow Charity Cup 1876–1966." *Recorde* 1 (2): 1–27.

Walters, G., and S. Chadwick. 2009. "Corporate Citizenship in Football: Delivering Strategic Benefits through Stakeholder Engagement." *Management Decision* 47 (1): 51–66.

Wilson, A. 1981. *The FA Charity Shield*. Association of Football Statisticians Report No. 16.

Wiseman, D. 1973. *Up the Clarets*. London: Robert Hale.

X.Y. 1897. "Football in '96–97.'" *New Review* 16: 574–576.

Young, P. M. 1964. *Football on Merseyside*. London: Soccer Book Club.

Still crazy after all those years: continuity in a changing labour market for professional jockeys

Wray Vamplew

ABSTRACT

Using the career of a leading modern rider as a focal point, this article examines the changes and continuities in the labour market for professional jockeys over the past century and a half. It looks at the rigours of the job via travel load, risk of injury and, above all, weight watching; at the rewards both monetary and psychic; at human capital formation; at drug and alcohol issues; and at power relations and disciplinary procedures.

Comment

My admiration for jockeys is unbounded. Not only do they risk life and limb every time they go to work, but they face the stress of public and private appraisal, constant weight-watching with its associated health risks and the demeaning struggle to gain employment in an over-supplied labour market.

An earlier version of this article was published under the same title in *Contemporary British History* 14.2 Summer 2000, 115–145. Although some amendments and minor additions have been made to the original text and notes, any references to 'now', 'today', etc. relate to the late 1990s. Since then, there has been relatively little historical work on jockeys published. Vamplew and Kay have looked at the amateur rider in National Hunt racing before 1914, Barbezat and Hughes have examined the labour market for jockey in the US, focusing on the period from 1880 to 1930, and Maynard has considered the Australian scene drawing on memories of his father's time as a jockey and focussing on the risks of the occupation and deaths through accidents and suicide (Vamplew and Kay 2006; Maynard 2013; Barbezat and Hughes 2014). We still know so little about the jockey in times past. How, for example, did the barely literate Fred Archer manage to arrange 667 rides in 1885?

In contrast, there has been a significant expansion in the literature on the modern jockey and their weight-loss practices, the medical problems, both physical and mental, they face in trying to reduce their weight, and the impact that weight watching has on their racetrack performance.[1] Injuries, employment conditions and industrial relations have also featured in recent research (Cowley, Bowman and Lawrance 2007; Winter 2008; Dabscheck 2013).

Although the bulk of the information relates to jockeys in the past decade or so, there is no reason to believe that this could not be applied to more historical periods.

Preamble

Lanfranco Dettori is not like other men: he travels over 200,000 miles a year in search of work; he weighs merely 115 lb; he is a millionaire. 'Frankie' Dettori is a jockey. In this article, his experiences are used to explore the working life of the professional jockey, at both the elite and journeyman level, and within the two branches of the industry, flat and jump racing.[2] It will be shown that, despite changes in the labour market, there has been a significant degree of continuity in a profession with a 250-year history.[3]

Supply and demand

The demand for jockeys is a derived one, stemming from the amount of racing taking place. In essence, the opportunities for any one jockey are dependent on the number of race days, the number of concurrent race meetings, the number of races on each card and the number of horses entered in each race. Rarely, until recently, have there been more than one or two meetings a day; normally no more than six or seven races feature on the card; and typically the fields have been in the range of 8–12 runners.[4] Turning to the supply side, at the start of their respective seasons in 1995, there were around 350 registered flat jockeys, some 230 of them apprentices, and some 350 licensed professional National Hunt jockeys, roughly 200 of them conditional riders, the jumping equivalent of apprentices.[5] Although today there are four to seven race meetings a day in summer and 300 more fixtures than ten years ago, the market situation remains one of a vast oversupply of labour. At times, as shown below, this has been aggravated by incursions from foreign riders and by gender changes in the profession.

When his mount *Lammtarra* won the *Prix de l'Arc de Triomphe* at Lonchamp in 1995, Dettori noted that the British national anthem was played to salute the success of a horse bred in America, trained and owned by Dubaians and ridden by an Italian: an indication of how globalized racing had become (Dettori 1997, 63). In 1990, the top ten jockeys in the British championship presented literally a league of nations, featuring three Irishmen, two Scots, two Welshman, an American, a South African and, of course, one Italian. Yet the regular international movement of jockeys is no modern phenomenon. It dates back well into the nineteenth century, coinciding with the development of railway networks in Britain and Europe (Tolson and Vamplew 1998, 41–43). British jockeys took advantage of the absence of Sunday racing in Britain to ride in France and Belgium. It is equally clear from the Racing Calendar that European riders, French jockeys in particular, came to England to participate in classic and other elite races, usually on mounts from European stables.

In the late nineteenth century, there was an American invasion of the British turf as racing faced increased political hostility in the US (Reiss 2011). In 1900, five of the top ten riders came from America, including the champion Lester Reiff, and in the next six years, the Derby, the blue riband of the British turf, was won five times by Americans. These men not only won a large number of races, they were also victorious in a high proportion of the races in which they had mounts: in 1900, Danny Maher, Johnny Reiff and 'Skeets' Martin topped 20%, Lester Reiff gained 26%, and Tod Sloan almost 27% (Vamplew 2004). Since then, there has been a constant flow of talented foreign riders, especially from Australia, including the 'Boy Wonder', Frank Wootton, champion jockey in 1909 at only

15, Frank Bullock, 'Brownie' Carslake, Edgar Britt, Rae Johnstone, four times champion 'Scobie' Breasley, George Moore, Bill Williamson and Ron Hutchinson, all of whom made their mark in British racing. More recently, Steve Cauthen came from the US to be champion three times in the 1980s and Michael Roberts from South Africa to top the table in 1992. These were high class imports whose presence drastically reduced opportunities for domestic riders. These developments were not matched in National Hunt racing, the Irish excepted, mainly because the earnings have not warranted it and also because jump racing is not such a major sport elsewhere in the world.

When Alex Greaves won the 1991 Lincoln handicap, Frankie Dettori finished in third place, two-and-a-quarter lengths behind her mount *Amenable*. Nineteenth-century jockeys faced no such competition from female riders. Victorian propriety may not even have allowed women to openly own horses.[6] Equestrian events have traditionally been one of the few sports where men and women compete on equal terms; but not in racing (Vamplew and Kay 2001). In Britain, the Jockey Club, for centuries a male fortress, did not allow women to race on the flat until 1972, compete against male amateurs until 1974 or race against male professionals until 1976, when forced to do so by sex discrimination legislation.[7] Opposition to women riders came from several quarters: conservative administrators who raised the economic smokescreen of the costs of providing separate changing facilities; chivalrous traditionalists who feared for the safety of women riders, especially over jumps; and many male jockeys, particularly the journeymen, who openly argued that women would be dangerous as they did not have the strength to control fractious horses but covertly feared more competition in an already oversupplied labour market (Ramsden 1973, 156). Arguments against the introduction of women jockeys were often patronizing, rarely substantiated and eventually overruled. Yet the removal of gender barriers has been more apparent than real. Although women have ridden winners in Britain, they have not yet, with the exception of Greaves, yet emerged as a threat to their male counterparts. Owners and trainers are still reluctant to employ female jockeys who are thus caught in a vicious circle of non-development: without rides, they cannot demonstrate their ability to win, but without a winning record, they cannot get the opportunities. This applied to the aspiring male rider as well, but with women, it is a prejudice to be overcome, not merely a rational comparison with the best male jockeys. Writing in the late 1980s, leading northern jockey Eddie Hide claimed that those women who were successful had generally relied on relatives to provide sufficient rides for them to gain experience and develop their skill (Hide 1989, 121). The great majority of Greaves's mounts came from Yorkshire trainer, David Nicolls, who was also her husband. In 1998, Sophia Mitchell remained the only professional female jump jockey. That season, she had 137 rides but only four winners, though she did not attribute this relative lack of success to gender, pointing out that 'there are a lot of jockeys worse off than me' (Sarah Potter, 'Chasing the Right Kind of Break', *The Times*, 5 June 1998).

In the stables, however, from where future jockeys might emerge, lasses are taking over from lads and recent staff training courses at both the British Racing School and the Northern Racing College have intakes dominated by females (Marcus Armytage, 'Girl Jockeys Preparing for Takeover' *Daily Telegraph*, 8 March 1997). Replacing stable lads with stable hands has proven economically viable as well as politically correct. Trainers appreciate – and exploit – female workers who love horses and are prepared to work long hours at menial tasks for little money simply to be with them. It is generally acknowledged that in some respects, girls make better grooms than boys as they are considered quieter and more reliable. Trainers also find them less militant. Susan Gallier, who worked as a stable hand in the 1980s in both France and Britain, felt that girls received preferential treatment as they were paid the same rate as the boys but were rarely asked to deal with a rampant colt or to unblock a stinking drain. That said boys were also more likely to be called on to ride trial gallops, an aspect of the job which provides valuable experience for the budding jockey. This is because many trainers adhere to the view that the very qualities that make women such good exercise riders – lightness and gentleness of touch – work against them as jockeys where full control of mounts is essential (Gallier 1988, 43–44).

One thing which flat-race jockeys can be thankful for is that they face no competition from amateur riders. Apart from novelty events, there are now no opportunities for amateurs to race against their paid counterparts on the flat. There are rare examples of successful amateurs in the nineteenth century such as 'Squire' Abington, but few amateurs were prepared to sacrifice the good life sufficiently to ride at flat-race weights. On the other hand, leading amateurs did win the National Hunt jockeys championship, the last being Harry Brown in 1919. Today amateurs can only compete against professionals over jumps if they have been awarded a permit as being competent to do so (Munting 1987, 135). Nevertheless, there are sufficient of them to reduce riding opportunities for the professionals. Of these, many are genuine amateurs who have no inclination to turn professional, but for some, it is a stepping stone towards professionalism. The Jockey Club has recognized this and now requires owners to pay them the equivalent of a riding fee when they put up an amateur who has had 75 rides in races open to professionals. They also suggest to successful amateurs that they consider turning professional, as they did to Peter Scudamore in 1979, who then went on to become joint champion National Hunt jockey in 1981–1982 (Lee 1980, 69).

Weight watching

During his winter holiday, Dettori's weight balloons out to 9 stone 2 lbs, but at the start of the racing season in March, he rides at 8 stone 5 lbs which, even with the lightest of saddles, necessitates turning the scales at 8 stone 3 lbs. To lose 13 lb is not easy, especially from a fit and already scrawny frame. That riding weight then has to be maintained for six to seven months if mounts are to be secured on a regular basis. Dettori has tried most options open to weight watchers including an American drug, Lasix, which brought about a five pound reduction in a matter of hours but had violent side-effects (Dettori 1997, 75). Like most elite jockeys, he has a sauna at home which can be supplemented by a similar facility at many racecourse to sweat off a vital pound or two just before a race. Records kept by Eddie Hide show that he had sweated off an average of 18 stone a season (Hide 1989, 229). The primary method of weight control is diet, which, according to Dettori, has 'become the most compelling factor in my life' (Dettori 1997, 73). Ex-champions Lester Piggott and Pat Eddery chose to eat very little, especially after they 'had conquered the hunger of the first few months'; they 'got used to having to go without', the former using cigars, the latter cigarettes to help suppress the appetite (Eddery 1993, 11; Piggott 1995, 16).

Fortunately for modern jockeys, they no longer have to rely simply on doing what their forefathers did. When Michael Turner became Chief Medical Adviser to the Jockey Club in the early 1990s, one of his early decisions was to treat jockeys as professional athletes and offer them scientific advice on nutrition and weight control. In the succeeding years, jockeys have also resorted more to the gym to help them lose weight and keep fit (Richard Evans, 'Dunwoody a Non-Runner in Retirement Stakes', *Daily Telegraph*, 22 March 1999).

In contrast, the nineteenth-century jockey relied on eating very little and a regimen of long walks in heavy clothes, Turkish baths and purgatives. Fred Archer, the champion jockey for 13 consecutive years from 1874 to 1876, once had to lose 12 lb in less than a week, an occasion on which yet again he resorted to 'Archer's Mixture', a devastating laxative developed for him by Dr J.R. Wright, a Newmarket physician. George Barrett was known to eat well then stick his fingers down his throat (Spencer 1900, 128). Such practices have not ceased. Ex-champion jockey turned television pundit, Willie Carson, notes that 'bulimia is not a secret in the weighing room' (Bob McGowan, 'Top Jockey's Great Race to Beat Eating Disorder', *Daily Express*, 27 March 1997).[8] Steve Cauthen, who rode a stone under his natural weight, exhibited bulimic behaviour and Walter Swinburn, who returned to racing following a horrific accident in Hong Kong which put him out for six months, has admitted to a 'persistent eating disorder' which forced him to take another 'temporary' retirement (Jamie Reid, 'Cool, Clear Walter', *Guardian*, 5 June 1998).

Almost by definition, there is no such person as a fat jockey: if riders cannot make the weight, then they do not have a job. Moreover, there is always the temptation to try and get an extra pound off so as to increase the chances of employment. Modern jockeys use a combination of diuretics, laxatives, rubber suits, saran warps, pre-race saunas and, despite Turner's advice, virtual starvation via appetite suppressants and self-discipline. Continued efforts by jockeys to keep their weight artificially low are dangerous to their health. Although Eddie Hide, who used to go running wrapped in sweaters and a mackintosh, found 'life more relaxing and easier once saunas became available', sauna-induced dehydration and long periods of inadequate nutrition reduce the ability to concentrate, affect the body's thermostatic qualities and blood flows, and deplete liver glycogen – all of which can lead to accidents and serious illness (Hide 1989, 50, 67; Gavin Evans, 'Medical Cabinet', *Guardian*, 15 May 1998). Leading flat rider, John Reid, was hospitalized by kidney stone caused by chronic dehydration (Joycelyn Targett, 'Slim Chance', *Sunday Telegraph Magazine*, 29 November 1998).

Certainly wasting contributed to the early deaths of Victorian riders, Tom French, John Charlton and Tom Chalenor, all of them Classic winners; John Wells, twice champion jockey; Archer himself; and in the early twentieth century, both three times champions, Danny Maher and Brownie Carslake (Tanner and Cranham 1992, 71, 129). Over time, the Jockey Club has raised the minimum weight to its present level of 7 stone 10 lbs in contrast to the 4 stone of 1850 and 5 stone 7 lbs of 1875.[9] In the nineteenth century, this was done to protect horses and owners rather than the jockeys. Too little weight implied insufficient strength to control a fractious mount which might have led to accidents or to erratic running in a tight finish, both of which could have financial consequences for those who owned valuable horseflesh. More recently, the legislation has recognized that, even for jockeys, average body weights have risen.

In the early nineteenth century, prior to minimum weight legislation, owners sometimes resorted to child riders. The official weight of little Kitchener when he won the Chester Cup in 1844 was a 'feather' (nominally four stone), but his actual body weight has been alleged at 2 stone 12 lbs. Such low weights imply very little strength, and if a horse proved troublesome, there was little that the diminutive rider could do. Fifteen-year-old George Fordham weighed only 3 stone 12 lbs when he won the 1851 Cambridgeshire but his horse ran on into Newmarket before he could pull it up. Five years later, in the Goodwood Stakes, *Chevy Chase* could not be controlled by his jockey, a little boy named Hearden, and he brought down seven other horses and put two jockeys in hospital for several weeks (Kent 1892, 122;

Astley 1895, 176; Tanner and Cranham 1992, 64). Although the days of the 'infant phenomenon' were legislated away, child riders continued well into the twentieth century before the minimum age was set at 15 in the 1960s (16 today). Eddie Hide was just 13 when he had his first official ride in 1950 and Lester Piggott rode his first winner at Haydock Park in 1948 aged only 12 (Hide 1989, 25–27; Piggott 1995, 11). It is worth noting that Hide, weighing just over four stone, found it difficult to control his mount which collided with the rails.

The whole system is artificial. At the elite level, some sports now resemble freak shows with seven-foot basketballers and 300-lb American footballers. Yet these athletes are not compelled to be so tall or so large: theoretically, and sometimes in practice, there is still room in these sports for the deviant normal-sized player. In horse racing, such a person has no place; at least not on horseback. Why jockeys have to be so small is not at all clear. In the mid-eighteenth century, nine stone seem to have been a minimum in racing for normal thoroughbreds.[10] The emergence of lighter weights probably owes something to gambling owners and most of them were – realizing that they gave an advantage in a race as well as lessening the risk that a valuable thoroughbred would break down. Such weights contradict the oft-used nineteenth-century rationale for horse racing as a racecourse test producing horses from which quality army remounts could be (half)bred. Put simply, army officers rarely weigh less than eight stone. There is more logic to the argument if applied to National Hunt racing where, perhaps because of its origins in the hunting field, average weights carried were normally two to three stone higher than on the flat (Vamplew and Kay 2006). However, paradoxically only flat racing qualified for the Sovereign's Plates, where racing was subsidized for such military breeding purposes (Kay 2000). Yet even modern jump jockeys have weight problems. Current champion, Tony McCoy, rides about two stone under his normal weight and lives on 'a near starvation diet' (McCoy and Duval 1998, 4). Striking a balance between sufficient strength and reduced weight is a continuing problem. Jockeys' weights are illogical, artificially imposed and dangerous to health, but they are unlikely to change as there are too many vested interests, including most existing jockeys who fear even more competition in the labour market if weight levels were raised significantly.

Industrial injuries

Dettori has ridden in only one National Hunt event, an invitation hurdle race at Cheltenham between flat and jump jockeys, in which he confesses he was 'terrified' (Dettori 1997, 94). And rightly so: Jockey Club figures show that a fall can be expected every 14 rides over jumps and hurdles and an injury every 80.[11] Imagine the state of mind of a jockey who has not fallen for 20 rides knowing that one is almost inevitable in the very near future. At least the jump jockey knows that most falls happen when his horse meets objects deliberately placed in its path and can be mentally prepared to take action. Flat racing has no such advance warning system and when a horse slips over at 35–40 miles per hour, often in the midst of other half-ton creatures, the consequences can be severe.[12] However, not all accidents occur during the race itself. The conclusions of local stewards' enquiries into flat-race accidents were published in the *Racing Calendar* from the late 1950s to the late 1960s and those for 1969 show that, while 60 falls occurred during the race, a further 17 took place in the parade ring, 35 on the way to the start, 44 at the starting gate and a further 12 after the race had finished.[13] So much can go wrong: a non-exhaustive review of accidents in flat racing in 1958 revealed that jockeys were injured by horses rearing in the parade ring, charging the starting gate, bolting, crossing legs, breaking blood vessels, running out at bends and striking the heels of another runner; as well as being pulled off by the starting gate and falling off because of a saddle slipping (*Racing Calendar* 1958). Although the domination of rides by the leading jockeys increases their chances of injury, it is the journeymen who have to ride the bad horses, of which, to quote Gur Lewis, one such rider, there are 'bad useless and bad horrible', the latter a dangerous mount. Yet the rides have to be taken: they might encourage the trainer to put you on a good horse and 'even if he doesn't, it's that fee in your pocket' (Magee and Lewis 1997, 130, 151). It has ever been the case. In contrast, leading jump jockeys with more rides available can afford 'to refuse the cash and be fit for a winner tomorrow' (Smith-Eccles 1987, 12).

All workers run the risk of industrial injury though for most the risk is minimal. For jockeys, however, serious injury at work is not a possibility or even a probability: it is inevitable. Every leading jockey, whether flat or National Hunt, has suffered serious injury during their careers. One survey of 700 jockeys found they aggregated over 1,000 fractures, mainly limbs (Gavin Evans, 'Medical Cabinet', *Guardian*, 15 May 1998). John Francombe, seven times National Hunt champion jockey, calculated that in 15 seasons, he lost 460 days through injury (Francombe 1985, 750. Terry Biddlecombe, champion jump jockey on three occasions in the 1960s, broke his shoulder blade six times, his wrists five times, bones in his left hand five times, his left collar-bone, elbow, forearm and ankle once each, as well as cracking two vertebrae, dislocating his right ankle, breaking a rib and chipping a bone in his shin; not to mention over 100 cases of concussion (Fitzgeorge-Parker 1971, 58–59). In Biddlecombe's day, a jockey could have a terrible fall but, if showing no signs of distress, be allowed to ride in the next race. Now Jockey Club regulations enforce a compulsory suspension of up to 21 days where concussion has occurred. This has come too late to prevent 'punch drunkenness' among several retired National Hunt riders (John Oaksey, 'Imaging Taking a Hammering' *Daily Telegraph*, 20 February 1998; Robert Philip, 'Therapist Harnesses Horse Power to Help the Wounded', *Daily Telegraph*, 1 February 1998). Since 1980, there have been seven deaths on the British turf, five of them in National Hunt racing (G. Rock, 'Silent Tributes Paid to Memory of Davis', *Observer*, 21 July 1996). Although comparative calculations are difficult because of inadequate measures of participation, it has been suggested that jump racing ranks below only mountaineering and aerial sports in risk of fatality (Magee and Lewis 1997, 28). Champion jump jockey, Tony McCoy, puts it succinctly: 'any time you walk to your car at the end of the day; that's not a bad day' (David Walsh, 'Fall Guys', *Inside Sport*, December 1997, 92). So far, Dettori's worst injury has been a broken elbow which put him out of racing for four months; but he is still only in his mid-twenties (Dettori 1997, 130).

Riding work is a way of becoming acquainted with the idiosyncrasies of the horses of particular trainers. For many mounts, however, jockeys have little or no knowledge of the animal which they are to pilot, an extreme example of this being Eddie Hide's 1973 Derby-winning ride on *Morston*, a horse that he had never seen until he entered the paddock. Since horses vary in temperament such ignorance is potentially dangerous, particularly as 'charm and placidity are not the qualities that win races' (Barnes 1988, 20). Thoroughbred racehorses are highly strung animals, inclined at the best of times to be fractious, especially when young. Inexperienced horses too can be dangerous but the 'schooling' of horses, particularly over hurdles and jumps, has never been a major priority in Britain. However, following the enquiry into the death of Richard Davis, who was crushed under an inexperienced horse which simply failed to rise at the first fence, the Jockey Club have insisted that unreliable jumpers are banned from the racetrack (J.A. McGrath. 'Bad Jumpers to Face Bans Under Safety Proposals', *Daily Telegraph*, 12 December 1996). Fortunately, Jockey Club minimum weight legislation and the coming of compulsory education put paid to that other dangerous youth, the child rider. Regulations on the licensing of amateur riders from 1879 also ensured that only 'gentlemen' of certain ability were allowed to compete against professionals, though, as with child riders, the rationale was to protect valuable horseflesh not the bones of the riders.[14] Jockeys have also developed their own risk-minimization procedures. Particularly in National Hunt racing, they will use the dressing room and 'the mill' at the start to discuss their plans through the first obstacle so as to avoid calamity in early traffic. During the race information on positions and gaps is readily exchanged: as Grand National winner Carl Llewelyn has pointed out, 'the more people are aware of everything in the race, the better' (Doust 1992, 89; Chris Madigan, 'Turf Life', *Total Sport* 37, January 1999, 66).

Until well into the twentieth century, little safety equipment was available to protect the rider. In 1923, crash helmets for jump jockeys became compulsory following the death of Captain Bennett at Wolverhampton but this was only for racing and was not enforced for training gallops until the 1970s (Munting 1987, 151). Body protectors too are now mandatory. Jimmy Thompson, along with Lester Piggott, was a prime mover in the introduction of goggles, though not until he lost an eye in an accident at Newcastle (Hide 1989, 21). As late as 1980, a majority of jockeys thought that 'the safety precautions provided for them were laughable', but much has been done in the past decade or so to lessen the risk of injury from course layout and construction (Lee 1980, 156). Turns have been made less stiff, heights of fences and hurdles have been regulated, and the jumps themselves redesigned to encourage horses to take off correctly (Magee 1995, 38). To its credit, the Jockey Club discontinued all-weather jumping on the grounds of safety in 1994 and, two years later, outlawed chase or hurdle racing on any going officially described as 'hard'. Since 1984, the Levy Board has increased its grants to replace concrete posts with plastic ones and to introduce light plastic running rails at fences and hurdles (Munting 1987, 143; J. Garnsey, 'Injured Jockey Blasts Jockey Club Policy', *Daily Express*, 20 September 1996; John Oaksey, 'Early Learning Essential to Improve Safety', *Daily Telegraph*, 11 April 1997).

Not until the mid-twentieth century was an insurance scheme established to look after the interests of professional jockeys.[15] Up to that point, distressed riders had to appeal to the trustees of various funds for assistance. The nineteenth century had seen the Bentinck Benevolent and Rous Memorial Funds both set up to honour distinguished turf administrators. In 1923, the Jockey Club inaugurated the Jockeys Accident Fund, but it was stressed that, despite its nomenclature, no jockey had a right to draw upon it. Jump jockeys had recourse to nothing but individual charity until the Rendlesham Benevolent Fund of 1902 made some provision for jockeys killed or injured whilst riding in National Hunt races. It was open only to licensed professionals, and payment was entirely at the discretion of the management committee. After the First World War, this was reinforced by the National Hunt Accident Fund which paid £1,000 in instances of death and £3 a week for 26 weeks for temporary disablement. The fund was initially financed by half of the jockeys' licence fees with supplementation after the 1920s from the Racecourse Betting Control Board (later the Horserace Betting Levy Board)(Munting 1987, 132–133, 142). During the 1963/1964, jumping season riders, Tim Brookshaw and Paddy Farrell, both broke their backs and a public appeal raised nearly £48,000 for them. Another £6,000 came in after the appeal had been closed and this was used as the basis for the Injured National Hunt Jockeys' Fund. In

1971, this was renamed the Injured Jockeys' Fund to incorporate flat-race jockeys, though, as might be anticipated, the demands on its resources have been dominated by those who ride over hedges and hurdles. As a registered charity, the Fund is dependent on public goodwill. By the mid-1990s, the pay out to jockeys, most of whom had to quit racing because of their injuries, totalled £3.4 million with a further £2.3 million outstanding in low-interest loans (Alcock 1978, 58–59; Injured Jockeys Fund 1996).

The Fund is not designed to cope with short-term injuries. For this, there is the Professional Riders Insurance Scheme which has emerged out of the Racehorse Owners Compensation Fund. It is financed by a mandatory levy on owners of 13% on all riding fees. This raises about half a million pounds a year of which about half is spent on weekly compensation for temporary injuries and most of the rest on premiums to insure all professional jockeys against death or career-ending injuries. The weekly benefits are paid on a sliding scale dependent on the number of rides the jockey had the previous season, ranging from £100 plus sickness benefit for less than 75 mounts to £1033 at the top level. However, what is being compensated for is the loss of riding fees not the share of prize money lost, and thus, some jockeys also subscribe to private insurance schemes, though premiums are not cheap and cover is limited. Although Lester Piggott, who retired in 1995, accepted that during his long career, there had been 'massive advances in racecourse safety', as well as better equipment and improved medical guidelines, he still maintained that riding 'remains a very dangerous and potentially lethal business' (Piggott 1995, 214–215). Serious injuries today are at an all-time high and, in early 1997, a record 31 jockeys were being paid weekly compensation under the Professional Riders Insurance Scheme (John Oaksey, 'Counting the Cost of Top Jockeys on Injured List', *Daily Telegraph*, 28 February 1997). In earlier days, with no such source of compensatory income, many of them might have been tempted to continue to ride whilst injured.

Trains and boats and planes ... and cars

In 1995, when both Frankie Dettori and his challenger for the championship, Jason Weaver, had more than 1000 rides in the UK, they travelled some 200,000 miles (Dettori 1997, 92). The vocation of jockeys is significantly different from most occupations in that the main place of work changes almost daily. Few race meetings last more than three days and most are single day affairs. In the pre-railways, jockeys had to travel to meetings by coach, on horseback, or even walking with their racing saddles tied to their waist. The coming of the railway eased travel problems but most top jockeys took advantage of the new mode of transport not to relax but to increase their workloads and earnings. Tommy Loates, for one, travelled 2000 miles and rode 33 times in 17 days in 1889, including successive days at Derby, Paris and Nottingham. Indeed, increasingly during the nineteenth century, leading jockeys took advantage of changes in race dates following the emergence of enclosed suburban courses to race in Britain on a Saturday and in France the next day. From the 1840s, full racing results, including the name of every rider in every race, are available in the *Racing Calendar* and this allows the tracing of individual work patterns. Nat Flatman, champion jockey in 1849 when the railway network was relatively undeveloped, raced on only 79 days of the season, but by 1899, Sammy Loates, the leading rider that year, was able to manage 179 days. Estimates of the respective distances travelled are 4270 and 10,770 miles (Tolson and Vamplew 1998, 42–43).

Two major points can be made about the workloads of the modern jockey. First, the vast majority would prefer it to be heavier. The top few jockeys monopolize the mounts available leaving the bulk of riders to join the demoralizing and stressful struggle for the remaining opportunities. Given that Dettori and other elite riders have a ride in most races at the meetings they attend, for the majority of jockeys there is more money to be made in riding work and schooling horses than in race riding (Chris Madigan, 'Turf Life', *Total Sport* 37, January 1999, 63). Second, to the initial travel convenience offered by the railway can be added that of the automobile, plane and helicopter, all of which have enabled top riders to race more frequently than in the past, often including both afternoon and evening meetings on the same day in their itinerary.[16] Generally, a top professional jockey may have to cover between 50,000 and 60,000 miles annually in Britain alone. As current champion Kieren Fallon puts it, 'all you do is live in the car and drive to racing'. Driving long distances is a routine part of a jockey's life, though motorways and ring roads have eased the hassle and, according to Eddie Hide, have helped halve the journey times between the 1950s and the late 1980s (Hide 1989, 34; Magee 1995, 115; Sue Mott, 'Fallon Keeps Tight Rein', *Daily Telegraph*, 30 May 1998). Nevertheless, Dettori is of the opinion that 'the motorways ... have finished off more jockeys than anything else', not in the sense of road fatalities and injuries – though this is surprising given the maniac, certainly risky driving, which comes through in all jockey biographies – but because the journeyman jockey has 'to flog halfway across the country to ride a useless horse with no possibility of winning' (Dettori 1997, 85; Magee and Lewis 1997, 12). The elite can afford to employ a chauffeur; the rest have to drive themselves or arrange lifts with colleagues. For the elite, there is also air travel. As early as 1946, Tommy Weston flew 1000 miles in a week to ride at York, Newmarket, Salisbury. Liverpool and Goodwood (Weston 1952, 179). Today, most leading jockeys have their own planes enabling them to leave home later, arrive fresher and get back earlier. Thanks to air travel most top flat-race jockeys also race for lucrative prizes on the continent most Sundays (thus freeing up Sunday rides at home for lesser jockeys). Flying has also allowed jockeys to race overseas both during the domestic close season – though this also occurred in the days when seafaring was required – and for short spells or even one meeting in Europe, America or Asia. In 1995, in addition to his UK rides, Dettori had mounts in France, Germany, Italy, the US, Australia, Dubai and Hong Kong. As the money in overseas racing has increased, winter contracts have provided quality jockeys with well-paid holidays. Only a minority of riders, however, can pursue this avenue, and it is one that is not so readily available to National Hunt riders because of the geographically restricted nature of the branch of the sport.

Earnings and emulation

When Dettori first came to England in 1985 at the age of 14 to work at the Newmarket stables of Luca Cumani, he was paid £12 a week plus board (Dettori 1997, 14). Now he earns a six figure sum because, like other top jockeys, he has the ability to make that split-second decision during a race which means the difference between winning and losing, between success and failure, between a horse being worth a few million or a few hundred thousand.[17] It is difficult to find accurate figures on earnings but some estimates can be made on the basis of the basic riding fee and the percentage of the prize money which placed jockeys receive. Even without the presents from grateful owners and backers, or the retainers to secure the services of the best performers, it is clear that, as in the nineteenth century, there is an earnings pyramid with rewards reflecting the skewed distribution of mounts and even more so that of winning rides. In his first week back after serious injury, Dettori won races worth over £400,000 from which he would receive his 4.5% (Dettori 1997, 186). Dettori also had a handsome retainer from the Dubai-based Godolphin training establishment. Along with perhaps four or five others, he makes an exceptional living from propelling half a ton of horseflesh faster than most of his rivals. Eddie Hide, writing in 1988, accepted that the very top jockeys were probably millionaires (Hide 1989, 205). Next come the two dozen or so who can ride perhaps 20 winners a season. They are followed by 'a large band of men who struggle to make ends meet', who earn relatively little and obtain most of their income from riding work rather than races (Hide 1989, 205; Dettori 1997, 30).

The money to be earned from jump and hurdle racing bears little comparison with that available on the flat. The basic riding fee is higher but the level of prize money substantially lower and always has been. As on the flat, a few outstanding individuals dominate the earnings pyramid. Champion jockey Tony McCoy paid his agent £17,000 in 1998 which suggests earnings of just under £200.000 (Charlie Brooks, 'Agent is the Central Source of Information', *Daily Telegraph*, 1 February 1999). Richard Dunwoody, champion in 1993 and 1994, may earn around the same whereas, in contrast, Guy Lewis who had 88 rides in 1996 actually made a loss after travel expenses, valet and agent fees, and equipment costs (Magee and Lewis 1997, 218). One estimate is that 250 rides and 20 winners are now required to show a surplus at the end of the season, a figure attained by around 30 jockeys. Dunwoody reckons 'only five or six of us make a good living' and overall 'very few jump jockeys make more than a very basic living' (Robert Philp. 'Dunwoody at Forefront of a Revolution', *Daily Telegraph*, 15 March 1999; Giles Smith, 'Dunwoody Still Down But No Longer Riding For a Fall', *Daily Telegraph*, 31 October 1998; Magee and Lewis 1997, 36).

Then, there is the matter of physic income from the applause of the crowd and the plaudits of the media. Dettori was not the first jockey to achieve 'superstar' status. Fred Archer, the long-legged 'Tinman' who won over a third of his 8,004 races, including 21 Classics, has that honour. Town criers announced his arrival; 'Stevengraphs' of his image had record sales; special trains brought adoring crowds to his wedding; and Newmarket virtually closed on the day of his funeral (Tanner and Cranham 1992, 78, 105; Humphris 1923, 76; Welcome 1990, 158–159). Nevertheless, Dettori inhabits a much more media-aware world in which he is used by racing to promote the sport not only to the initiated but also by appearances on pop music programmes and in other non-racing venues. His behaviour has broken the mould and taken some of the stuffy insularity out of English racing. Until Frankie's era riders rarely exhibited excitement, emotion or even enthusiasm for their job. Dettori's trademark flying leap from winning mounts, fractured English, and charismatic flamboyance have endeared him to the racing public. Yet even stars can crash to earth both literally and metaphorically. In September 1996, to the delight of Ascot racegoers, Dettori galloped into turf history as the first jockey to win all seven races on the card. A season later he looked ridiculous when dumped by his mount *Sea Wave* as it left the starting stalls in the Prix Neil at Longchamp, and he also felt the sting of public criticism when his riding tactics cost *Swain* victory in the Breeders' Cup (Sue Mott, 'Under the Whip', *Daily Telegraph*, 9 January 1999). But the crowd and punters do not pay the jockey's wages. The rider is more concerned with the reaction of owners and trainers. There is a racing aphorism that good jockeys lose fewer races that they should have won than do other riders. This is appreciated by trainers such as Henry Cecil who stood by Kieran Fallon after his poor performance on *Bosra Sham* in the 1997 Eclipse Stakes. Fallon went on to become champion jockey. A general loss of form is more worrying than a momentary lapse in judgement. Adrian Maguire, number one National Hunt rider for the Jackdaws Castle stable, was forced to resign his position and go freelance in 1998 when owners put pressure on trainer David Nicholson to replace him with Richard Johnson who had ridden twice as many winners (Brough Scott, 'How Maguire Suffered in the Battle of Jackdaws Castle', *Sunday Telegraph*, 3 January 1999).

In racing success breeds success and it is often easier to remain at the top than to get there. Owners wish to have a fashionable jockey on board their animals so if he – or increasingly his agent – is a good judge of horseflesh more winning rides will come his way. One notable change over the past two decades, and particularly in the 1990s, has been the emergence of the jockey's agent, first used in Britain by Willie Carson. Lester Piggott, renowned for 'jocking off' other riders from animals he fancied in big races, finally succumbed and employed Anna Ludlow, a Newmarket businesswoman, as his agent. Today even some apprentices, no longer subject to the restrictions of the old indenture contract, have agents (Piggott 1995, 277). Prior to this development, a top jockey could spend as much time on the phone trying to secure rides as on the horses themselves. One can only wonder how barely literate Fred Archer managed to arrange his 667 rides in 1885. The use of agents who offer trainers their complete client list obviously reduces the opportunities for spare mounts for lesser riders. In the nineteenth century, a retainer from an owner guaranteed rides, but, over time stable retainers from public trainers were seen as more attractive as they were less reliant on the whims of an individual owner. However, a retainer does mean that a jockey has to accept all mounts supplied, good or bad, and many riders view going freelance as a chance to be more selective, though it has a downside in that he 'must try to keep all his contacts sweet so that none of his sources of mounts dries up' (O'Neill 1985, 82). Here, the agent can usefully shoulder the burden. What agents do not do is remove the need for the ambitious jockey to study form, to watch races in which he does not have a ride, and to replay videos in the evenings so that he is aware of the potential opposition in his next races. This also enables him to learn the characteristics of his own future mounts: Is it a horse which needs 'covering up' during a race; does it run better on hard or soft ground; does it have finishing speed? For the aspiring jockey, the key is getting a chance to ride in a race. As Dettori puts it, 'ability, natural light weight, temperament, and the right attitude to work are helpful but do not guarantee success. You also need opportunity' (Dettori 1997, 30). It may come from the misfortune of others, unable to ride through injury, or due to successful networking, but it has to be seized. In particular, winning a televised race can get a rider noticed and set his mobile phone ringing.

Money and fame tempt many to try but few turtles reach the sea. Director of the British Racing School, Rory MacDonald, estimates that nine of ten budding apprentices fail to become full professional jockeys.[18] Little has changed since 1900 when of the 187 registered apprentices only 75 became jockeys and a mere 23 (12%) continued as such for more than three years.[19] As they receive weight allowances in recognition of their inexperience, outstanding apprentices and conditional riders can do well. In 1923, Charlie Elliott was champion jockey whilst still an apprentice, as was Elijah Wheatley 18 years before him. Under the scheme brought in 1991, the allowance is progressively reduced, disappearing after a total of winners reaches 85. Losing one's 'claim' to an allowance is a major rite of passage after which the young rider has to compete on ability alone. Even a leading apprentice has no guarantee of success. Lester Piggott, Pat Eddery and Dettori himself all went on to become champion jockeys, but who recalls David Coates or Richard Dicey, joint champion apprentices in 1968?

Both historically and contemporarily, most elite jockeys have come from families associated with racing. Dettori's father, Gianfranco, was champion jockey in Italy 13 times. Journeymen National Hunt riders too generally have equestrian backgrounds. Nevertheless, particularly in flat racing, there is room for the uninitiated. Steve Donaghue, winner of six Derbies, ran away from a Warrington wire works at the beginning of the century; victor in five Classics, Geoff Lewis came to racing from being a pageboy at a London hotel; and leading apprentice Royston Ffrench had never ridden before he attended the British Racing School. That said, those with families associated with the sport have the advantage of early training and later support by relatives who know the industry.

Successful jockeys have to possess many skills, including being smart out of the stalls, balance on the horse, rapport with their mounts, judgement of pace, the ability to look behind while keeping a horse running straight, using the whip both left- and right-handed and being able to transfer it from one to the other if necessary during a hard finish. Some stables, especially those with ex-jockeys on the staff, taught apprentices how to race ride. Indeed where an apprenticeship promised the trainer half the boy's earnings it was in his interest to do so. Men such as Frenchie Nicholson, Sam Armstrong and Major Sneyd, a first rate but hard teacher from whose stables graduated brothers Doug and Eph Smith as well as Joe Mercer, earned a reputation as well as an income from their ability to produce good, young riders. Other trainers, perhaps the majority, saw apprentices as simply cheap, stable labour (Nicholson 1966, 206–208; Smith 1968, 24–25, 38–39; Francombe 1985, 27; Baerlein 1987, 21). Until two decades ago, apprentices were indentured to a trainer with whom they had to stay until they completed their articles. Today, they have the freedom to switch stables, though, at the insistence of the Jockey Club, they are not allowed to race ride for the remainder of the season unless both trainers agree. This is rarely implemented. The old apprenticeship system has now gone, along with what many believed to be overharsh discipline, but, with nothing to tie an apprentice to a stable, the incentive to pass on advice and give young riders a chance has been weakened (Weston 1952, 13; Hide 1989, 238–239). Indeed, most apprentices are now virtually freelance riders, and though trainers no longer take half their earnings, they no longer pay half their expenses.

Based on an assumption that the traditional system of training – if indeed it could warrant such a designation – was failing to produce riders capable of matching foreign jockeys coming to ply their trade in Britain, an enquiry by John Marriage QC in the early 1980s recommended the establishment of an apprentice training school. The British Racing School at Newmarket, and to a lesser extent, the Northern Racing College at Rossington Hall near Bawtry took on this task. The Northern Racing College, however, has always given priority to training stable staff and recently the British Racing School has also gone down this track though with other courses being offered to apprentices in which they are taught the essential skills required before riding in public and how to improve their race and work riding. When the apprentices lose their seven-pound allowance, they are given a three-day intermediate course dealing not so much with riding as with career management, money matters, interview techniques, fitness and diet.

That is the extent of the teaching available. Once apprentices become fully fledged jockeys they are on their own; all further skills acquisition is very much a matter of independent learning. As Eddie Hide put it, good jockeys 'keep learning'. To some extent, this involved tips from admired senior riders; Edgar Britt taught him to hold the reins shorter on a tight track and Frankie Durr to catch hold of the mane in the stalls to give the horse full freedom when it jumped out (Hide 1989, 60, 80). Otherwise, it was down to experience. Racing itself was the best way to appreciate that different tracks required different skills: that Brighton's long, uphill finish was a different proposition to the sharp, ill-cambered final bend and short run-in at Catterick; that Chester's sharp left-hand bends do not suit big horses; and that the steep and perilous descent to Tattenham Corner at Epsom can cause tired horses to drop back and impede other runners.

As this suggests, many skills were acquired or refined simply via 'learning by doing'. At times, however, new skills had to be developed as a matter of urgency. In 1965, the introduction of starting stalls in flat racing meant that the experience of jockeys who knew how different starters operated the gate and had the ability to manoeuvre horses ready for the off was rendered redundant virtually overnight. Now what had to be learned was the art of keeping horses ready for the opening of the stalls and being prepared to go instantly from a standing start. In the 1980s, the introduction of all-weather tracks on which a smooth run was all-important necessitated the development of new tactics. Some riders grasped the essentials quicker than others, and it was on such tracks at Wolverhampton, and particularly Southwell, that Alex Greaves established herself as 'Queen of the Sands'. More recently, furore has erupted over the new restrictions placed on the use of whips. Jockeys propel their mounts mainly by physical effort and skill, using legs, hands and heels, sometimes their voice, but the only material aid permitted is the whip. Recently, the Jockey Club, under the pressure of public opinion, has taken exception to 'excessive' use of this implement and it has taken many riders some time to come to terms with what is now required (Richard Evans, 'Whip Ban to Carry More Sting', *Times*, 12 January 1999). Yet having to adjust to innovation is nothing new. In the late nineteenth century, a whole new style of riding had to be learned when the American invasion threatened the livelihood of British jockeys. The Americans were masters of their craft but the key factor was their riding style. Crouching along the horse's neck, they rode with the saddle pushed forward, reins and stirrups shortened, and knees bent. This not only provided a better weight distribution on the horse, it also offered less wind resistance. For a while, there was a possibility that the American jockeys would dominate British racing, but then, many local riders adopted the American style and were able to compete more effectively (Vamplew 2004).[20]

Power relationships

In 1996, when Dettori won the 2000 Guineas, he was fined £500 for his flying leap from the saddle, performed illegally before his horse had left the track; he was also suspended for eight days for excessive use of the whip (Dettori 1997, 120). The Jockey Club has never been in awe of leading riders. In 1901, when suspicion of corruption fell on Lester Reiff he was simply told not to bother to reapply for his licence. In the 1920s, Derby-winning jockey Charlie Smirke was banned *sine die* (in actuality for five years) for not trying at the start of a two-year-old plate. More recently, record-breaking National Hunt champion Tony McCoy received five suspensions totalling 33 days for excessive use of the whip and was sent to the British racing School to learn how to modify his technique. Although its role in the running of racing had been diluted in the past decade, the Jockey Club remains the paramount disciplinary authority in the sport. These days jockeys can be represented by solicitors when brought before the Portland Square stewards, but in the past even natural justice had no place in that establishment. Until very recently, the stewards retained the right to refuse a licence to any jockey without having to specify a reason. Even in 1999, amidst allegations of race-fixing, there has been debate about the legal and moral authority of the Club in forcing jockeys to pay for racing's discomfiture by suspending riders who had been arrested but not charged, let alone convicted. Suspension for riding offences is more common that in Archer's era, especially since the introduction of the patrol camera in the 1960s, and, more recently, of a totting up system under which, once 12 days have been accumulated under one head of offences, another 14 days ban is automatic. In contrast to Archer who, despite his aggressive riding, received only 14 days suspension in his career, the modern top jockeys expects at least a compulsory fortnight's holiday almost every season (Tanner and Cranham 1992, 12). Additionally fines are levied on jockeys for a variety of offences. On the more positive side, it was the Jockey Club which took steps in the nineteenth century to protect the income of riders by insisting that riding fees were deposited by owners with the clerk of the course before the race took place; and in 1969, it determined that jockeys should receive a guaranteed percentage of prize money which was paid to them by Weatherby's, the Club's administrative arm.

Nevertheless, the attitude of the Jockey Club towards riders remained almost feudal well into the twentieth century. A television documentary in 1982 revealed that the stewards at York treated senior jockeys such as Willie Carson and Eddie Hide like errant schoolboys, demanding that they stand to attention while being questioned and insisting on being called 'Sir' by the riders but addressing them by their surnames. The resultant outcry led to the Club adopting the courtesy of calling jockeys 'Mister' (Francombe 1985, 86; Hide 1989, 243). Until the past two decades or so, the Jockey Club has shown little inclination to being ex-jockeys into the regulatory process. The application form for the position of Stewards' Secretary in the 1970s asked candidates to supply their 'rank and regiment' and, when Eddie Hide applied for the position in the mid-1980s, the successful applicant was the one individual with virtually no racing experience, though he was a former household cavalry officer (Hide 1989, 8–9). More recently, several retired jockeys have been employed by the Club as inspectors and safety officials.

Jockeys are involved in several other power relationships within the sport. Apprentices, like stable lads, have been subject historically to the almost absolute power of the trainer. More recently, that power has been curtailed by the development of trade unionism within the stables and, so some trainers argue, by the indentured apprenticeship becoming defunct. That said, many trainers and owners still believe in a master and servant relationship. Dettori may be a millionaire, but he tips his cap to the owner of his mount and calls him 'Sir' when he enters the saddling enclosure, a symbolic reminder of the power relationship between employer and employee. Anthropologist Kate Fox has argued that the body language indicates that this is a vestigial gesture rather than an expression of genuine deference, particularly since syndicalization has to a degree democratized ownership. Be that as it may, jockeys Francome and Hide both attest that 'tact' and 'diplomacy' are vital components of success and that 'chatting up' owners and trainers 'can be the most important part of the job' (Lee 1980, 57; Francombe 1985, 42; Hide 1989, 237; Fox 1997, 16). Owners do not like to acknowledge that they have purchased a dud and would rather blame the jockey than his mount (Smith-Eccles 1987, 46). According to Jeff King, rider of over 700 National Hunt winners, loyalty by owners to the jockeys they employ 'is not one of this sport's most obvious qualities' (Lee 1980, 116). Hence, the occurrence of what Derby-winner Bill Rickaby describes as 'the series of sackings which plague almost every jockey's career' and what Michael Caulfield, executive manager of the Jockeys Association, labels a working life of confidence-sapping mental abuse (Rickaby 1969, 16; Lee 1980, 116; Smith-Eccles 1987, 46; Caulfield interviewed by the author, 2 June 1999). More recently, the friction between owner and rider surfaced over the issue of sponsorship. The Jockeys Association secured sponsorship for its members to be displayed on their breeches and polo neck, but the Racehorse Owners Association insisted on individual owners having a veto which could deprive riders of an extra £10 a mount (Chris McGrath, 'Savill Stalls on Jockeys Logos', *Times*, 15 December 1998).

Although jockeys are in competition for mounts, wins and prize money, and 'jocking off' has become more prevalent since agents began to do the scrambling for rides, inside the weighing room, a jockey's sanctuary from which all others are excluded, the atmosphere resembles that of a team sport (Fox 1997, 32). Mutual support, trust and good fellowship abound within a group bonded by the risk and excitement of their occupation. Francome says it is the possibility of being injured that creates the 'wonderful camaraderie' amongst jump jockeys. It is a rare professional sport where in 1982 a potential champion (John Francombe) simply refused further rides once he had equalled the total of the existing leader (Peter Scudamore) who had been sidelined for the rest of the season with a broken arm when 20 wins ahead (Francombe 1985, 72, 108–110). Nevertheless, it was not until the 1960s that this solidarity manifested itself into organized form, most particularly in the founding of the Jockeys Association in 1969 via an amalgamation of the northern and southern sections of the Flat Race Jockeys Association and the Professional National Hunt Jockeys Association, all of which had developed a few years earlier. The Association has concerned itself with matters of racecourse facilities and safety and also operates a pension fund, savings plans and insurance services. Although it negotiates with the Racehorse Owners Association on riding fees, in many respects, it is more of a guild than a union, with a prime aim of maintaining the highest standards of integrity among its members. When confrontations have occurred, they have been flashpoint combinations of riders rather than premeditated strikes, as when jockeys refused to race at Beverley in 1989 and at Haydock in 1996 because of what they judged to be dangerous riding conditions ('Jockey Club Rules under the Microscope', *Daily Express*, 20 February 1997). Despite, or perhaps because of, its lack of militancy, jockeys do not have representation on the British Horseracing Board, unlike the owners and the racecourse operators.

Corruptive influences

No mention of racing scandal is associated with the Dettori name. He has been accused of losing through misjudgement and over confidence but never by deliberately stopping a horse. Although Dettori says that he has never been asked to pull a horse in Britain, there is no doubt that a subculture of corruption has long existed in racing (Helena de Bertodano, 'Life after the Ascot Seven', *Sunday Telegraph*, 11 May 1997). Because of its connection with gambling, racing has always been subject to corrupting influences. Knowing that a jockey will not be trying to win on a particular horse gives a gambler an advantage in the betting markets. Most jockeys understand that in an overcrowded labour market, riding to orders was crucial to their future employment prospects: and those orders were not always to win (Weston 1952, 26; Robert Philp. 'Aintree Anti-Hero Savouring the Lucky Life of Ups and Downs', *Daily Telegraph*, 25 March 1996). Neither the extent of corruption in racing nor the degree of involvement of jockeys can be quantified. Malpractice certainly occurs. Racing writer Danny Hall acknowledges that 'no-one with the remotest connection to the turf believes that racing is scrupulously clean', but few accept that up to 30% of races are fixed, as was alleged by the disillusioned and dispirited Lewes trainer, Roger Hoad (*Daily Express*, 28 February 1998; Richard Evans, 'Hoad Risks Disciplinary Charges', *Times*, 19 February 1998). Owner Stan Hay notes that

> racing may have its problems, but its stables are nowhere near as dirty as some of those in other areas of public life ... none of us can pretend that racing is completely clean, but nor is it as bent as some other sports wracked by drugs and gambling scams. Nor indeed is it any more corrupt than the financial services industry, whose various disgraces over the last decade far outstrip anything that racing has so far produced' (Stan Hay, 'Odds and Sods', *Independent*, 19 January 1998).

All that can be asserted is that, for some riders, losing is a more certain way to make money than trying to win. Even those jockeys anxious to create a positive image for their sport do not deny that corruption occurs, though they stress that elite jockeys are not involved (Francombe 1985, 127). Jockeys would be fools to risk riding doped horses – the game is dangerous enough anyway – but making sure that a horse does not feature in a finish is still relatively easy even with the race patrol camera and Jockey Club regulations on riding out. This may not be at the behest of gamblers but simply riding to orders so as to deceive the handicapper. Nevertheless, Gut Lewis notes that 'it's an open secret in the weighing room that some jockeys have close associations with big punters' (Magee and Lewis 1997, 127). If this becomes less of a secret, their careers might be at risk: at one point, John Francombe was suspended by the Jockey Club for six weeks as his relationship with bookmaker, John Banks, was seen as being damaging to the interests of racing (Francombe, 1985, 16).

In 1992, Dettori had his license to ride withdrawn by the Hong Kong racing authorities after he had been caught in possession of cocaine (Dettori 1997, 35). This use of drugs seems to have been a youthful indiscretion rather than related to his occupation. For other jockeys, however, drug and alcohol abuse is a product of a stressful life. Few would argue with Dettori's claim that 'being a jockey is a pressure job, and when things don't go well, you take your losers home' (Dettori 1997, 2). No one is immune. In the year he was champion jockey Doug Smith once went over 100 rides without a winner. Nevertheless, a good jockey with plenty of rides can expect most losing streaks to end relatively quickly; a lesser rider might have to wait some time, all the while having his confidence sap away. John Reid, a leading rider, talks of getting 'grumpy' with his family (Joycelyn Targett, 'Slim Chance', *Sunday Telegraph Magazine*, 29 November 1998). Graham Thorner, National Hunt Champion in 1971, reckoned 'the worst thing about the job was the periods of depression when I couldn't ride a winner' (Lee 1980, 51). Moreover, every time jockeys race they are subject to public and employer appraisal; they are constantly watching their weight; and they anticipate injury each time they get on a horse. No wonder so many jockeys appear to have used alcohol to escape reality. Jem Snowden is said to have turned up a week late for Chester races; Charles Marlow to have lost a two-horse race for the 1850 Doncaster Cup on the odds-on favourite through lack of sobriety; and, after a morning at the brandy bottle, Bill Scott is alleged to have been so drunk at the 1846 Derby that he did not realize the race had started (Vamplew 1975, 164; Tanner and Cranham 1992, 55).[21] In the modern era, both Walter Swinburn and Steve Cauthen have acknowledged having drinking problems. National hunt riders, with notable exceptions, such as teetotallers Tony McCoy, Jonjo O'Neill and John Francome, see drinking as part of the social life associated with their sport. And regard it as a means of winding down. Whether the stress or the culture of their working lives contributed to jockeys resorting to alcohol more than other workers remains conjectural in the light of current research (Lee 1980, 11; James Lawton, 'A Lifetime of Agony' *Express Sport*, 18 January 1998; Jamie Reid, 'Cool, Clear Walter', *Guardian*, 5 June 1998).[22]

The effects of alcohol are often aggravated by a lack of food. Nutrition expert Professor Michael Lean suggests that 'alcoholism is a probable effect of being starved' (Joycelyn Targett, 'Slim Chance', *Sunday Telegraph Magazine*, 29 November 1998). Allegedly both Cauthen and Swinburn were bulimic. Yet, although the idea of a drunk or drugged jockey aboard a horse is a frightening one, the Jockey Club took no action on this issue till October 1994 when, at the instigation of Michael Turner, their new chief medical adviser, a protocol was developed for banned substances. These included marijuana, cocaine, amphetamines and alcohol, the threshold of the latter initially being set at the drink-driving limit but later reduced to half that level (Jockey Club 1994). Some 600 tests have revealed no alcohol abuse, but one apprentice and two conditional riders have been suspended for recreational drug use, though it should be noted that amphetamines, the banned substance in two of the cases, speed up the metabolism and can be used for weight loss (Letter from Michael Turner to the author 25 March 1999; 'Drugs Ban Costs Walsh Young Jockeys Title', *Daily Express*, 15 May 1997; 'McCarthy is First Jockey to Fail Test', *Guardian*, 10 October 1995).

Retirement

In his autobiography, Dettori remarks on riding alongside the incomparable Lester Piggott when the latter was approaching his sixtieth birthday and almost 50 years in the saddle. Willie Carson was in his mid-fifties when he had his last ride as, in earlier decades, were Scobie Breasley, Frankie Durr, Charlie Smirke and Gordon Richards. Clearly, experience counts in Britain's 'horses for courses' scenario. Retirement comes earlier over the sticks. By the age of 30, the elder statesman stage has been reached. John Francome called it a day at 32 after a fall too many at Chepstow in 1985, and eight-times champion Peter Scudamore did likewise at 34. When Simon McNeil retired in 1998 aged 42, he had been the oldest jump jockey around (Marcus Armytage, 'Old Stager McNeil is Making a Fresh Start', *Daily Telegraph*, 28 November 1998). Lack of rides ends most jockeys' careers: loss of nerve, injuries and weight problems the rest. Some never made the grade: others could no longer sustain their performance. Most jockeys try to remain connected with racing. Jonathan Haynes, condemned to a wheelchair by a fall at Southwell, explained 'racing is all I know' (Lee 1980, 159).

Yet it must be emphasized that most of the skills they possess are specific to the racing industry and are not easily transferable to other occupations. Some move on to become trainers though they find business sense as vital as horse sense if they are to be successful. Others, particularly the failed apprentices, return to the stables where, unlike the market for jockeys, there is always a labour shortage, becoming work riders or stable hands hoping to supplement their income by 'doing a good horse' or perhaps rising to become a senior lad (Gallier 1988, 55; Tony Stafford. 'Taxing Time for Lowly-Paid Stable Staff', *Daily Telegraph*, 2 February 1999). For the articulate and successful, there are media opportunities. Others have secured positions as clerks of courses, racecourse inspectors, agents and valets. For the younger ones today, there is the Jockeys Employment and Training Scheme initiated by the Jockeys Association to provide some of the basic skills required to secure employment when they finally opt out of race riding. Talk of retirement used to be taboo in the changing room but times have changed and career advice and training are now more readily accepted (Fox 1997, 33).

Piggott finally retired aged 59. Dettori, at 27, can look ahead to a long and prosperous career. Nevertheless, his millionaire status has not been earned easily. Although his income is higher than most jockeys, Dettori is less unique when it comes to problems faced by professional riders. Like other jockeys, he has to watch his weight carefully; his work site is constantly changing necessitating significant travel; he faces appraisal of his work by both the public and his employers every time he goes out to ride; and almost each season he can expect to be sidelined by injury and suspension. Indeed jockeys are extraordinary sportspersons. They contrast with other professionals in terms of their physique, age, gender and the danger of their occupation. In what other job are participants expected to peak five or six times a day – even more if there are evening meetings – for six and increasingly seven days a week, risk serious injury every time they go to work, and all the time restrict themselves to a diet designed to keep their weight well below the norm? Yet, like Dettori, most of them believe that 'it is a wonderful game' (Brough Scott, 'Dettori in Seventh Heaven', *Sunday Telegraph*, 29 September 1996). They share his view that 'racing is my life, it is everything. It is my good times, my bad times, my happiness, my sadness, everything' (Helena de Bertodano, 'Life after the Ascot Seven', *Sunday Telegraph*, 11 May 1997).

Epilogue

At the age of 44, Dettori is still a successful major rider though he no longer challenges for the championship. In December 2012, he began a six-month suspension from riding after admitting recreational use of cocaine. In 2013, his contract as stable jockey for Godolphin Racing was not renewed and he went freelance before becoming retained rider for Sheikh Joaan Al Thani. He rides at 8 stone 6 lbs, only a pound more than in 2000.

Notes

1. For examples, see Leydon and Wall (2000); Caulfield and Karageorghis (2008); Tolich and Bell (2008); Warrington et al. (2009); Dolan et al. (2011); Wilson et al. (2014).
2. The starkest contrast can be gained from a reading of Dettori (1997) and Magee and Lewis (1997).
3. For basic histories of flat and National Hunt racing (see Vamplew 1975; Munting 1987; Huggins 2000; Huggins 2003). Useful background material can also be found in Vamplew and Kay (2005). Unless otherwise specified, information on jockeys in general is mainly derived from annual editions of the *Racing Calendar*, the official organ of the racing authorities, *Ruff's Guide*, and similar commercial publications, with supplementary information from the racing press. On the veracity of the Racing Calendar see Kay (2009).
4. Occasionally, particularly at major holiday times, there could be up to twelve meetings on the same day, providing more mounts for the ordinary jockey. National Hunt meetings are more likely to be called off because of adverse weather conditions but, in the last decades, some financial offset has come through that branch of the sport now being an all year round affair. Nevertheless a long freeze can be disastrous for the journeyman jockey without a retainer who relies on a few rides to pay the mortgage.
5. Apprentices are young riders learning their trade while formally tied to a trainer and able to claim a weight allowance because they have ridden insufficient winners.
6. This now appears to be a partial myth (Kay 2009, 360–362).
7. To avoid confusion, it should be noted that the Jockey Club had nothing to do with jockeys but was essentially a group of influential owners who set the rules of racing (see Vamplew 2003).

8. At the time of writing the initial article, there was a substantial scientific literature on athletes and eating disorders but the bulk of it pertained to female sports participants with little specifically on the problems faced by jockeys. An exception was King and Mezey (1987).
9. In 2002, it was raised to 7 stone 12 lbs and by a further two pounds in 2013.
10. Information supplied by Iris Middleton from her research on horse racing in eighteenth-century Yorkshire.
11. Based on information supplied by Dr. Michael Turner. A further breakdown suggests a fall every eight mounts over fences and every 27 over hurdles. In contrast, on the flat, there is a fall only every 300 rides.
12. The ratio of falls to injuries in flat racing is 4.34:1 but 6.36:1 in National Hunt.
13. The underestimation of accidents in National Hunt racing is likely to be less than on the flat as jump horses are generally older, more experienced, and hence less fractious. Moreover, starting stalls, a cause of many accidents, are not employed in jump racing.
14. In 1961, permits were introduced into National Hunt racing with Class A being required for races open only to amateurs and Class B for all steeplechase and jump races.
15. The Workmen's Compensation Act of 1897 did not apply to jockeys on several counts: many earned more than £250 a year; they worked on premises not under the control or management of their employer; and most were casually employed for a purpose not directly connected with their patron's trade or business (see Wilson and Levy 1939, 101–102; Hanes 1968, 103).
16. On 4 July 1981, Paul Cook rode the winner of the 2.45 at Sandown, the 5.00 at Bath, and the 7.50 at Nottingham (Tanner and Cranham 1992, 222).
17. When Pat Eddery's mount, *El Gran Senor*, failed by a short head in the 1984 Derby its stud value fell from £80 to £30 million in a matter of seconds (Jamie Reid, 'Cool, Clear Walter', *Guardian*, 5 June 1998).
18. Interviewed by the author 18 March 1999.
19. Calculated from data in the *Racing Calendar*.
20. Eighty years later, as an apprentice, Dettori spent two winters in America learning the even more streamlined 'flatback' riding style (Karter 1995, 29).
21. For other allegations of alcoholism (see Frances Collingwood, 'The Tragedy of Thomas Loates', *The British Racehorse*, October 1967, 427–428; Mortimer 1978, 174, 219; Tanner and Cranham 1992, 116).
22. Michael Caulfield, then Executive Manager of the Jockeys Association, in an interview with the author 2 June 1999 suggested that the real alcohol problem with jockeys emerges post retirement as income, status and self-esteem all decline.

Acknowledgement

I am grateful for help towards the research costs of this paper from the Wellcome and Leverhulme Trusts and for comments received at various conferences and seminars at which earlier versions were presented. Especial thanks are due to Michael Turner, Chief Medical Adviser to the Jockey Club; Rory MacDonald, Director of the British Racing School; Jim Gale, Director of the Northern Racing College; Michael Caulfield, Executive Manager of the Jockeys Association of Great Britain; Dede Brown, Curator of York Racing Museum; and fellow researchers John Tolson, Joyce Kay and Iris Middleton.

Disclosure statement

No potential conflict of interest was reported by the author.

References

Alcock, A. 1978. *They're off: The Story of the First Girl Jump Jockeys*. London: J. A. Allen.
Astley, J. 1895. *Fifty Years of My Life*. London: Hurst and Blackett.
Baerlein, R. 1987. *Joe Mercer: The Pictorial Biography*. London: MacDonald.

NUMBERS AND NARRATIVES

Barbezat, D., and J. Hughes. 2014. "Finding the Lost Jockeys." *Historical Methods: A Journal of Quantitative and Interdisciplinary History* 47 (1): 19–30. http://dx.doi.org/10.1080/01615440.2013.821876

Barnes, S. 1988. *Horsesweat and Tears*. London: Heinemann Kinswood.

Caulfield, M. J., and C. I. Karageorghis. 2008. "Psychological Effects of Rapid Weight Loss and Attitudes towards Eating among Professional Jockeys." *Journal of Sports Sciences* 26 (9): 877–883. http://dx.doi.org/10.1080/02640410701837349

Cowley, S., B. Bowman, and M. Lawrance. 2007. "Injuries in the Victorian Thoroughbred Racing Industry." *British Journal of Sports Medicine* 41: 639–643. http://dx.doi.org/10.1136/bjsm.2006.032888

Dabscheck, B. 2013. "Sweated Labour, Literally Speaking: The Case of Australian Jockeys." *Sporting Traditions* 30 (2): 47–70.

Dettori, F. 1997. *A Year in the Life of Frankie Dettori*. London: Mandarin.

Dolan, E., H. O'Connor, A. McGoldrick, G. O'Loughlin, D. Lyons, and G. Warrington. 2011. "Nutritional. Lifestyle, and Weight Control Practices of Professional Jockeys." *Journal of Sports Sciences* 29 (8): 791–799.

Doust, D. 1992. *Sports Beat*. London: Hodder and Stoughton.

Eddery, P. 1993. *To Be a Champion*. London: Coronet.

Fitzgeorge-Parker, T. 1971. *Steeplechase Jockeys: The Great Ones*. London: Pelham.

Fox, K. 1997. *The Racing Tribe*. Oxford: Social Issues Research Centre.

Francombe, J. 1985. *Born Lucky*. London: Pelham.

Gallier, S. 1988. *One of the Lads*. London: Stanley Paul.

Hanes, D. J. 1968. *The First British Workmen's Compensation Act 1897*. New Haven, CT: Yale University Press.

Hide, E. 1989. *Nothing to Hide*. London: MacDonald.

Huggins, M. 2000. *Flat Racing and British Society 1790–1914*. London: Cass.

Huggins, M. 2003. *Horseracing and the British 1919–1930*. Manchester, NH: Manchester University Press. http://dx.doi.org/10.7228/manchester/9780719065286.001.0001

Humphris, E. M. 1923. *The Life of Fred Archer*. London: Hutchinson.

Injured Jockeys Fund. 1996. *One Fall Can End a Jockey's Career*. Newmarket: Injured Jockeys Fund.

Jockey Club. 1994. *Protocol and Rules for the Testing of Riders for Banned Substances*. London: Jockey Club.

Karter, J. 1995. *Frankie Dettori: The Illustrated Biography*. London: Headline.

Kay, J. 2000. "Closing the Stable Door and the Public Purse: The Rise and Fall of the Royal Plates." *The Sports Historian* 20 (1): 18–32. http://dx.doi.org/10.1080/17460260009445827

Kay, J. 2009. "Still Going after All These Years: Text, Truth and the Racing Calendar." *Sport in History* 29 (3): 353–366. http://dx.doi.org/10.1080/17460260903043310

Kent, J. 1892. *The Racing Life of Lord George Cavendish Bentinck*. London: Blackwood.

King, M. B., and G. Mezey. 1987. "Eating Behaviour of Male Racing Jockeys." *Psychological Medicine* 17: 249–253. http://dx.doi.org/10.1017/S0033291700013131

Lee, A. 1980. *Jump Jockeys*. London: Ward Lock.

Leydon, M. A., and C. Wall. 2000. "New Zealand Jockeys' Dietary Habits and Their Potential Impact on Health." *International Journal of Sport Nutrition and Exercise Metabolism* 12: 220–237.

Magee, S. 1995. *The Channel Four Book of Racing*. London: Hamlyn.

Magee, S., and G. Lewis. 1997. *To Win Just Once: The Life of the Journeyman Jump Jockey*. London: Headline.

Maynard, J. 2013. "Bodies on the Line." In *The Cambridge Companion to Horseracing*, edited by R. Cassidy, 83–93. Cambridge: Cambridge University Press. http://dx.doi.org/10.1017/CCO9781139012768

McCoy, T., and C. Duval. 1998. *The Real McCoy*. London: Hodder and Stoughton.

Mortimer, R., R. Onslow and P. Willett. 1978. *Biographical Encyclopedia of British Flat Racing*. London: MacDonald and Janes.

Munting, R. 1987. *Hedges and Hurdles*. London: J.A. Allen.

Nicholson, G. 1966. *The Professionals*. London: Sportsman's Book Club.

O'Neill, J. 1985. *Jonjo*. London: Stanley Paul.

Piggott, L. 1995. *Lester*. London: Partridge.

Ramsden, C. 1973. *Ladies in Racing*. London: Stanley Paul.

Reiss, S. 2011. *Sport of Kings and Kings of Crime: Horseracing, Politics and Organised Crime in New York 1885–1913*. Syracyse: Syracuse University Press.

Rickaby, B. 1969. *First to Finish*. London: Souvenir Press.

Smith, D. 1968. *Five Times Champion*. London: Pelham.

Smith-Eccles, S. 1987. *Turf Account*. London: Queen Anne Press.

Spencer, E. 1900. *The Great Game*. London: Grant Richards.

Tanner, M., and G. Cranham. 1992. *Great Jockeys of the Flat*. London: Guinness.

Tolich, M., and M. Bell. 2008. "The Commodification of Jockeys' Working Bodies: Anorexia or Work Discipline?" In *A Global Racecourse*, edited by C. McConville, 101–114. Melbourne: ASSH.

Tolson, J., and W. Vamplew. 1998. "Derailed: Railways and Horseracing Revisited." *Sports Historian* 18 (2): 39–49.

Vamplew, W. 1975. *The Turf*. London: Allen Lane.

Vamplew, W. 2003. "Reduced Horse Power: The Jockey Club and the Regulation of British Horseracing." *Entertainment Law* 2 (3): 94–111. http://dx.doi.org/10.1080/1473098042000275792

Vamplew, W. 2004. "Sporting Innovation: The American Invasion of the British Turf and Links 1895–1905." *Sport History Review* 35: 122–137.

Vamplew, W., and J. Kay. 2001. "Horse Racing." In *International Encyclopedia of Women and Sports*, edited by K. Christensen, A. Guttmann, and G. Pfister, 537–544. New York: Macmillan.

Vamplew, W., and J. Kay. 2005. *Encyclopedia of British Horseracing*. Abingdon: Routledge.

Vamplew, W., and J. Kay. 2006. "Captains Courageous: Gentlemen Riders in British Horse Racing, 1866–1914." *Sport in History* 26: 370–385. http://dx.doi.org/10.1080/17460260601065961

Warrington, G., E. Dolan, A. McGoldrick, J. McEvoy, C. MacManus, M. Griffin, and D. Lyons. 2009. "Chronic Weight Control Impacts on Physiological Function and Bone Health in Elite Jockeys." *Journal of Sports Sciences* 27 (6): 543–550. http://dx.doi.org/10.1080/02640410802702863

Welcome, J. 1990. *Fred Archer: A Complete Story*. London: Lambourn.

Weston, T. 1952. *My Racing Life*. London: Hutchinson.

Wilson, A., and H. Levy. 1939. *Workmen's Compensation*. London: Oxford University Press.

Wilson, G., M. B. Hawken, I. Poole, A. Sparks, S. Bennett, B. Drust, J. Morton, and G. L. Close. 2014. "Rapid Weight-Loss Impairs Simulated Riding Performance and Strength in Jockeys: Implications for Making-Weight." *Journal of Sports Sciences* 32 (4): 383–391. http://dx.doi.org/10.1080/02640 414.2013.825732

Winter, J. 2008. "Industrial Relations-Lite? The Management of Industrial Relations in the UK Thoroughbred Training Industry." In *A Global Racecourse*, edited by C. McConville, 87–100. Melbourne: ASSH.

Successful workers or exploited labour? Golf professionals and professional golfers in Britain 1888–1914

Wray Vamplew

ABSTRACT

Golf was one of the fastest growing recreational sports in Britain before 1914. It created a market for professional golfers as shopkeepers, teachers, green-keepers, and craftsmen. A database of 3000 players was used to examine their social and economic experience at club and competitive level, and this experience was then compared to that of professionals in horseracing, cricket, and football. Golfers were the first sportsmen to permanently organize themselves with the establishment of the Professional Golfers' Association in 1901, which provided welfare services and promoted tournaments, thus actively and uniquely assisting the development of the industry within which its members worked.

Comment

Like most nineteenth-century definitions of professional sportsmen the appellation 'professional golfer' was not simply a label for those who played for money. Many gentlemen golfers (often partnered by a professional) played matches for money but they did not forfeit their amateur status. Initially the term implied a golfer who was available to caddy for gentleman golfers, though caddying inferred not just carrying their clubs but also advising them on their play. By the end of the period under study here the *Golfer's Handbook* for 1913 provided an instructive set of definitions of the professional and the amateur. It cited the Royal & Ancient's Rules of Golf Committee who, in answer to a query 'what constitutes a professional golfer?' answered that 'the term "professional golfer" is usually applied to players who receive payment for teaching or playing the game'. The amateur definition was more profuse:

> an amateur is one who, after attaining the age of sixteen years, has never carried clubs for hire [thus excluding the more mature caddy]; has never received any consideration, directly or indirectly, for playing or for teaching the game; and has never played for a money prize in any competition.

It added that 'no amateur may, without forfeiting his status, receive directly or indirectly from the promoters of any match or tournament any consideration for playing in such a match or tournament.' Presumably this still allowed amateurs to play against each other for wagers (*Golfer's Handbook* 1913, 105–106).

Anyone studying the history of the professional golfer is indebted to the path-breaking work of Peter N. Lewis in his *Dawn of Professional Golf* and to Alan Jackson's *British Professional Golfers.* I am grateful to Jessica Macbeth and Orla Gilmore for research assistance; to Dr Joyce Kay, Dr Jane George, Peter Lewis and participants at the Australian Historical Conference in Newcastle for comments on earlier drafts; to the many golf club secretaries who answered queries and sent information; and to the Royal & Ancient Golf Club, the British Golf Museum, and the Professional Golfers Association for access to libraries and archives. Financial assistance towards the research costs of this paper was obtained from the Carnegie and Leverhulme Trusts, the Arts and Humanities Research Board and the Faculty of Management at the University of Stirling.

This is a revised version of a paper published under the same title in the *Economic History Review* 61.1 (2008), 54–79. Most academic work on golf history since the first publication of this article has focused on gender and other forms of discrimination (George, Kay, and Vamplew 2007; Vamplew 2008, 2010; George 2009; Dee 2013) or on the golf club as a social or cultural institution (Ceron-Anaya 2010; Vamplew 2012).

Introduction

In the four decades before the First World War golf was one of the fastest growing recreational activities in Britain. From less than a 100 clubs in the 1870s the total rose to almost 3000 by 1914. Many of these employed a professional to teach members, repair balls and clubs, sell equipment and look after the course. These golfers formed one of the largest groups of professional sportsmen in Britain.[1] Perhaps of more significance, they were the first sportspersons to successfully and permanently organise themselves to protect their interests with the formation of the Professional Golfers' Association (PGA) in 1901. This article examines how the rising demand for their services influenced the professionals' social status and economic position and the effect that collective action had on their welfare. This will be done by examining the duties and work load of the professional golfer, their social and geographical origins, their sources of income, the extent to which they changed employers, and the labour and social relations between the professionals and their employing clubs. The focus is on professional golfers as a whole but a distinction will be drawn between the experiences of the club professionals and those of the elite tournament players. Both groups, however, were members of the PGA and how this community of interest affected their working lives will also be scrutinized. Where possible comparisons will be made with three other major professional sports of the time: cricket, horseracing and association football. The former both have a long history of paying participants but soccer was a newcomer to the professional ranks, only accepting that players could be paid in England in 1885 and seven years later in Scotland.

In employment numbers, golf's 941(+) professionals on the eve of the First World War ranked behind football which had 4740 registered paid players in England and a further 1754 in Scotland, but ahead of racing's 699 (419 on the flat and 280 over the jumps) and cricket's 191 first-class players (plus between 200 and 400 in the leagues) (Vamplew 1976, 159; Munting 1987, 129; Russell 1997, 45; Vamplew 2004a, 208).[2] However, in terms of the number of potential employers, golf and racing respectively had almost 3000 clubs and just over 3000 owners (divided almost equally between flat racing and National Hunt); soccer in

England had 158 clubs who hired professionals with a further 32 Scottish Football League clubs and perhaps a similar number at non-League level; and cricket had its 16 first-class county clubs and possibly up to 400 league and other teams who might have employed one paid player each.[3] Information on working conditions, economic rewards and some other aspects of the labour market in the comparator sports is available in synthesised form.[4] Material on strikes and informal labour relations is generally limited and random, though an official history has been published for the Professional Footballers' Association, founded in 1907 as the Association Football Players Union (AFPU), the only other sports labour organisation to have been established before 1914.[5]

The research for this paper has centred on the creation of two databases. One, essentially drawing on the statistical work of Jackson, deals with the career lengths and mobility between clubs of some 3000 professionals who obtained their first appointment between 1888 and 1914.[6] The second, of necessity much smaller as it relies mainly on material from published club histories and information supplied by club secretaries, details the contractual relationships between professionals and their employers.[7] This quantitative approach has been supplemented with information from the PGA Archives and the golfing press.

The club professional

Professional golfers did not just play golf. The letter of appointment that the Nottingham club sent to Tom Williamson in 1896 provides a glimpse into the demands made upon one early professional. He was to be engaged temporarily as 'clubmaker etc.' on the following terms:

(1) That you shall be at the service (so far as your other duties will permit) of any member of the club to play with him or coach him at a charge of 1s.6d. a round (18 holes) including caddie; same charge to apply to a round of the Ladies Links, whether with a member of the club or the ladies club.

(2) That you should take charge of the Clubhouse and be responsible for its safety.

(3) That you should take the management of the caddies and the caddies shelter.

(4) That you should conduct the draw on Medal days.

(5) That you should assist in keeping the course and greens in order, giving your services upon them for eight hours a week, these hours to be given on such days and at such times as the Committee, or the Greenkeeper on their behalf may require.

(6) That you may receive from the club 5/- a week.

(7) That you should take all profits from making, mending and selling clubs and balls.

(8) That this engagement may be terminated at any time by 14 days' notice on either side (Collins 1989, 37–39).

A useful source that has thrown some light on the work of other club professionals is the *Golfers' Handbook and Yearbook* in which several advertised their skills and wares to a wider audience than their immediate club members. That for 1907, for example, carries over 40 two-page adverts depicting moustachioed men and, alongside their portraits, their sales promotion.

This was not yet the age of mass production of golf clubs and all professionals were expected to make and repair clubs. Many emphasised the high quality of their products. Percy Hills (North Manchester), for one, reported that he paid timber merchants an extra 20% so that he could select his own wood. Others distinguished their products by quoting testimonials or by claiming that they had a secret ingredient for the golf bag, be it O. Gibson's (Westward Ho!) long fishing-rod drivers, Ernest Morgan's (Barnsley) 'special mashie niblick for approaching', or Alex Weir's (Turnberry) 'non-slicing drivers and brassies'. In contrast Jonathon Randall (Sunridge Park) advertised that 'golfer's own ideas [would be] made to order'. Many of them, aware that golfers had favourite clubs, offered to provide exact replicas when a replacement was sought. Most appreciated that the club golfer did not want to wait for his new woods or his re-gripped trusty driver. So repairs would be 'promptly executed' (John Aitken, Royal Portrush) and 'all orders despatched same day as received' (James B. Batley, Bushey Hall). Generally it was emphasised that large selections of all kinds of clubs were kept on hand so that callers and orders could be dealt with immediately, though this had financial implications for the professional who needed capital to pay for such stock.

Few of the clubmakers did all the work themselves, though several, including John McAndrew (Glasgow North Western) and J.H. Oke (Sutton Coldfield), noted that personal attention would be given to all orders. Others, such as John Aitken, pointed out that repairs would be carried out 'by experienced workmen only' and that, in the case of David Anderson (Bromley and Bickley), his clubs were 'not made by boys but by practical workmen'. Here is another aspect to the job of being a golf professional: that of employing labour.

Several advertised themselves as coaches. Jack Carr (Finchley) highlighted that he was an 'instructor' while George Coburn (Sandwell Park) said 'teaching [was] a speciality'; Ernie Gray's (Littlehampton) forte was 'wooden clubs and teaching'; Alan Tribble (Raynes Park) was an 'expert teacher'; Edward Hardman (Newark) gave 'best attention ... to tuition'; J.H. Oke described himself as a 'first class instructor' who had won the Canadian Open in 1904; and Reginald Wilson (Berkhamsted) proclaimed that his 'tuition [was] a great success'.

These advertisements provide an outline of what the club professional had to do: make clubs, invent clubs, repair clubs, sell clubs and other equipment, train assistants and apprentices, run a workshop, and coach amateur golfers. They were placed by men who had made the grade and were at reputable clubs. Elsewhere there might be other jobs to do such as organising the caddies if there was no separate caddiemaster, acting as greenkeeper especially at the nine-hole courses and smaller clubs, working as a bar steward sometimes with mother or wife as cook, cleaning the toilets, being in charge of the telephone, collecting fees, starting the monthly medal competitions, and even looking after the club horse as was the case with poor Thomas Winton at Muswell Hill. This was outside his formal working hours, but the horse was vital to course maintenance ("Minutes of Muswell Hill." *Golf Club*, May 1, 1897).

Determining what the professionals did is easier than finding out where they came from. There are two conventional wisdoms in golf history about the recruitment of professionals. One is that they mainly emanated from Scotland where the game had been longer established than in England and the other is that they began as caddies (Lowerson 1989, 196). Neither can be substantiated with hard evidence. There is logic behind the belief that caddying was a route to professionalism. Caddies could absorb the skills of the game by watching practitioners; they were often given old clubs by their employers; and there was the possibility of patronage from club members impressed by their ability. The register of 21 caddies at the Royal & Ancient Golf Club (R & A) in St Andrews in 1870 includes three who went on to win the Open, but many caddies at that time were as much playing professionals as advisors to club members. By 1891, when caddies were more likely to be just club carriers, an extract of 31 names from the register includes only one who went on to be a club professional (Stirk 1989, 30; Mackenzie 1998, 43). From the other side of the coin the proportion of professionals who had been caddies has never been quantified: the information is simply unavailable. Although star player George Duncan reckoned that 'there are few champions among the professionals who haven't caddied' and Ted Ray, another leading player, was

NUMBERS AND NARRATIVES

clear that only a 'minority of professionals had not in their youth been caddies', all that can be suggested here is that of the sample of 19 elite golfers in Table 6 the majority seem to have taken the caddying route to professionalism (*The Professional Golfer*, August 12,1923, Duncan 1951, 4). The background of these leading professionals also lends credence to the Scottish hypothesis as 10 of them emanated from north of the border.[8]

Actually getting a position could come from responding to an advert, gaining the ear of a member with influential friends at other clubs, or performing well in a tournament. George Duncan received an attractive offer from Hanger Hill after beating both James Baird and Harry Vardon in the Manchester Courier Cup in 1906 (Duncan 1951, 25). The same Duncan obtained one of his earlier positions at Timperley by playing a round with the three other short-listed candidates and demonstrating his skill to the appointing committee (Duncan 1951, 23). Playing skills involved not just knowing how to drive, pitch and putt but having the ability to do this in all weathers and on different terrains from windy seaside links to inland mud baths. Experience was the best teacher, but assistants might pick up ideas from the professional who employed them and caddies by observing those players for whom they carried clubs.

As in many occupations, family could be used for learning skills and securing employment. Clearly some golfing families stand out. Looking at opposite ends of the alphabet for example, there are the Auchterlonies and the Whitcombes. David Auchterlonie set up a clubmaking business that employed four of his sons. Two other sons, Willie and Laurence, respectively won the Open and the United States Open ("The Auchterlonie Brothers." *Golf Illustrated*, March 8, 1907, 206). As for the Whitcombes, brothers Charles, Reginald and Ernest all played in the 1935 Ryder Cup but they began their careers before the First World War. Their father was a greenkeeper and their mother was stewardess at Burnham Golf Club. Ernest became a caddiemaster at 17 and a club professional at 19; Charles became his assistant in 1910; and Reg became an apprentice clubmaker in 1912 (Fry 1994, 11–29). Some indication of the extent of kinship among professional golfers can be suggested by identifying those professionals in the data base with the same surname. A sample of 566, based on the surnames beginning with the letters C, O, and P, shown in Table 1 reveals that 64.7% of professionals shared their surname with at least one other professional. A sampling of a modern telephone directory for the same letters gives a lower percentage of 55.4 which suggests that there may be an element of kinship within golf.[9] However, except for a few men traceable through biographies and club histories, it cannot be proved that those sharing a common surname were sons, siblings, nephews or cousins. Moreover, the approach adopted ignores the female influence. Jack White, Open winner in 1904, had uncles on his mother's side of the family who were well-known golfers (Davie Grant and Ben Sayers) but who would not be identified by this method. Ultimately, of course, there is a lack of hard evidence to establish that family actually mattered. It may be of relevance that in the few cases where parental attitude is known, those elite golfers with families in

Table 1. Possible kinship in professional golf.

Initial letter	Number of professionals	% with same name	Telephone directory sample	% with same name
C	326	67.5	333	56.1
O	46	60.9	44	45.5
P	194	60.3	195	56.4
C+O+P	566	64.7	572	55.4

Source: Calculated from data in Jackson (1994) and BT, *The Phone Book: Central Scotland and Trossachs* 2003/2004.

NUMBERS AND NARRATIVES

the sport such as Willie Auchterlonie and Willie Park were supported in their endeavours whilst George Duncan's policeman father and ploughman James Braid senior initially were not in favour of their sons taking up a career in the game.

It is ironic that professional golfers who gained their jobs because of their skill at playing the game then had little opportunity to play tournament golf because of the other demands on their time. The working hours of Tom Chisholm at Royal Eastbourne were defined as 'from early morning until everyone had ceased to use the course for play'; William Fernie at Glamorganshire had to start at seven in the morning and remain till the last member had finished playing; and Thomas Ball at West Lancashire was instructed 'to occupy his spare time as the secretary directs'. William Lowe at Mullion was allowed to keep any fees he received for playing golf but 'on the understanding that all time taken up by playing during working hours shall be made up'. How he would find the space in his working calendar to do this when he was also steward and caddiemaster is not clear. And all this was expected for 14 shillings a week! W. Walker of Richmond was not untypical in being expected to be on the course at 7.30 am to start the men at work, at his workshop by 9.30, and be available (apart from an hour at lunch) until dusk. If not in his workshop he had to leave word on a slate where he could be found and was not to be absent from the course at any time other than specified. John Wilson at Cathkin Braes was scheduled to be at work from 7 in the morning to 7.30 in the evening in the summer but wrote to the secretary to object that he was kept hanging around while a few members sat and smoked in the clubhouse. He was told to employ an assistant if he wanted an evening off (Edwards 1973, 6; Milton 1987, 118; Crampsey 1988, 20–21; Brennard 1990, 23; Corrigan and Reynolds 1990, 62; Casley 1995, 22).

There was no real off-season for golf professionals. Although demands on their time might vary with the weather and holiday periods, few courses closed for the winter once effective drainage became affordable or for the summer as mowing equipment improved. However, the working week of the professional was affected by the coming of Sunday play at many courses. Whether golf should be allowed on a Sunday was a major topic of debate within clubs, though of course the professional had no say in the matter (Lowerson 1984, 212–214). Traditionally this was his one day off in the week. At Olton, when Sunday play came in 1901, no caddies were allowed and the professional was not required to be in attendance. However, Fred Foord's contract at Pennard specified that, although he did no work on the course on Sundays, Christmas Day or Good Friday, he was expected to be in attendance on general holidays and usually on Sunday mornings and Saturday afternoons. Increasingly, as was specified in James Bradbeer's contract at Porters Park, Monday became the day off for the club professional (Cadney 1991, 15; Grant 1995, 106; Moreton 1999, 181).

To improve their positions professionals often had to shift geographically. As Table 2 shows there was a degree of mobility among golfers with over 20% of those who remained professionals for more than two years serving at least three clubs in their career. Why some moved on is easy to explain. After D.Y. Pinkerton resigned from Redhill & Reigate, the committee then decided to purchase a spade, a scythe, a roller and a wheelbarrow! (Lee and Kemp 1986, 38). More generally some moved up the hierarchy of clubs to enjoy the enhanced status (and possibly money); others opted for larger clubs where they were likely to be concerned solely with teaching, playing and running the shop. At the smallest clubs the professional often also undertook greenkeeping, usually having to devote all morning to mowing greens and scything fairways. The intermediate stage was to be the club professional

NUMBERS AND NARRATIVES

Table 2. Player mobility.

No. Clubs	1888–1899				1900–1912			
	All players	%	Pro for >2 years	%	All Players	%	Pro for >2 years	%
1	673	68.9	362	54.3	1186	59.9	908	53.3
2	127	13.0	127	19.1	410	20.7	410	24.1
3	73	7.5	73	11.0	233	11.8	233	13.7
4	58	5.9	58	8.7	86	4.3	86	5.1
5	20	2.0	20	3.0	39	2.0	39	2.3
>5	26	2.7	26	3.9	26	1.3	26	1.5
	977	100.0	666	100.0	1980	100.0	1702	100.0

Note: Players are included in the period in which their first appointment occurred.
Source: Calculated from data in Jackson (1994).

Table 3. Time spent at each club.

Period	1st	2nd	3rd	4th	5th	6th	7th
1888–1892	6.2	7.6	6.8	6.2	9.3	4.2	8.2
1893–1897	5.6	7.6	6.9	8.7	6.0	7.6	5.3
1898–1902	8.2	8.9	8.5	8.1	8.3	3.7	10.0
1903–1907	6.3	7.2	8.6	7.6	7.5	5.7	5.6
1908–1912	6.3	7.2	8.6	7.6	7.5	5.7	5.6

Note: Players are included in the period in which their first appointment occurred.
Source: Calculated from data in Jackson (1994).

with responsibility for the course but having the manual work done by other employees (Northerner. 1924. "Is Greenkeeping Part of a Professional's Job?" *The Professional Golfer*, March, 14; Northerner 1933).

In having the freedom to change his employing club, the golfer had an advantage over his fellow professional in cricket or football. Nevertheless it is clear from Table 2 that, despite the overall rising demand as the number of golf clubs increased, most professionals served only one club, even allowing for the substantial proportion that gave up the game. There is also no evidence that players flitted from club to club. As Table 3 shows most seem to have served several years before moving on.

Sometimes mobility was forced on the professional. His relationship with the club was one of master and servant in which dismissal could occur at any time. James Gowans was fortunate to have a generous three months' notice clause in his contract with Flempton, as the majority of professionals had only a week or a fortnight's grace (Nunn 1995, 8). Most club professionals would be aware that their employment was, even if not specified as clearly as in James Cunninghame's contract with Coventry Hearsall, only 'as long as he gives satisfaction to the committee' (Newbould 1994, 21). Unsurprisingly George Duncan lost his job at Conway when he opted for a Saturday afternoon game of football rather than a round of golf with a club member (Duncan 1951, 11). W. McKinley, the first professional at Olton, was sacked partly because of his poor coaching ability. More common a reason was the state of the greens. This was why Old Colwyn sacked F. Tottey in 1909, though within 18 months his replacement Peter Paxton, a founding executive member of the PGA, had also gone because of 'certain deceptions and irregularities' ("Minutes of Old Colwyn." *Golf Club*, December 28, 1909; January 14; May 26, 1911). Charlie Wingate, later to be a driving force in the Midlands section of the PGA, was dismissed after 18 months at Handsworth

NUMBERS AND NARRATIVES

Table 4. Age at appointment and retirement.

1st appointment	Number	Age at 1st appointment	Age at retirement
1888–1892	31	25.5	53.3
1893–1897	62	21.2	53.5
1898–1902	86	22.0	46.6
1903–1907	69	22.7	45.8
1908–1912	37	23.2	48.1

Source: Calculated from data in Jackson (1994).

Table 5. Career lengths.

Period[a]	No. of Prof.	Career in years	No. of Prof.[b]	Career in years[b]
1888–1892	291	11.7	220	14.8
1893–1897	617	10.4	387	15.3
1898–1902	366	16.9	327	18.7
1903–1907	638	13.6	528	16.1
1908–1912	780	11.2	641	13.2

Source: Calculated from data in Jackson (1994).
[a]Before 1888 information can be found for only 36 professionals.
[b]Excluding those who served no more than two years.

owing to the unsatisfactory condition of the links and the manner in which he had carried out his duties (Neale 1995, 35).

Those that survived the wrath of irate committees could last longer than professionals in many other sports. The photographs and portraits of the grandees often disguise the fact that many professionals were young men. Of the 19 elite players discussed in the following sub-section, six gained their first jobs as club professionals while still teenagers and four more before they attained their majority. More generally Table 4 suggests that the early 20s was the normal age of a first appointment. Most professionals could then anticipate a career of over decade and, when those who left the trade within two years are discounted, a decade and a half was a typical career length, slightly less for those most affected by the First World War. Some lasted much longer: indeed, as one put it 'the great consolation about our profession' is that compared to other sports 'we can go on playing long after we have reached the age of 40' (Lynxman. 1920. "Leaves from a Professional's Diary." *Professional Golfer*, January, 6). Tables 4 and 5 suggest that many did so.[10]

During his career a long-serving professional might earn perhaps £200 a year. Clubs paid their professional a weekly retainer but he was allowed to earn extra money from the shop, from teaching, and from the fees paid for services of caddies. Very quickly a standard retainer of a pound a week emerged. For the 1880s (seven observations), the 1890s (38), and 1900–1914 (52) 20 shillings was both the mode and median retainer. Variations can generally be explained in terms of the degree of responsibility held, the provision of housing, and fees charged for tuition. The retainer guaranteed a weekly income because revenue from sales and teaching could fluctuate and would certainly be lower in the winter months.

Teaching took two forms, instruction by the hour or, more commonly, playing a round with a member seeking hints and advice. Generally the prices were not usually for the professionals to determine but were laid down by the club committees. Here, on the basis of 40 observations, there were significant variations between clubs. Nine holes with the professional could cost between 6d and 1/6d and 18 holes between 1/- and 3/- though with 2/- and 2/6d being the most common price. Private coaching cost between 1/6d and 2/6d an hour with a few professionals willing to offer half-hour sessions. According to James Sherlock,

NUMBERS AND NARRATIVES

professional at Stoke Poges, 'giving instruction' to club members was 'the most important duty a professional has to perform'. He admitted that not all club professionals could be good teachers but most could render 'first aid to those golfers going wrong' (Sherlock 1912, 173, 176). Restrictions were placed on the amount of teaching that a professional could under-take. T.B. Whitehead was allowed to teach the ladies at Ilford only after 5 pm on Saturday and 1 pm on Sundays; T. Chisholme at Chorleywood was allowed to tutor ladies at any time but had to return to the club should a member require his services. These examples might simply reflect the subordinate position of women in most clubs, but Charlie Brookes could only teach at Bakewell on Wednesday afternoons; and the incumbent at Lansdown had to give any tuition fees earned before 2 pm to the club ("Minutes of Ilford." *Golf Club*, April 2, 1913; Brockway 1993, 17; Cohen et al. 1993, 5). As teachers they were not really like the club or public school cricket coach as they were still able to earn money from competitions and demonstrations. In this sense perhaps the club professional was more akin to the pro-fessional swimming teacher, though the latter rarely supplemented their incomes by also acting as salesmen.

Making and repairing clubs plus selling balls could net him between £70 and £150 per year. Although the manufacture and particularly the remoulding of gutta percha balls was undermined by the coming of the rubber-cored ball in the early twentieth century, club-making remained relatively immune until the legalisation of steel shafts in the interwar years opened up the possibility of mass production (Vamplew 2004b). The *Golfer's Handbook* advertisements show that some of the club professionals were enterprising businessmen. Both Tom Hood (Royal Dublin) and John McAndrew (Glasgow North Western) maintained a second shop in their respective city centres. Percy Hills (North Manchester) advertised for shippers 'who will make money by sending a postcard for quotation'. James Batley (Bushey Hall) had an agent in London and Thomas Renouf (Manchester) employed them in Manchester, Silloth, Wigton and Carlisle. The prices of balls and clubs were generally decided by the professional but increasingly he was selling in a competitive market. The move of department stores into the selling of golf equipment damaged the income of some professionals, but Josh Taylor, club professional at Acton and brother of star player J.H., went too far when he claimed this had 'literally killed the professional out of the business' (Taylor 1912, 135).

There was a limit to earnings at a club which was set by the time allocated to particular tasks. If he was cutting the grass then the professional could not be making clubs; if he was in the workshop then he could not be out teaching; if he was out teaching then he had to pay for an assistant to cover for him in the shop (some clubs offered an allowance of five shillings a week towards this); and if he was supervising the caddies then he was unavailable for other work, so the penny or two from their fees – or the half-crown a week as given to Tom Fernie at Aldeburgh – was in essence compensation for lost income (O.F.T. 1982, 17).

Elite players

All professional golfers began their work at club level. A few emerged from the ruck and became successful tournament players, though they continued to be attached to clubs. At the top of the pyramid was the famous triumverate of Harry Vardon, John Henry 'J.H.' Taylor, and James Braid who between them won 16 of the 21 Open Championships from 1894 to 1914. But there were others and, for the purpose of this study, an elite golfer was defined as a player who won or was a runner-up in one of two major tournaments for professional

NUMBERS AND NARRATIVES

Table 6. Elite British professional golfers 1889–1914.

[A]	[B]	[C]	[D–I]	[J]	[K]	[L]	[M]	[N]
Willie Auchterlonie	Scot	Yes	1 0 0 0 0 0	?	?	91	?	?
Tom Ball	Eng	?	0 1 1 0 2 0	57	20	37	4	5
James Braid	Scot	Yes	5 3 4 1 1 3	526	26	79	2	45
George Duncan	Scot	Yes	0 0 1 1 2 0	187	18	?	6	4
Willie Fernie	Scot	Yes	0 2 0 0 0 0	?	22	66	3	37
Sandy Herd	Scot	Yes	1 2 1 1 0 2	281	22	75	4	20
Andrew Kirkcaldy	Scot	Yes	0 1 0 0 0 0	98	32	74	2	24
Hugh Kirkcaldy	Scot	Yes	1 0 0 0 0 0	?	26	32	3	2
Charles Mayo	Eng	?	0 0 0 1 1 2	44	20	35e	3	12
Willie Park jnr	Scot	Yes	1 1 0 0 0 0	?	16/18	?	3	?
Ted Ray	C I	Yes	1 1 0 3 0 3	177	21	60	4	26
Fred Robson	Eng	?	0 0 0 1 0 0	24	15/21	53	5	8
Douglas Rolland	Scot	?	0 1 0 0 0 0	?	28	48	4	11
James Sherlock	Eng	?	0 0 1 0 0 0	?	20	57	3	12
J.H. Taylor	Eng	Yes	5 5 2 1 3 0	529	19	67	4	39
Alfred Toogood	Eng	?	0 0 0 1 0 0	?	19	64	9	24
Harry Vardon	C I	Yes	6 4 1 0 2 2	544	20	67	4	34
Tom Vardon	C I	Yes	0 1 0 1 0 1	?	16	41e	4	11
Jack White	Scot	Yes	1 0 0 0 0 0	109	17	c60	7	?

Notes: [A] Golfer.
[B] Birthplace. CI indicates Channel Islands.
[C] Worked as a caddy.
[D] Open winner (1889–1914).
[E] Open runner-up (1889–1914).
[F] News of the World winner (1903–1914).
[G] News of the World runner-up (1903–1914).
[H] Winner of Belgian (1910–1914), French (1906–1914) or German (1911–1912) Open.
[I] Runner-up Belgian (1910–1914), French (1906–1914) or German (1911–1912) Open.
[J] Number of exhibition matches played.
[K] Age at which professional career began. Slash indicates assistantship.
[L] Age at retirement from professional golf. 'e' indicates emigrated.
[M] Number of clubs served.
[N] Years at last club.
Sources: Lewis (1995); Jackson (1994); Leach (1907); Herd (1923); Howell (1990); MacAlindin (2003); Taylor (1943); Duncan (1951); Park (1896); Kirkcaldy (1921). Other information was obtained from *Golf Illustrated* and secretaries of the clubs that employed these professionals.

players, the Open Championship (a stroke-play contest began in 1860 but here considered from 1888) and the *News of the World* competition (a match-play contest begun in 1903).[11] This revealed 19 elite professionals, data on which appear in Table 6. When European Open championships began this group also dominated proceedings: with only one exception no other British player came first or second in the continental events.[12]

Using data from golfing periodicals, Lewis has calculated that eight players (seven of those in Table 6 plus Frenchman Arnaud Massy) won over 40% of the tournament prize money available from British events between 1894 and 1914 (Lewis 1995, 166–167). Topping the group was Harry Vardon with £1750 though George Duncan had a higher average income from tournaments of £22.26 (Lewis 1995, 166). That Jack White was ranked eighth in the list with £226 shows that the bulk of players could not rely on tournaments as a major source of earnings. Perhaps uniquely among sportsmen at this time, arrangements to pool prize money and thus cut down on income fluctuations were not uncommon. George Duncan and Abe Mitchell, one of the best golfers not to win a major title and later Captain of the first British Ryder Cup team, had a partnership that lasted 13 years (Duncan 1951, 42). Those who were successful in tournaments could do well via the exhibition matches that they were asked to play, usually by clubs celebrating their opening or some anniversary by

NUMBERS AND NARRATIVES

Table 7. Travel schedule of James Braid.

1897	Place	1901	Place	1910	Place
14/5	Wallasey	4/4	W. Cornwall	7/4	Northamptonshire
15/5	Southport	12/4	Eltham	16/4	Bearsden
19–20/5	Hoylake	9–11/5	Richmond	18/4	Paisley
22/6	Halifax	22/5	Penarth	19/4	Troon
28/6	W. Middlesex	30/5–1/6	Musselburgh	25/4	Skegness
3/7	Acton	5–6/6	Muirfield	2/5	Burnham
7/7	Mitcham	12–14/6	Islay	5/5	Cirencester
19/8	Filey	15/6	Bogside	9/5	Stockport
15/9	Dudley	17/6	Pollock	26/5	Nottingham
2/10	North Surrey	18/6	Glasgow	1–2/6	France
8/10	Scarborough	19/6	Stirling	4–5/6	Belgium
15/10	Rochford	1/7	Blackheath	9/6	Godalming
13/11	Epsom	11/7	Blairgowrie	11/6	Bishops Stortford
		13/7	Dornoch	20–24/6	St Andrews
		18/7	Lytham	25/6	Oban
		20/7	West Lancs	29/6	Solihull
		27/7	Warlingham	2/7	Brookwood
		14–15/8	Cromer	9/7	Rothesay
		16/8	Sheringham	12/7	Romford
		21/8	Prestwick	14/7	Colchester
		22/8	Troon	16/7	Northwood
		24/8	Nairn	20/7	Stoke Poges
		26/8	N. Berwick	23/7	Byfleet
		28/8	Hunstanton	29–29/7	Belgium
		19/9	Norwich	4/8	Peebles
		24/9	Galashiels	6/8	Wemyss Bay
		25/9	Hawick	22–23/8	France
		28/9	St Andrews	8/9	Newcastle
		9/10	W. Bromwich	10/9	Glasgow
				12/9	North Berwick
				17/9	Manchester
				22/9	Brighton
				24/9	Leeds
				1/10	Woking
				26/10	Brighton
				Early/11	Wales

Source: MacAlindin (2003); Lewis (1995).

bringing high quality golf to their members. These provided virtually guaranteed income. Between the mid 1890s and 1914 Vardon averaged 27 exhibition matches a year but never played more than 12 tournaments; for Braid the respective figures were 25 and 11 while Taylor also averaged 25 exhibitions but only played an annual 7 or 8 tournaments. Poor Jack White was unable to fully capitalise on his 1904 Open victory because of illness, though his later adverts in the *Golfer's Handbook* continued to note that he would play exhibition matches 'at usual fees'.

Tournaments and exhibitions led to considerable travel for the elite player. Table 7 shows the expansion of James Braid's activities as he established himself as one of the leading players. Such workloads were not untypical. In 1914 rising star George Duncan played 43 matches in 27 places plus 7 tournaments before the end of July (Lewis 1995, 50). It should not be forgotten that between such engagements even the elite players were expected to return to their clubs. As the tournament circuit expanded and more clubs also hosted exhibition matches, a writer in *Golf Illustrated* commented that 'the professional golfer of today requires in addition to superlative skill, a constitution of iron to stand the strain' (*Golf Illustrated*, March 27, 1908). Even five years earlier Harry Vardon had noted that 'the game

NUMBERS AND NARRATIVES

[was] a great strain. We never get a rest' (*Golf Illustrated*, August 7, 1903). But it was by choice. No club forced their professional to undertake arduous travel. Although Josh Taylor maintained that 'from a health point of view there is nothing to beat' being a professional golfer, his remarks may have been more pertinent to club professionals like himself than to the travelling elite (Taylor 1912, 133). Was it just coincidence that Jack White, Douglas Rolland and Harry Vardon all suffered serious health problems?

A few golfers travelled even further afield to undertake lucrative overseas tours. Vardon went twice to the States in 1900 to publicise his 'Vardon Flyer' ball at the behest of Spalding, from whom it was rumoured he had a £800 per annum four-year endorsement contract. On the first trip between January and May he earned over £1000 and, after returning for the Open, his second sojourn which lasted six months brought him at least £4000. J.H. Taylor also went to America in 1900 where, on top of his earnings for matches and exhibitions, he gained a £2000 contract to write magazine articles. Andrew Kirkcaldy, Jack White and Sandy Herd toured Mexico in 1905; George Duncan took a six-week visit to the States in 1911; and Vardon and Ted Ray joined forces for another American tour in 1913 where four to five months brought them over £3250 in appearance money alone (Duncan 1951, 40–41; Lewis 1995, 73–80). The growth in the popularity of golf in Europe also led to invitations to most elite professionals to play in France, Germany, Italy, Belgium and Switzerland (Lewis 1995, 80–83).

Leading tournament players of course traded on their reputations, well aware that many club golfers would buy their instruction books and equipment, either out of hero worship or in the belief that somehow the magic would rub off. If we return to the *Golfer's Handbook* adverts of 1907 we find James Braid and Harry Vardon listing their Open Championship victories, Vardon also pointing out that he was the only player to have won both the British and the United States' titles. Presumably Willie A. Anderson felt that genes would out as he had no major tournament victories himself but pointed out that his father had been 'thrice champion'. J.H. Taylor said nothing about himself but maintained that his clubs had a 'worldwide reputation' and indeed one of his stores was across the Atlantic in New Jersey. Others offered different services, but still stressed their excellence as players. Willie Fernie reminded readers that he was Open Champion in 1883 and had won a further 34 tournaments. What relevance this had to his expertise as a golf green specialist or to his seed and manure business is conjectural. He also used his Open victories to argue successfully on his appointment to the Felixstowe Ferry club that he should do no 'work with spade or scythe, for it is very much against the playing' (Savage 1980, 4). Additionally most stars – and even some ordinary club professionals with specialist local knowledge – received invitations to advise on the planning and development of courses. Jack White actually advertised that he laid out courses; others waited to be approached or relied on word of mouth. So profitable was this line of activity to Willie Park that he virtually opted out of serious tournament play to concentrate on such work (Park 1920, 4–5). Unfortunately he also invested unwisely in developing a new course at Huntercombe which failed and forced him into bankruptcy (*Times*, April 26, 1912). Endorsing equipment and consumer products like tobacco also brought in money.

For some a reduction in tournament play came because of illness (White and Rolland), or a preference to concentrate on other golf-related activities (course design by Park and club-making and instruction in the case of Willie Auchterlonie), but most seem to have cut back on such commitments as they entered middle age. Both Tom Vardon and Charles

Mayo, respectively aged 41 and 35, migrated to the United States to take up club positions. Tom Ball died in 1919 of war wounds. Most of the remaining elite professionals became long-serving club professionals, giving lessons and running the shop, though hopefully receiving due respect from their pupils and customers. None matched Braid's 45 years at Walton Heath, but Taylor served 39 at Royal Mid Surrey, Fernie did 37 years at Royal Troon, and Vardon 36 at South Herts. Success in tournaments thus paid off in the long run at club level.

Power and paternalism

According to J.H. Taylor, the recipe for being a successful club professional combined several ingredients including 'clean living', 'acute technical knowledge which he imparts intelligently to his pupils' and, significantly, being 'courteous to his employers' (Taylor, J. H. 1914. "Aims and Aspirations of a Professional." *Golf Magazine*, 22). Except perhaps in Scotland, golf was mainly a game of the middle classes, organised on the basis of private club membership. Golf clubs were institutions for the socially privileged. In the words of *Golf Illustrated* of July 1906, 'golf as played today by the average club member is certainly not a poor man's game'. A writer in *Golf Illustrated* in November 1906 noted that 'prevailing opinion' was that golf was 'an expensive game suitable only for the moneyed and leisured classes' (cited in Lewis 1995, 16). It was these classes whom the professional served at his club. The relationship was one of master and servant, of employer and employee. For some professionals golf brought economic prosperity; for none of them did it bring social equality.

Late nineteenth-century British class distinctions carried over into golf. Professional players were not allowed to use the clubhouse and the social chasm between them and the club members was recognized and was not to be crossed. Whilst being willing to play – and indeed pay for – a round of golf with their club professional as part of their golf education, club members had little intention of mixing socially with the professional. The *PGA Journal* editor recalled the days before the First World War when 'snobbery was acute and ... to become a professional was equivalent to being sentenced to a kind of social ostracism' (*PGA Journal*, September 1934, 4).

In 1911 Harry Fulford, the Bradford professional and Honorary Secretary of the Northern Section of the PGA between 1906 and 1909, wrote an attack on the management of the Open (Fulford, H. 1911. "The Open." *Golf Illustrated*, December 8). He noted in this *Golf Illustrated* article that 'there are many points in connection with the running of the Championship that do not appeal to the professional'. Although recognising the need to have a controlling body, he protested about the 'autocratic dealings towards us'. He felt there was a total disregard for the comfort of the professional players: 'any shed or hurriedly-constructed compound is thought good enough for him to disrobe in.' He was, however, reminded in the same issue by the editor, Garden Smith, that:

> the whole meeting is practically a free gift to them from the members and that it entails a great expenditure of time, labour and expenses, both on [the part of] delegates and on the club over whose course the tournament is played.

Clubs could be good to their pros. Those who suffered serious ill-health often had subscription fund opened for them. In 1909 David Stephenson received £270 from such lists at both his former club (Hunterscombe) and his current one (Prince's, Sandwich) (*Golf Illustrated*, November 26, 1909). Clubs might pay for their professional to enter and travel to the Open Championship and to the regional stages of the *News of the World* tournament or allow the assistant professionals and clubmakers time off to play in local PGA events. L. B. Ayton of Rye was allowed to play in the Open and the *News of the World* events 'as of right' and 'other competitions with permission'. However, Tom King at Royal West Norfolk was not allowed to play in any tournament between mid-June and the end of September (Vidler 1984, 45; Coleridge 1992, 610).

Winners of major tournaments could expect additional rewards from their home club. Harry Vardon received a 'purse of sovereigns' from Ganton after his 1896 Open Championship win. Tom Ball was given a cheque for over £25 from West Lancashire for his victory in the *News of the World* in 1909. For his Open wins in 1908 James Braid received £140 from Walton Heath and £60 more than this when he repeated the feat two years later (*Golf Illustrated*, November 5, 1909; Lewis 1995, 31). Nor was it unusual for a popular professional to receive a testimonial when he left his club for another. Ilkley Golf Club gave Tom Vardon £50 when he left, while his successor, Douglas McEwan, was given £53 by Musselburgh Golf Club as a leaving present. On the occasion of his marriage, George Duncan received a clock, ornaments and a cheque from the members of his club at Timperley. It was not just the big names that fared well. When T.B. Whitehead, the Ilford professional, married, the members presented him with £9 and, when he emigrated to America six years later, over £20 was raised as a farewell gift 'in acknowledgement of his good services to the club'. Similarly Northumberland opened a subscription list, limited to 2/6d per member, to provide a wedding present for John Douglas Edgar in 1907. Mid-Herts gave Arthur Catlin £2 towards his removal expenses when he left to join another club ("Minutes of Northumberland." *Golf Club*, January 1907; "Minutes of Ilford." *Golf Club*, April 16, 1909, November 18, 1915; Gregory 1992, 22; Lewis 1995, 31). But all this was the smiling face of paternalism. 'Impudence', 'ingratitude', and 'indiscipline' are all subjective concepts capable of being interpreted quite differently by player and club official or member, but power lay with the latter. Although the 1909 AGM at Bishop Auckland recorded that the engagement of J. Martin from Bathgate GC had been 'of great benefit to the Club', a year later he was asked to apologise to the Secretary about his language when asked to re-position some tees and also given a final warning to maintain the course in better order. He was given notice the following March over his poor timekeeping and insolence ("Minutes of Bishop Auckland." *Golf Club*, September 14, 1909, October 6, 1910, March 1, 1911).

The PGA

There was little that the individual professional could do to protect himself but collectively there was a possibility. The two decades before the First World War saw widespread development of trade unionism in Britain. British workers joined unions in unprecedented numbers from a total of 1,559,000 in 1893 to 4,145,000 in 1914 (Jackson 1984, 50). Although professional sportsmen demonstrated a marked reluctance to follow suit and organise themselves into groups to protect their interests, by 1914 two such organisations for sportsmen were in existence, the AFPU founded in 1907 and the pioneering PGA, set up in 1901 (Vamplew 1985, 232–247).

In spring of that year the editor of *Golf Illustrated* published an article sympathetic to the cause of the professional which eventually led to the formation of the PGA ("The Case for the Professional." *Golf Illustrated*, April 19, 1901; "The Professional's Lot." *Golf Illustrated*, March 22, 1901). Both 'A North of England Professional' and 'A Professional in North Wales' responded by suggesting that a collective organisation be established but that this would require a first-class professional as leader such as J.H. Taylor (*Golf Illustrated*, April 19, April 26, 1901). He had already condemned 'the growing practice' of clubs offering the right to sell balls and repair clubs to the highest bidder rather than allow the resident professional to retain this customary right (*Golf Illustrated*, April 26, 1901).[13] In September, with the support of other leading players, he took the initiative in establishing the London and Counties Golf Professionals' Association to serve south-eastern England. By December this organisation had transmogrified into the PGA with a national remit.[14] Specifically its objectives were: to promote interest in the game of golf; to protect and advance the mutual and trade interests of all its members; to hold meetings and tournaments periodically for the encouragement of the younger members; to institute a Benevolent Fund for the relief of deserving members; to act as an agency for assisting any professional or club maker to obtain employment; and to effect any other objects of a like nature as may be determined from time to time by the Association (Cousins 1974).[15] The PGA was not the first organisation of professional golfers in Britain. It had been preceded by the Midlands PGA, set up in 1897 by professionals in the Birmingham area to organise local tournaments, but this group of 37 players opted to merge into the larger organisation as did the Northern Counties PGA which had been formed in January 1902 (*Golf*, December 10, 1897; "Minutes of Midlands." *PGA*, vol. 1, 1899–1914, *passim*; held in PGA Archives, The Belfry, Sutton Coldfield).

From the beginning it was emphasised that the organisation had 'no desires of a revolutionary nature' and that they wanted 'to work in complete harmony with their patrons' (*Golf Illustrated*, December 20, 1901, November 7, 1902). Unlike in football there were no mobility or wage restrictions to be fought against. The PGA took pains not to label itself as a union and did not regard its primary function as 'wage raising'. Harry Fulford, a foundation member and an activist within the Northern Section, argued later that they were aware that the golfing public would not have stood for such action and executive member Josh Taylor 'truly believed that the PGA would be committing suicide if it attempted to enforce any terms that smack of trade unionism' (*PGA Journal*, October 1926, 16; May 1927, 21; November 1919, 9). Whereas greenkeepers were indispensable, clubs could organise their own sales of equipment, manufacturers could do repairs and golf schools could offer instruction.

Hence the PGA never concerned itself with contract negotiations between a golf club and its professional. Instead it focused its attention on benevolent activities and establishing a quasi labour exchange for professional golfers. In some sports the authorities had taken up welfare functions. Cricket had the Cricketers' Fund organised by the MCC and horseracing the Rous and Bentinck Funds both under the trusteeship of the Jockey Club. Golf, however, had no supreme authority till 1897 when the Royal & Ancient Golf Club took the lead in the establishment of a rule-making body (Behrend, Lewis, and Mackie 2001, 63–71). It was concerned solely with the practice of golf and not at all with charitable purposes. There was thus a welfare gap to be filled into which the new organisation slotted. Regular appeals were made to clubs for contributions to the benevolent fund and statements of donations and the number of professionals and their families helped were published in *Golf Illustrated*, which by 1910 was promoting itself as the official organ of the PGA.

There were obstacles to the formation of the PGA. Golf professionals were isolated geographically; they negotiated contracts individually with a separate employer; and they were in competition with each other both for club positions and at tournament level. Nevertheless, it was able to secure members because of the benevolent scheme and labour exchange facility. Neither of these activities faced opposition from employers and indeed influential patrons were secured to back them (*Golf Illustrated*, October 25, 1901). At the conclusion of the first PGA-organised tournament held at the Tooting Bec course, the Club president not only presented J.H. Taylor with the trophy but also with five guineas collected by the members for the PGA Benevolent Fund. He commented on the 'great pleasure that he and his fellow-members had in hearing of the professionals' movement' and that they were in 'full sympathy' with 'the more practical objects of the association'. Indeed 'in affording its members a day's recreation and providing a cup for competition, the Tooting Bec Club desired to show their general appreciation of the professionals' objectives.' Such attitudes helped the Association become large enough to adequately finance its activities.[16] Rates of turnover within the sport were sufficiently low (relative to most other sports) to encourage continual membership. Moreover, star players, without whom the PGA would have been seriously weakened, were supportive of the organisation. This may have been altruism by men who had been caddies and ordinary club professionals themselves, but elite players continued to be attached to clubs – at this time there were no independent tournament professionals - and possibly they realised that they would end their careers back at the clubs. The stars were also kept onside by the Association's decision not to prohibit elite players from giving paid demonstrations in stores such as Harrods. This was controversial in that it undermined the potential income of fellow but lesser professionals by encouraging club golfers to purchase their balls and other equipment from sources other than the pro shop (*Times*, March 28, 1914).[17]

Arguably, however, the key factor in strengthening the union was the grip that it developed on tournament organisation. At the first meeting of what was to become the PGA, it had been proposed that two annual tournaments should be held, one for professionals and the other for assistants. Although the latter did not come into existence till 1910, the Tooting Bec Cup, a 36-hole, stroke-play event, was inaugurated on 15 October 1901, the first – but far from the last – competition to be held under the auspices of the Association. In the eight years before the first PGA-organised tournament, professional golfers had about 13 tournaments a year in which they could play, with average prize money of just over £55. With the exception of the Open Championship these were mainly irregular events. By 1913 an incipient tour had been established with 31 tournaments averaging nearly £90 in prize money (Lewis 1995, 93–95). Much of this development was attributable to the PGA which organised tournaments at national, regional and local level and actively sought sponsorship for them. Between 1902 and 1914 over half the professional tournaments played in Britain were national or regional ones sanctioned by the Association and 30% of the rest were district events run by branches of the PGA (Lewis 1995, 96–98). A key aspect of these tournaments was that with relatively few exceptions only PGA members were eligible to enter. Whereas the Open was just that – open to all players – these PGA-sanctioned events were virtually closed shops, thus ensuring that those professionals who wished to play in high-level tournaments were obliged to join the Association. It is clear from extant PGA minutes of the 1920s that golf clubs were keen to host tournaments. A few perhaps were looking for gate-money; possibly for others this was a continuation of their traditional patronage of the professional; but it can also be seen as a means to establish a higher position within the hierarchy of golf clubs. In promoting tournaments, the PGA was actively – and possibly uniquely within sports – assisting the development of the industry within which its members worked.[18]

NUMBERS AND NARRATIVES

What role the PGA played in determining the economic position of the professional is conjectural. Its benevolent fund provided a safety net in case of illness or unemployment and it offered a facility to assist members in finding positions. Moreover, *Golf Illustrated*, a permanent feature in most clubhouses, became the official organ of the Association whose views were thus well-publicised at club level. However, the Association did not involve itself in the negotiations between a professional and his club and the norm for a retainer was established before the PGA came into existence. Yet it was able to enforce the professional's right to ball sales by not allowing clubs to host a PGA-sanctioned event unless they complied with this demand. Once the PGA stepped in as an organiser all club professionals had the chance to play competitive golf and, if good enough, rise through the local and regional championships to participate in major national tournaments. Success here could lead to new job offers and the financial rewards from the less-pressurised exhibition matches.

This contrasts significantly with the situation in horseracing, cricket and football. In the former two sports there were no labour organisations. Elite jockeys secured the bulk of mounts and had no community of interest with the 'also ran' riders. In cricket there were two major labour disputes, one in 1881 involving seven Nottingham professionals and another in 1896 when five England players demanded a pay increase, both of which ended in defeat for the players due to the hard line taken by the relevant committees and a lack of support from other players (Sissons 1988, 174–180). In football, although its benevolent activities and quasi employment agency work were possibly the equal of the PGA, the AFPU never really rivalled the golf association as a labour organisation (Harding 1991, 46–47, 108; Taylor 2005, 93). Whereas all golf professionals who wished to play in tournaments were virtually obliged to join the PGA, in March 1914 the AFPU encompassed only about a sixth of eligible professional footballers (Harding 1991, 110). At its height membership had never been more than 50–60% [possibly as low as 30%] even with the backing of many stars who felt that the maximum wage prevented them earning their full economic rent.[19] That football, unlike golf, had a vast reserve army of potential professionals may have contributed to the weak support, but so too might have the failure to achieve any breakthrough on the twin issues of wage limitation and the monopsonistic retain and transfer system. Neither the Football League (FL), increasingly holding financial responsibility for English elite professional football, nor the Football Association (FA), which itself had brought in the first maximum wage legislation, would budge on these matters. And the FA held a trump card. In golf the PGA operated a closed shop and determined who could enter most tournaments, but in football the FA determined who could play at all. It had the ultimate sanction in that it could de-register players and thus exclude them from the game. This it used as a weapon against APFU members when the Union exhibited signs of militancy and affiliated with the General Federation of Trade Unions, went to law over players' compensation cases without FA consent, threatened a withdrawal of labour, and encouraged players to wear union badges on their football shirts (Dabscheck 1991; Harding 1991, 55–57, 59, 64, 94). Inevitably this undermined the political operations and economic ambitions of the Union which, according to one football historian, 'was never more than a marginal body' in the period under review (Taylor 2005, 162).

Relations between the PGA and the clubs that employed its members never reached the nadir of football where the AFPU Chairman remarked in 1909 that 'we look upon the clubs as the enemies of the players' (Dabscheck 1991, 227). And certainly the R & A, the acknowledged ruling body in golf from the 1890s, never sought to destroy the labour organisation in golf as the FA attempted to in football during a major industrial confrontation when it declared a lockout of union members (Dabscheck 1991, 222). Nor did the R & A ever intervene to prevent fund-raising activities by the PGA unlike both the FA and the FL who respectively, in 1911 and 1912, refused permission for the annual football match whose gate-money was used to finance AFPU benevolent activities (Harding 1991, 101). In golf, in contrast, clubs vied to host PGA tournaments, the R & A consulted the PGA on matters concerning the Open Championship, club members donated to the PGA benevolent fund, and the PGA never considered a collective withdrawal of labour (Behrend and Lewis 1998, 118, 150; Holt, Lewis, and Vamplew 2002, 26–27).

Comparisons with other sports

Although information on other sports is limited in its detail, this section will attempt to assess the extent to which the social and economic experiences of the professional golfer differed from those of the jockey, cricketer and footballer. Overall the average club professional with his annual income of around £200 was economically neither better nor worse off than his peers in other sports. Horseracing offered the greatest rewards. A top jockey could earn several thousand pounds in a season and a moderately successful one probably a thousand or so, but, in a market vastly oversupplied with labour, the great majority of riders had a few mounts at three guineas a time and rode no winners at all (Vamplew 2004a, 216–217). In cricket a regular first team county professional could earn £150–£200 over a year and a leading player up to £300 (Sissons 1988, 114). This comprised a basic wage, match fees, win bonuses, talent money and ground collections, an income 'to a large extent derived from a payments-by-results system' (Sissons 1988, 93). The imposition in football in 1901 of a maximum annual wage of £208 actually reduced the earnings of a few star players. By 1910, when the introduction of biennial increments for long service raised the limit to £5 a week, perhaps a third of League professionals were paid at this level (Taylor 2005, 103). To what extent illegal payments lifted actual earnings is unknown but they would have gone only to the elite performers; most professional footballers would have been happy to have been raised to the maximum permitted (Taylor 2005, 111–112). If they lasted long enough – 5 years in football, at least 10 in cricket – a benefit, if awarded, could raise their career earnings by about £2 a week, but the vagaries of the climate meant that it was an unreliable source of income in cricket (Sandiford 1991, 113; Taylor 2005, 106–110). Both the cricket and football incomes cited above assume winter and summer pay respectively, but this was not guaranteed except by the wealthier clubs and for the better players. Cricketers, footballers and jockeys all had close seasons in which, depending on their wage guarantee, they might have to seek alternative sources of income. Golfers, in contrast, worked all year round at their trade, concentrating more on club and ball manufacture in winter when tournament play ceased and the demand for teaching fell away.

The benefit was a discretionary payment and thus another weapon in the armoury of the employers, already strong because of restrictions on player mobility. In having the ability to change his employing club, the golfer had an advantage over his fellow professional in cricket or football. He was free to move from one appointment to another, unlike the cricketer, who, from 1873, had to serve a two-year residential qualification if he wished to change counties, or the footballer who, virtually a bonded man, was subject to the highly restrictive retain and transfer system (Sissons 1988, 85; Taylor 2005, 98–101). The only way to be a paid cricketer and not be subject to the severe mobility restrictions was to opt out of first-class cricket and play as the professional in a league club, but, of course, the status was lower as might be the economic reward (Dixon and Garnham 2003–04, 104–108).[20] A similar situation pertained in football, though Taylor has argued that the oppressive elements of the retain and transfer system have been overemphasised by historians and that generally clubs did not stand in the way of players who were determined to move on. However, his examples are few and all are after 1914 (Taylor 2005, 100).[21] Apart from a few elite riders who held lucrative retainers, jockeys had no restrictions on whom they rode for but for most this equated to seeking work in a casual labour market.

In one respect golf professionals were much better off than their counterparts in racing, football and cricket. Apart from the elite tournament-playing golfers there was little travel involved in their job. This contrasts with jockeys who often travelled the length and breadth of the country to take rides and with footballers and cricketers who played half their games away from their home ground (Tolson and Vamplew 2003, 95–96).[22] However back at the club the golf professional put in longer hours of work each week than the others; and this without a close season. He also did it for more years than football professionals. The career lengths of golfers contrasted significantly with football, a much more physically-demanding sport where mean careers of those who lasted more than two years as Football League professionals was less than four seasons. However, golf careers were on a par with those in county cricket, particularly for batsmen, and in horseracing where, after the initial shakeout that meant only 1 in 8 apprentices lasted beyond a third season as a licensed jockey, the majority had a career of over 10 years and a quarter of them over two decades.[23]

More research is needed on the social mobility and inter-class relationships of the professional sportsman before 1914. On the basis of limited biographical material, it can be speculated that perhaps a few stars rose to the level of the lower middle class but that most professionals remained solidly working-class. For them there may have been the psychic income of public adulation and esteem in the local community, but opportunities for interaction with their social superiors would be severely curtailed. The golfer could play a round of golf with his social superiors but he could not join them in the clubhouse afterwards. Cricketers too could play alongside the middle-class amateur in the first-class game but they travelled to the match separately and stayed in different hotels, changed in separate dressing rooms, entered the pitch through separate gates, and suffered the symbolic subordination of having their initials after their names on the official scorecards in contrast to the prefix of the amateurs (Birley 1999, 185). The middle-class amateur was a disappearing figure in league football and professional players rarely came into contact with the middle-class in the game except when called before the committee on disciplinary matters (Taylor 2002, 27). In horseracing the doffing of the jockey's cap to owners and trainers showed who held the social reins (Vamplew 2000, 135).

To some extent attitudes towards the professional sportsmen may have been influenced by beliefs of their social practices. There was certainly a perception that alcohol featured too much in their social lives. Fluid replacement after a long day in the field and evenings away from home with colleagues no doubt contributed to the drinking habits of the professional cricketer and although 'nine drunks and a parson' as a description of the professionals in the Yorkshire cricket team in the 1880s is an apocryphal exaggeration, it does indicate the stereotypical view of the paid player (Birley 1999, 135). For professional footballers the 'alleged fondness for alcohol was a difficult image to shake off' (Taylor 2002, 33). No doubt this owed something to the insecurity of the job coupled with the added stress of simultaneously trying to entertain and compete whilst enjoying the unholy combination of reasonable wages and substantial free time.

Stress for jockeys, men who also had a reputation for insobriety, came from constant weight-watching, the struggle to obtain mounts, and the anticipation of inevitable injury. Champion riders such as George Fordham and Tommy Loates were definitely alcoholics but below them were many lesser riders also with drinking problems (Collins and Vamplew 2002, 104–105). Possibly stress-related drinking was lower in golf where rising employment opportunities lessened the pressure on the professionals, particularly as the bulk of them did not have to compete on the course to make their living. Even tournament players whose earnings could fluctuate wildly had their club retainer to fall back upon.

The authorities in cricket, football and racing all prohibited professionals in their sport from gambling. No such ban was in operation in golf, but, despite gambling among golfers, no accusations of associated corruption appear to have arisen. Possibly this was because of the master–servant relationship in which the views of the amateurs with their emphasis on etiquette was dominant.[24] Cricketers' whites reflected the purity of their sport once the MCC had intervened to end the gambling associated with the Georgian game. Again the exemplar role of the amateur players and captain could have been a factor in a sport where 'the idea that the players were private servants of the county clubs was widely held' (Sissons 1988, 88). It might be argued that there was also a strong master-servant relationship in horseracing where allegations of gambling and corruption by jockeys were commonplace, but here there was no amateur code of ethical behaviour to be adhered to; nor did amateur riders commonly race with professional jockeys or take lessons from them (Dizikes 2000, 136–152; Huggins 2000, 192–193; Vamplew and Kay 2005, 14–16). In football corruption actually occurred in collusion with the employers who were sometimes willing to circumvent the maximum wage legislation to placate star players (Taylor 2005, 111–112). Whether the infrequent incidents of bribery of opponents, such as the high profile case of Welsh international, Billy Meredith who was suspended for a year by the FA, were associated with gambling or the desire to win trophies (as with Meredith) or avoid relegation has not yet been investigated by scholars (Harding 1998, 105–117).

Conclusions

Professional sportspersons often have career structures and working lives different from the majority of other skilled workers. They retire earlier, face greater public appraisal of their work performance, have more erratic income flows and often have to change their place of work on a regular basis. In golf, however, a distinction can be drawn between the elite tournament player and the journeyman club professional, groups referred to by one of the foundation PGA members respectively as 'professional golfers' and 'golf professionals' because of the differences in their experiences (Fulford, H. 1952. "Fifty Years of the PGA." *Golf Magazine*, January, 38).

The origins of most professionals is unclear but, whether they learned their skills as caddies or gained their positions via their Scottish background or family connections, most had little time to play competitive golf. They were too busy teaching, maintaining the course or manufacturing equipment. Only the stars played regularly in tournaments. Once established the club professional could anticipate a career of around 15 years but this was substantially less than that of the successful tournament player, whose skill and experience compensated for ageing muscles until middle age and who then often became a respected club professional for another decade or more. During their careers the erratic nature of earnings was felt mainly by the tournament players whose prize money was dependent upon performance, but they still had their club retainer as a reliable source of income. Absolute incomes were clearly greater for the elite professional. As was pointed out by a commentator in 1903, whereas the leading players were winning a lot of money in tournaments, the rank and file were not: 'and', he added, 'what of the smaller men, those who are just second and third rate players? They have to depend not upon their prowess with the club, but upon the profits drawn from their workshops' (*Golf Illustrated*, January 23, 1903). To play in contests and to advise on the construction and development of courses, the tournament professional had to travel to different work sites whereas the club professional was relatively immobile on a day-to-day basis. It was the tournament player too who faced the greater public appraisal. Although golf was not yet a major gate-money sport, spectators could be attracted in large numbers to watch the tournament and exhibition play of the professional golfer. For the golfing professional any appraisal was more at a one-to-one basis as a teacher though, if responsible for course maintenance, all club members would have a view on their performance.

Yet despite their different work experiences, the elite played an important role in the future of the journeymen. This was partly by helping them gain 'respect' if not respectability, but mainly because they supported the idea of a players' association which, without the star players, stood little chance of success. That they were willing to join with the club professional to form the PGA may be attributable to the fact that both at the start and end of their careers the tournament player was a 'golf professional' and remained attached to a club even when participating extensively in elite activities. The PGA itself provided welfare functions but was also able to gain its members the monopoly right to sell golf balls at clubs. Additionally by organising the bulk of professional golf tournaments it provided its members with an opportunity to earn extra income and showcase their golfing talents whilst simultaneously, by the enforcement of a closed shop on entrants to these competitions, it strengthened its own position among both professional golfers and golfing professionals.

In the context of other sports professionals, and indeed of most working-class occupations of the time, it is difficult to describe the golf club professional as exploited labour. Certainly like cricketers, footballers and jockeys he faced social restrictions. Yet his reputation was possibly higher than that of his counterparts in other sports. Although a few had drinking problems, generally the golf professional was regarded as reliable, respectable and honest. Economically the situation was much better. He had a guaranteed retainer and, though this was often eaten into by payments to assistants when he was out teaching or away at a tournament, his annual income was at least the equivalent of his counterpart in cricket and football, and, as might be anticipated for a skilled craftsman, substantially above that of the unskilled labourer. At times spokesmen for the PGA claimed that clubs were reducing retainers or claiming the right to profits from ball sales, but these seem to be instances of special pleading or isolated individual circumstances. It certainly does not fit the aggregated statistical evidence provided in this article. Admittedly working hours were long, a six-day week was the norm, and generally there was no off-season, though quiet times could be utilised to make clubs and, till the coming of the rubber-cored variety, manufacture balls. Possibly offsetting the earnings level was a lack of job security, but turnover rates and career length data do not suggest overly frequent movement or an inability to obtain a new position. For the more skilled and temperamentally suitable player

Notes

1. A lower limit to the number of professionals can be determined from those listed in the *Golfer's Handbook*. These total 679 in 1907 and 941 in 1913. An upper limit would be set by the number of golf clubs in existence – estimated by Lewis at 161 in 1885, 959 in 1895, 1939 in 1905 and 2844 in 1914 – though not every club had a course of its own and not every club with a course employed a professional (Lewis 1995, 8).
2. The figure for league cricket professionals is an 'educated estimate' following discussions with Neil Garnham, Jeffrey Hill, and especially Jack Williams, all of whom have written academically on league cricket.
3. The number of owners was based on a count of registered colours (compulsory from the 1890s) in the *Racing Calendars* (1913). Football club estimates are from Russell (1997, 45) and the *Scottish Football Annual* (1913–1914). The cricket figures are based on estimates by Jack Williams (personal communication).
4. On football see Lanfrachi and Taylor (2001), Russell (1997), Taylor (2005); for cricket see Birley (1999) and Sissons (1988); and on horseracing see Huggins (2000), Vamplew (2000) and Vamplew and Kay (2005).
5. Harding (1991) which makes use of earlier work by Dabscheck (1979).
6. The numbers in the following tables fall short of this figure as information on some players was inadequate for the particular statistical purpose.
7. Of some 400 histories consulted, 207 yielded useable information. A further 86 pieces of information containing contractual data were obtained by contacting the clubs that employed the foundation members of the PGA.
8. That three of them also came from Jersey is less easily explained.
9. Given the weaknesses of establishing kinship it was felt that detailed sampling of pre-1914 material would serve little purpose.
10. The career lengths of those whose ages are given in Table 4 are clearly longer than the larger numbers dealt with in Table 5. They are a skewed cohort in the sense that we know more about them.
11. This was the first occasion in which private enterprise, apart from golf clubs themselves, had given golf professionals from all over the country a chance to compete for a national prize.
12. The French Open began in 1906, the Belgian in 1910, but the German event was run for only two years from 1911. The other British victor was J.D. Edgar who migrated to the United States and won the Canadian Open but was later murdered in a robbery.
13. Once the PGA was set up, having the exclusive right to the profits from the sale of golf balls at a club was made a condition of membership.
14. For fuller details see Holt, Lewis, and Vamplew (2002, 1–10).
15. Cousins had access to the early minutes of the PGA which have since gone missing. A simpler version appeared in *The Golfers' Year Book* 1905, 249 which stated that the objectives were 'to promote the interests of professional golfers by holding tournaments for the encouragement of younger players, to assist those who are out of work in obtaining employment, and to relieve cases of distress by the establishment of a Benevolent Fund'.
16. Passing references in *Golf Illustrated* give membership numbers as 1901 = 70, 1902 => 300, 1908 = 574 and 1914 = c800.
17. At one stage, in 1908, another form of collective action was considered, that of a golfers' co-operative trading society. The underlying idea was that bulk purchasing could lower costs and hence raise profits. However, at the time less than a 100 professionals expressed interest and

the idea was shelved for a decade or so ("Minutes of Midlands." *PGA*, September 16, 1908; "Minutes of PGA." January 23, 1921).

18. There were earlier experiences in mid-Victorian cricket. Professional cricketer William Clarke founded the All-England Eleven which toured the country playing matches for a share of the gate-money. Clarke's success spawned other itinerant teams and over two to three decades the professional cricketer helped popularise the sport and further his earning power. However, the touring teams were in competition with each other and not part of an overall collective. The economic experiment ended when first-class county cricket became organised in which amateurs and professionals played alongside each other but with amateurs firmly in control in the committee rooms (West 1988). The others concerned overseas cricket trips, to the United States and Canada in 1859 led by George Parr and to Australia in 1861 under Heathfield 'H.H.' Stephenson. Both were successful commercial ventures organised by professionals (Light 2005, 70).

19. Different sources offer different estimates (Harding 1991, 85; Taylor 2005, 141).

20. Hill (1987, 74) has argued that local esteem would be high and incomes could be greater than in county cricket but there was no mass migration of first-class professionals to the leagues which suggests a preference for the first-class game.

21. For a discussion of mobility of football players within Britain see Lanfrachi and Taylor, (2001, 38–45).

22. George Ulyett, the Yorkshire professional cricketer, was an extreme example who during his career travelled an estimated 258,000 miles, of which 157,000 occurred in his five tours to Australia (Sissons 1988, 115).

23. For details of these calculations and their deficiencies see Vamplew (2004a, 227–238).

24. For a general discussion on the role of etiquette in the evolution of rules in sport see Vamplew (2007).

Disclosure statement

No potential conflict of interest was reported by the author.

References

Behrend, J., and P. N. Lewis. 1998. *Challenges and Champions*. St Andrews: Royal & Ancient Golf Club.

Behrend, J., P. N. Lewis, and K. Mackie. 2001. *Champions and Guardians: The Royal & Ancient Golf Club 1884–1939*. St Andrews: Royal & Ancient Golf Club.

Birley, D. 1999. *A Social History of English Cricket*. London: Aurum.

Brennard, T. 1990. *Richmond Golf Club: A Centenary History 1891–1991*. Richmond: Club.

Brockway, E. 1993. *The Lansdown Golf Club*. Bristol: Club.

Cadney, D. 1991. *The Story of Olton Golf Club*. Worcestershire: Grant.

Casley, D. 1995. *Mullion Golf Club 1895–1995*. Mullion: Club.

Ceron-Anaya, H. 2010. "An Approach to the History of Golf: Business, Symbolic Capital, and Technologies of the Self." *Journal of Sport & Social Issues* 34 (3): 339–358.

Cohen, L., A. Kingman, M. Faulks, and A. Lipson. 1993. *Bakewell Golf Club; The First Century*. Bakewell: Club.

Coleridge, J. 1992. *1892–1992 The Royal West Norfolk Golf Club*. Norwich: Club.

Collins, J. 1989. *The Nottinghamshire Golf Club*. Nottingham: Club.

Collins, T., and W. Vamplew. 2002. *Mud, Sweat and Beers: A Cultural History of Sport and Alcohol*. Oxford: Berg.

Corrigan, P., and R. Reynolds. 1990. *The Glamorganshire Golf Club 1890–1990*. Glamorgan: Club.

Cousins, G. 1974. "The PGA Story: And Now Nationwide." *Golf Trade Journal* February, 6.

Crampsey, R. A. 1988. *The History of Cathkin Braes Golf Club 1888–1988*. Cathkin Braes: Club.

Dabscheck, B. 1979. "'Defensive Manchester' a History of the Professional Footballers Association." In *Sport in History*, edited by R. Cashman and M. McKernan, 227–257. St Lucia: Queensland University Press.

Dabscheck, B. 1991. "'A Man or a Puppet?' The FA's Attempt to Destroy the Association Football Players' Union." *International Journal of the History of Sport* 8 (2): 221–238.

Dee, D. 2013. "'There is no Discrimination Here, but the Committee Never Elect Jews': Antisemitism in British Golf, 1894–1970." *Patterns of Prejudice* 47 (2): 117–138.

Dixon, P., and N. Garnham. 2003–04. "Cricket Club Professionals in Victorian and Edwardian County Durham." *Sport in History* 23 (2): 94–108.

Dizikes, J. 2000. *Yankee Doodle Dandy*. New Haven, CT: Yale University Press.

Duncan, G. 1951. *Golf at the Gallop*. London: Sporting Handbooks.

Edwards, L. 1973. *The West Lancashire Golf Club*. Liverpool: Club.

Fry, P. 1994. *The Whitcombes*. Worcestershire: Grant.

George, J. 2009. "'An Excellent Means of Combining Fresh Air, Exercise and Society': Females on the Fairways, 1890–1914." *Sport in History* 29 (3): 333–352.

George, J., J. Kay, and W. Vamplew. 2007. "Women to the Fore: Gender Accommodation and Resistance at the British Golf Club before 1914." *Sporting Traditions* 23 (2): 79–98.

Grant, P. M. 1995. *100 Years on the Cliff: The Complete History of Pennard Golf Club*. Pennard: Club.

Greenfield, S., and G. Osborn. 1998. "From Feudal Serf to Big Spender: The Influence of Legal Intervention on the Status of English Professional Footballers." *Culture, Sport, Society* 1 (1): 1–23.

Gregory, B. 1992. *The History of Mid-Herts Golf Club*. Wheathampstead: Club.

Harding, J. 1991. *For the Good of the Game*. London: Robson.

Harding, J. 1998. *Football Wizard*. London: Robson.

Herd, S. 1923. *My Golfing Life*. London: Chapman and Hall.

Hill, J. 1987. "First-class Cricket and the Leagues: Some Notes on the Development of English Cricket, 1900–40." *International Journal of the History of Sport* 4 (1): 68–81.

Holt, R., P. N. Lewis, and W. Vamplew. 2002. *The Professional Golfers Association 1901–2001*. Worcestershire: Grant.

Howell, A. 1990. *Harry Vardon*. London: Hutchinson.

Huggins, M. 2000. *Flat Racing and British Society 1790–1914*. London: Cass.

Jackson, M. P. 1984. *Industrial Relations*. London: Croom Helm.

Jackson, A. 1994. *The British Professional Golfers 1887–1930: A Register*. Worcestershire: Grant.

Kirkcaldy, A. 1921. *Fifty Years of Golf*. London: Fisher Unwin.

Lanfrachi, P., and M. Taylor. 2001. *Moving with the Ball*. Oxford: Berg.

Leach, H. 1907. *Great Golfers in the Making*. London: Methuen.

Lee, J. H., and L. H. Kemp. 1986. *Redhill & Reigate Golf Club Centenary 1887–1987*. Redhill: Club.

Lewis, P. N. 1995. *The Dawn of Professional Golf*. New Ridley: Hobbs and McEwan.

Light, R. 2005. "'Ten Drunks and a Parson'? The Victorian Professional Cricketer Reconsidered." *Sport in History* 25 (1): 60–76.

Lowerson, J. 1984. "Sport and the Victorian Sunday: The Beginning of Middle-class Apostasy." *British Journal of Sport History* 1: 202–220.

Lowerson, J. 1989. "Golf." In *Sport in Britain: A Social History*, edited by T. Mason, 187–214. Cambridge: Cambridge University Press.

MacAlindin, B. 2003. *James Braid Champion Golfer*. Worcestershire: Grant.

Mackenzie, R. 1998. *A Wee Nip at the 19th Hole*. London: Collins Willow.

Milton, J. 1987. *A History of Royal Eastbourne Golf Club*. Eastbourne: Club.

Moreton, J. 1999. *Porters Park Golf Club*. Hertfordshire: Club.

Munting, R. 1987. *Hedges and Hurdles*. London: J.A. Allen.

Neale, R. L. 1995. *A History of Handsworth Golf Club*. Birmingham: Club.

Newbould, D. 1994. *Coventry Hearsall Golf Club*. Coventry: Club.

Northerner. 1933. "Brief Biographies." *The PGA Journal*, April, 12.

Nunn, P. 1995. *100 Years of Golf at Flempton*. Flempton: Club.

O.F.T. 1982. *Aldeburgh Golf Club; The First Hundred Years*. Ipswich: Club.

Park, W. 1896. *The Game of Golf*. London: Longmans Green.

Park, W. 1920. *The Art of Putting*. Edinburgh: J and J Gray.

Russell, D. 1997. *Football and the English*. Preston: Carnegie.

Sandiford, K. A. P. 1991. "The Birth of the Professional Cricketer's Benefit Match." *International Journal of the History of Sport* 8 (1): 111–123.

Savage, E. J. 1980. *The Story of Felixstowe Ferry Golf Club*. Felixstowe: Club.

Sherlock, J. 1912. "From the Professional's Point of View." In *The New Book of Golf*, edited by H. Hutchinson, 171–234. London: Longmans Green.

Sissons, R. 1988. *The Players*. Sydney: Pluto Press.

Stirk, D. 1989. *Carry Your Bag, Sir*. London: Withweby.

Taylor, J. H. 1912. *The Art of Golf*. London: Hutchinson.

Taylor, J. H. 1943. *Golf: My Life's Work*. London: Jonathan Cape.

Taylor, M. 2002. "Work and Play: The Professional Footballer in England c1900–c1950." *Sports Historian* 22 (1): 16–43.

Taylor, M. 2005. *The Leaguers*. Liverpool: Liverpool University Press.

Tolson, J., and W. Vamplew. 2003. "Facilitation Not Revolution: Railways and British Flat Racing 1830–1914." *Sport in History* 23 (1): 89–106.

Vamplew, W. 1976. *The Turf*. London: Allen Lane.

Vamplew, W. 1985. "Not Playing the Game: Unionism in British Professional Sport 1870–1914." *British Journal of Sport History* 2: 232–247.

Vamplew, W. 2000. "Still Crazy after All These Years: Continuity in a Changing Labour Market for Professional Jockeys." *Journal of Contemporary British History* 14 (2): 115–145.

Vamplew, W. 2004a. *Pay Up and Play the Game*. Cambridge: Cambridge University Press.

Vamplew, W. 2004b. "Sporting Innovation: The American Invasion of the British Turf and Links, 1895–1905." *Sport History Review* 35: 122–137.

Vamplew, W. 2007. "Playing with the Rules: Influences on the Development of Regulation in Sport." *International Journal of the History of Sport* 24 (7): 843–871.

Vamplew, Wray. 2008. "Child Work or Child Labour? The Caddie Question in Edwardian Golf." www.idrottsforum.

Vamplew, W. 2010. "Sharing Space: Inclusion, Exclusion, and Accommodation at the British Golf Club before 1914." *Journal of Sport & Social Issues* 34 (3): 359–375.

Vamplew, W. 2012. "Concepts of Capital: An Approach Shot to the History of the British Sports Club before 1914." *Journal of Sport History* 39 (2): 299–331.

Vamplew, W., and J. Kay. 2005. *Encyclopedia of British Horseracing*. Routledge: Abingdon.

Vidler, D. 1984. *Rye Golf Club: The First Ninety Years*. Rye: Club.

West, G. D. 1988. *The Elevens of England*. London: Darf.

Empiricism, theoretical concepts and the development of the British golf club before 1914

Wray Vamplew

ABSTRACT

Golf took the concept of the club from traditional voluntary organizations along with the ideas of committee structures, mechanisms for ensuring exclusivity and a place, both geographically and socially, for communal conviviality. It became one of the fastest growing recreational activities of late nineteenth and early twentieth-century Britain and the first participant sport to expend and invest large sums of money. By means of a model constructed around the development of the British golf club before 1914, this paper offers a new approach to examining the history of associativity in sport. It uses five concepts of capital – physical, financial, cultural, social, and human – and argues that their formation in the context of club development should not be explored in isolation of each other.

Comment

This is a modified version of 'Concepts of capital: an approach shot to the history of the British sports club before 1914', originally published in *Journal of Sport History* vol. 39 no. 2, Summer 2012, 299–231. The article encapsulates the results of a project described in the author's Howell address at the 2009 NASSH Conference in Asheville. Thanks go to Jessica MacBeth, Orla Gilmore and especially Jane George for research assistance; to the Arts and Humanities Research Board, the Leverhulme Trust and the Carnegie Trust for financial aid; to the many golf club secretaries who responded to queries; to Peter Lewis at the British Golf Museum for his knowledge, constant support and access to the library of the Royal & Ancient Golf Club; and, above all, to the authors of the many golf club histories whose work has provided the information central to this paper.

Three things remain on the research agenda. The first is to make this analysis more sophisticated by expanding on the simple definitions of capital used here and explore the concepts in greater depth. For example it might be possible to combine aspects of cultural and social capital as was done by Humphreys in her study of golf tourism (Humphreys 2011, 105–128).[1] More too could be done on the fact that both social and human capital, unlike physical and financial capital, are not depleted by use, rather the reverse as experience is gained. The second is to apply the concepts to other aspects of the golf club such as volunteering and communal conviviality. As volunteers, golf club members, unlike those at tennis and bowls clubs, had no role in the maintenance of the playing surface: the sheer size of it required paid labour. However, they had a role in organizing fund-raising and social activities, often the same thing. Others volunteered their professional expertise, such as solicitor Alexander Travers Hawes who helped ensure that Chislehurst's course, which was on common land, was protected and the experienced architect on Alwoodly's committee who designed their new club house (*Golf Illustrated*, August 20, 1909, 223). Communal conviviality is an aspect of golf that should not be underestimated: dinners, dances, soirees, smokers for men, the annual garden party and drinks at the bar all served to draw individuals into social relationships whilst also contributing to financial capital formation. The third line of research is to develop this approach into a general model of club development so that comparisons can be made with clubs in other sports. In doing so, hopefully it will distil the typical from the atypical and make a contribution to the emerging history of the sports club.[2]

Introduction

Background

Golf likely originated in the Low Countries but it was popularized in Scotland from the seventeenth century, primarily as a short game – little more than putting – played in church yards and other limited areas by a broad spectrum of the population using minimal and often basic equipment (Gillmeister 2002; Hamilton 1998). However, as golf developed into a longer game it required larger amounts of land and became a less democratic sport. The club, with its ability to raise funds collectively, became the instrument of golf expansion, much of which took place south of the border in England, first as Scottish golfing outposts but later as clubs dominated by English players. Golf became one of the fastest growing recreational activities of late nineteenth and early twentieth-century Britain. From only a few thousand who played the game at the beginning of the 1880s, by 1914 some 350,000 golfers were 'spoiling good walks' all round the country. Most of these players were members of a club, that traditional British organizational institution in sport and other activities (Clark 2000). Golf clubs, however, were more than a means of leisure. In the words of one supporter:

> A golf club whose ground is used for the recreation of a large section of the inhabitants of a district, that supplies a 'living space' for the dwellers in its neighbourhood, gives employment to many of the poorer classes, brings money into the district, and increases the building value of the land around, is a public amenity. (A London Golfer 1909)

Hence determining the development of the golf club can contribute not just to sporting history but to wider historical themes.

Most private golf clubs followed one of three major development models as illustrated by the respective histories of Douglas Park, North Hants and Betchworth Park. The former was the brainchild of William Gibson who on 22 June 1897 sent a letter to a number of friends and neighbours inviting them to form a club at Douglas Park, Milngavie. Eleven turned up at a meeting. Two weeks later a committee had been elected and a lease of 50 acres taken. Arrangements were made for the land to be drained and a clubhouse to be built and on 2 October a 9-hole course was opened with 56 members enrolled (MacCabe 1981, 1). North Hants represented those clubs who wished to begin on a larger scale. Here, in December 1903, a self-chosen group sent a circular to 'selected' inhabitants of Fleet, a residential community centred around large Victorian properties occupied by prosperous families, and senior officers from nearby Aldershot Garrison. The prospectus promised not only an 18-hole course 'equal to any inland course in the country' but also 'first-rate lawn tennis courts and croquet grounds, surrounded by well-laid out gardens and pleasure grounds, with fine trees and abundance of shade.' Dinner was to be served in the clubhouse on most nights and a number of bedrooms would be available for members and their guests (Littlewood 2004, 1–7). Then there were those like Betchworth Park which opted to start off as a limited liability company. One F.S. Phillips circulated a letter inviting support to form a company to take a lease from Lord Francis Hope of Deepdene House. Sixteen respondents then met, taking the advice of a solicitor and accountant on the terms and issues of bonds and shares. They established the company in February 1912, appointed the famous golf architect H.S. Colt to lay out the course, and by August had 53 subscribers, each of whom took a minimum of £50 in debentures towards the estimated cost of over £4000. The clubhouse and course were opened in September 1913 (Hogan 1991, 4–7).

Whether starting off small or large, whether ambitious to expand or content to remain as they were, all clubs required land, funds, members and a labour force. These resources form the focus of this article, which will explore the pre-1914 history of the British golf club utilizing a framework based on five concepts of capital, those referring to the physical, financial, human, social and cultural versions. As with many social science concepts, definitions of capital can be complex, multi-faceted, and sometimes opaque. Here, however, for the sake of progressing an argument, broad definitions will be employed. Hence physical capital formation will be considered as those improvements to natural resources which create productive assets that help procure revenue. Financial capital will be regarded as the money source such as share purchase, debentures, loans and even donations that pay for these fixed assets and also the working capital that covers operating costs. Human capital formation embraces those aspects of the labour force which enhance productivity such as the acquisition of skill, competencies, knowledge and experience as well as improved physical and mental health. It can also encompass self-improvement for non-economic reasons such as simply wanting to be fitter or more culturally aware.

Transferring these concepts to the golf course it will be asked what did it cost to develop a course and the associated club facilities which enabled the club to offer services and goods for sale. It will be queried how the money was raised to pay for this and for the wages of the greens staff who maintained the course and the purchase of the materials which they used for that purpose. It will be considered how improvements were made to the human capital stock: the workforce that prepared the greens, made and repaired the equipment and carried the players' clubs. However, economic forms of capital do not explain everything and hence the paper will also look at social capital – the development of networks between individuals which can benefit them socially and economically – and cultural capital which can be considered as reputation or status-enhancing activities.

Notwithstanding that every golfer might regard their own club as being unique in some way – perhaps the difficulty of the back nine, or the way the prevailing wind can wreak havoc on a bad day, or simply the conviviality dispensed at the 19th hole – the aim of this paper is to produce a collective history of the British golf club. Rather than attempt to summarize the chronological development of numerous clubs, here it will be endeavoured to ask how the 'typical' club fared using these concepts of capital formation as an exploratory and explanatory mechanism.

NUMBERS AND NARRATIVES

Table 1. Estimates of golf clubs in Britain 1870–1914[a].

Year	Total	Year	Total	Year	Total	Year	Total	Year	Total
1870	74	1880	117	1890	375	1900	1357	1910	2729
1871	79	1881	119	1891	479	1901	1418	1911	2765
1872	82	1882	130	1892	589	1902	1503	1912	2799
1873	85	1883	138	1893	716	1903	1613	1913	2839
1874	89	1884	147	1894	838	1904	1764	1914	2844
1875	91	1885	161	1895	959	1905	1939		
1876	95	1886	171	1896	1072	1906	2130		
1877	98	1887	202	1897	1153	1907	2304		
1878	107	1888	237	1898	1224	1908	2456		
1879	111	1889	290	1899	1276	1909	2667[a]		

Source: *Golfing Annual* (1888–1910), *Nisbet's Golf Year Book* (1905–1914), Lewis (1994, 11–14, 1995, 168).
[a]Includes all clubs in *Golfing Annual* 1909/10 with no foundation date attached.

A note on sources

The study is based on a survey of some 2000 primary data sets of individual golf clubs derived from golfing yearbooks and secondary material from over 400 club histories, supplemented by information from articles in the golfing press and other contemporary publications. To prevent excessive references only club-specific information is documented.

The quality of club histories varies greatly. Some, usually written by trained historians – amateur or professional – provide analysis, context and critique. Others simply quote extensively from the minutes, poor history but useful for the project. The worst can contain 'many anecdotes … about personalities, some a trifle eccentric' (Littlewood 2004, x). Some authors are fortunately able to draw on club minutes, though often those for the foundation period have disappeared, lost to fire, water and the whims of the committee. Yet historians must be aware that archives are sites of power that privilege some information above others. The committee minutes reveal the views of those running the club, not necessarily those of the membership.

The use of golf yearbooks, which give information on all clubs at a point in time, helps provide a broader picture of many of the issues discussed below. These are generally factually reliable in that a template was used to solicit information, but there could be omissions as they were dependent on club secretaries submitting material before the publication deadline. A check on the following year usually allowed any deficiency to be corrected.

Like all newspapers, the golfing press was aimed at a specific market, an objective which may have influenced its contents and approach. Additionally in 1910 *Golf Illustrated* became the official organ for the Professional Golfers' Association (PGA) which gave a voice to one faction within the golf club's labour force. Caddies, however, remained a silent subordinate group: an inquiry into the welfare of golf caddies in Edwardian Britain took evidence from golf club secretaries but not from a solitary caddie (Agenda Club 1912).

Establishing the numbers

As Burnett and Lewis noted 'counting golf clubs is an inexact science' (Burnett and Lewis 1996–97, 114). Inherent flaws in the primary sources render it impossible to present a definitive figure for the number of golf clubs in any given year. Basic figures can be obtained from the *Golfing Annual* (1888–1910) and *Nisbet's Golf Year Book* (1905–1914) which list clubs in existence in the particular year covered and, in many cases, their [alleged] foundation dates. However the editors were reliant on individual clubs sending in annual returns so what the data show are the minimum number of clubs that existed in a given year, though Lewis, at the time Director of the British Golf Museum, had 'a clear impression that most golf clubs were listed' (Burnett and Lewis 1996–97, 114). A best fit of known information is shown in Table 1 and, whilst absolute accuracy is not claimed, it suggests that the great golf boom began in 1887; that there was a hiccup at the turn of the century before the advent of the rubber-cored golf ball stimulated even more players to take up the game (Vamplew 2005, 122–137). At its height, between 1891 and 1896 and again between 1904 and 1909, on average a new club was being established every two or three days.

Not all these clubs had their own courses. Some were no more than ladies sections of existing clubs being given a degree of independence; others were golfing societies composed of members of professions, firms, educational establishments and political parties brought together by a love of golf but who hired the facilities of other clubs. The majority, however, possessed courses and usually an accompanying clubhouse. Overall Lewis has estimated that in 1889, 202 clubs had a course attached. This had risen to 532 by 1894 and to 1801 by 1914, respectively around 70, 63 and 63% of all known clubs (Lewis 1995, 168).

The number of golfers is harder to determine. On the basis of clubs that listed their membership in the 1887/88 *Golfing Annual* (59% of known clubs) there were around 24,000 club golfers in 1888. A similar calculation for 1898 suggests this had grown to 185,000. In 1904 one estimate reckoned that the average membership of a club with 18 holes was 275 and for 9 holes 106, in total some 169,000 golfers but this covered only 58% of clubs so the actual figure was nearer 291,000 (*Golf Illustrated*, February 26, 1904). Using a similar calculation for 1914 gives an estimate of around 350,000.

As for the workforce, Garden Smith, editor of *Golf Illustrated*, reckoned on at least 20,000 caddies in 1909 while the Caddies Aid Association, set up by a group of golf club secretaries in 1911, estimated that 12,000 caddies were 'employed regularly' (Smith 1909; *Times*, November 12, 1912, 16). Higher up the employment scale, the *Golfer's Handbook* lists 941 professionals in 1913 but, as many clubs with their own course employed a professional, the actual number would be larger.

Physical capital

Golf can be played without a clubhouse to change in, without a professional to offer instruction and without caddies to carry the equipment, but there is one essential ingredient: land. Golf is a land-hungry sport with a typical 18-hole course taking up 80–100 acres. Finding land was not usually a major problem. Much marginal agricultural land had no real exchange value as it was too unproductive to yield any viable crops except at times of agrarian inflation, not a descriptor applicable to the late Victorian economy. The demands of golf clubs commodified such acreage and many landlords found that not only could they get more rent for golfing ground than for farming but also there was, for some, an added bonus of 'increased revenue ... because of the demand for the adjoining land as building sites' ("A Chat about Golf" 1903, 268). In the late Edwardian years many clubs near large towns were granted leases primarily 'to ripen the land for building purposes' (*Golf Illustrated*, September 3, 1909, 269).

Some clubs played upon common or open land, which had often been used for other recreational purposes. The alienation of this by golfers, who demanded more space than the footballers or cricketers, sometimes led to disputes and protests. By the early 1890s the Commons Preservation Society opined that 'golf clubs practically monopolize the commons' (cited in Lowerson 1995, 145). Although exaggerated, this complaint highlighted a growing problem: customary local expectations as to recreational and grazing use of common land being over-ridden by golf clubs and their members. Lowerson documents incidents at Chorley Wood in Hertfordshire, on the Isle of Wight, at Lincoln, Royal Epping Forest, Rushmore Heath near Ipswich, Weybridge, Wimbledon, Yeovil, and the two-decade struggle at Mitcham in Surrey, all of which ultimately ended in legal or negotiated settlements in favour of the golfers (Lowerson 1995, 144–151). Money and a membership that included solicitors and politicians generally won out. Sometimes, however, the golfers opted to move. Coventry used to play on Whitley Common but could not cope with the dual pressures of increased public use as the city grew and utilization of the land by the Royal Artillery for field training. The decision to move may also have been influenced by objections from the freemen to the rough being cut as it restricted the food supply for their cattle (MacLean 1987, 6–7). At York a move from Dringhouses to Strensall was motivated by a combination of poor drainage and interference from people exercising horses (Pearson 1990, 14).

Most courses, however, were laid out on private land, sometimes obtained free or on favourable terms from a supportive landowner, farmer or fellow player. Other landlords, however, often imposed restrictions. In 1893 the Earl of Jersey said he would not let ground to Ealing if Sunday play was introduced. Braemar's lease too precluded Sunday play. For Huntley, although the rent at Castle Parks owned by the Duke of Richmond and Gordon was minimal, their aristocratic landlord did not permit golf during the summer months. Leicestershire, like several clubs, played in the under-utilized area in the centre of a racetrack, but was constrained by a restrictive covenant in their lease from the New Leicester Club and County Racecourse Company that 'there be no damage to the racecourse' which effectively prevented the construction of bunkers. Olton secured a favourable lease from Major Alston but the course had to be closed for four days each year to accommodate his shooting party (Brailsford 1996, 149; Cadney 1991, 26; Charman 1990, 3; Scott 1992, 1; Soulsby 2002, 8). Many of the early clubs held subleases from tenant farmers for whom agriculture could take priority over play. When they retained silage rights this led to tension between the desire of the club to keep the rough down to acceptable limits and that of the tenant for a good crop of hay. At West Lancashire the grass was left so long by the local farmer that the 1884 Summer Meeting had to be postponed (Edwards 1973, 2). Moreover, although grazing animals could keep the grass short and fertilize the ground, they could also cause damage, particularly to putting surfaces.

The length of lease was vital to future planning. Longer leases sometimes could suit both partners, a guaranteed future for the club and a guaranteed income for the landlord. If a long-term lease could not be secured then neither course nor clubhouse was safe. A number of clubs near larger towns held their courses on short leases, sometimes annual ones, from speculative developers and often had to move on as the builders expanded residential construction (*Golf Illustrated*, September 3, 1909, 269). The members of Sunningdale and Park Langley were fortunate that their local developers appreciated 'the power of golf as an attraction to prospective residents' (*Golf Illustrated*, January 28, 1910, 217). When a course was leased the clubs showed massive deference to the landowner and he or she was almost automatically club president, prize presenter, ribbon cutter etc. The clubs could not risk a falling out. Renegotiating leases was often a fraught occasion. In 1892, Alexander Mitchell, the tenant farmer occupying the land that Ballater wished to use for its course, offered the relevant area gratis, but 11 years later when the club wanted to expand to 18 holes he demanded £3 an acre in rent and in 1911 he initially refused to consider an application for further land though he later settled for £125 per annum and £20 in compensation. When West Hert's lease expired their landlord, Lord Essex, sold the land containing four of their holes and the clubhouse (*Golf Illustrated*, August 6, 1909, 171; MacPhee 1992, 15–23). All said and done it was far better to own the property. This brought security but it required a capital outlay rather than an annual rent.

Having access to land was not enough; the land had to be made into a course. The costs of laying out a course increased as there was a move inland away from the free-draining sandy links of the coastal courses. Making playable courses on the heavier clay soils necessitated expenditure on drainage. Few courses were as fortunate as North Hants where the subsoil meant that 'after a night's rain the links come up smiling and "mud golf" is unknown' (*Tatler*, October 7, 1908). Additionally hazards that had occurred naturally on the links often had to be created elsewhere. Golf courses could have been constructed simply as a test of the skill and endurance of the players, but, especially as inland ones developed, there was also a challenge to the designer to create an aesthetically pleasing landscape. The Scottish links wilderness became less appreciated than a romanticized rural England. Golf provided a means to enjoy the countryside, though in a form tamed by greenkeepers. Some of the early courses, particularly links, were, apart from the putting surfaces, almost as nature intended; but later ones, created by the emerging profession of golf architects, were artificial 'natural' environments.[3] The rural landscape, natural or constructed, offered a challenge to the urban achiever as the countryside became part of the (sub)urban adult playground. Nevertheless golf presented a pastoral experience, but not too wild a one, culminating on each hole with 'the supreme object of suburban veneration: the perfect lawn' (Holt 1998, 79).

For many clubs the costs of constructing a course were not one-off. Few courses remained unchanged for long. The main change was the expansion of the number of holes, usually from 9 to 18. Additionally many courses had to be redesigned, some significantly so, with the advent of the rubber-cored golf ball which, by offering players more distance, rendered obsolete those holes geared towards the gutta-percha ball (Vamplew 2005). Many others simply had to start again as around 45% of clubs moved at least once before 1914, generally for one of four reasons. First, the club wished to extend the course to 18 holes which could accommodate more players simultaneously; this usually necessitated either the securing of adjacent land or a shift to a new course altogether. Second, there were problems with the landlord (or his tenant, for often clubs held sub-tenancies). Third, the club wanted the security of a longer lease; or, fourth, an opportunity arose to purchase land of their own.

On top of the initial capital outlay, the assets had to be maintained. A glance at the 'Trade List' in the *Golfer's Handbook* for 1913 shows the many purchasing decisions that had to be considered by the committee. Among the 50 products advertized by some 200 manufacturers were badges, bamboo sweepers, ball scoops and troughs, club house furnishings, fences, flags and pins, grass seed, horse boots, lawn mowers, lawn rollers, lockers, manure, medals, sand, stationery, spades and shovels, stoves, weed extractors, weed killer, and worm exterminators (*Golfer's Handbook* 1913, 893–906).

Another major investment in land improvement was the clubhouse, which, apart from perhaps the provision of changing and storage facilities, was not actually necessary to the playing of golf. However, what appealed to some members was its sociability, a haven from work and family where they could settle in their favourite chair and enjoy a drink or participate in a hand of cards or a game of snooker. Often costing more than the course

NUMBERS AND NARRATIVES

itself, some were palatial but others, as at Bishop Auckland, initially lacked basic amenities. Here, in the absence of a piped water supply, caddies were organized to carry water from a spring near the 18th tee. The first clubhouse at Flempton and Bury St Edmunds was an old railway carriage; that at Silloth the former pavilion of the North Cumberland Tennis Club purchased along with mowers and chairs for £17.10s. Pioneering players may have been content with a tin shed – literally so at Biggar where it was built by a member who was the local blacksmith at a cost of £10 – in which to change but later golfers demanded better and more expensive facilities (Longstaff 1994, 33; Nunn 1995, 5; Pearson and Cusack 2002, 6; Ward and Ward 1995, 10). Crail progressed from having a local farmer dispense beer, lemonade and pies from a shed near the first tee, to purchasing a pavilion from a tennis club and converting it into a clubhouse in 1895 to, nine years later, constructing a stone-built clubhouse. At Silloth the pavilion gave way to a new-build costing £1000, which was expanded in 1908 to provide female players with a room above a new boiler room which supplied central heating to the club premises. At socially ambitious clubs thousands could be expended on off-course facilities. Royal Liverpool spent £8000 in the 1890s; Leeds began in 1896 with a cottage adapted for £3 but spent £3500 on a replacement in 1909. Others became quasi country clubs taking over historic mansions for the purpose. Stoke Poges, with its 1000 members, occupied the estate of that name; Shirley Park was created in 1914 around Lord Elsdon's former house; and Park Langley adapted Langley Park mansion, turning the ballroom into a dining room. It burned down in 1913 but a new one was built at a cost of £26,000 (*Golf Illustrated*, November 29, 1912, 233; Lowerson 1989, 193–194; MacDonald 1985, 36, 44, 1986, 15; Pearson and Cusack 2002, 10, 16).

Some clubs opted to offer more than golf. At Ilford the club professional was instructed to engage six extra men to make up ground near the eighth tee for the purposes of tennis courts. Ashford Manor added a new smoking room and a billiard room in 1907 and also set up tennis, croquet and bowls sections which shared a pitch and putt course. Shirley Park had nine tennis courts, a separate putting course and a boating lake. Some attempted to develop a cross between a gentleman's club and a proto country club. This involved the provision of overnight accommodation, dinner for members and their guests, card and billiard rooms, tennis and croquet lawns, and even, as at North Hants, 'a romantically situated and picturesque lake' (General Committee Minutes of Ilford Golf Club, January 8, 1909 (Club Archives); Historian 1966, 27; Lowerson 1982, 67–68; *Prospectus of North Hants Golf Club 1904*).

What was the collective cost of creating golf facilities across the nation? The basic price paid for land was an agricultural one. Clubs were not in competition with each other for land; thus the opportunity cost was generally that of agricultural earnings which, as farm product prices fell, made golf clubs a growing option for landowners. In 1904, it was estimated that some 89,000 acres with a rental value of £82,140 was devoted to golf (*Golf Illustrated*, February 26, 1904). If there is any veracity to this, then, using the proportion of clubs with courses and allowing for those with less than 18 holes, the succeeding decade would take a further 55,000 acres with an actual or opportunity cost of around £50,000. Estimated lease buy out over 21 years (a typical golf club lease period) would equate to about £2.6 million being the real cost of land devoted to golf by 1914. As for building upon this land, designing, constructing and extending golf courses with irrigation, drainage and quality greens did not come cheap. One estimate is that by mid-Edwardian Britain some £2 million had been spent on golf clubs and courses (Leach 1906, 422). Using another, but uncited, reference Lowerson has maintained that by 1910 course creation alone cost about £200 a hole (Lowerson 1989, 194). Allowing for inflation (using the Consumer Price Index) this would suggest that some £4 million had been spent in this way since 1870. Then there was the clubhouse. Omitting extreme examples at either end of the spectrum such as Biggar's £10 shed and Langley Park's £26,000 rebuild, on the basis of a sample of 123 clubs the average cost of constructing a clubhouse was around £1350. Assuming all clubs with a course in 1914 possessed a clubhouse, this would suggest some £2.4 million had been spent on such off-course facilities. So how was all this financed?

Financial capital

The purchase of clubs, balls and appropriate attire was an individual spending decision, but establishing a course and a clubhouse necessitated collective financing. Many golf clubs began as small-scale sporting enterprises, in essence private partnerships between members. They could almost be regarded as sporting co-operatives, though the middle-class membership might shy away from that term. Initially for many small clubs all the funding that was required was a combination of entry fees and annual subscriptions, but as clubs grew more ambitious, or increasingly as they wished to begin on a larger scale than their predecessors, subscriptions might cover operating costs but not the new clubhouse, course extension, or the long-term lease. This persuaded up to an estimated tenth of clubs before 1914 to adopt limited liability company status by which they could raise money through the issue of shares and their members gain some personal financial protection from the risk. Indeed golf clubs were in the vanguard of joint stock company formation in the sporting world. This came in three forms, all mainly composed of the club membership: those that were limited by guaranteed amount, those that were owned by holding companies or property trusts; and a very few that went fully public. Lowerson hazards that some of these such as Moortown (Leeds) and Oakdale (Harrogate) had members of slightly lower social standing who had less money to risk and were also in a more competitive land market than most clubs (Lowerson 1982, 67–68).

The bulk of clubs remained private membership organizations and it was the members that basically funded club development and operations. Committeemen, or particular individuals within the committee, often provided loans to clubs, both short and long term. Debentures, often used to fund the building of a clubhouse or extend the course, were spread more generally across the membership. These were sometimes made more attractive by granting an extra vote at meetings, reducing the annual subscription over the period of the debenture or guaranteeing representation on the all-powerful club committee. Sometimes assistance came in the form of guarantors for loans from banks. At Woking each member provided a guarantee of £5 though this liability was terminated 12 months after leaving the club. When more funds were needed, but not so much as to warrant the issue of shares and debentures or major loans, members were called on for extra financial aid. The initial appointment of a professional at Beverley & East Riding was only made possible by a special levy of five shillings on each member; the unanticipated costs of Leicester clubhouse was paid for by donations from members; members of Mid Herts paid an extra subscription to meet the legal expenses incurred in defending the club's rights to play on common land; and when Bristol & Clifton spent more than its income in 1892 each of the member guarantors had to pay £3.50 (Charman 1990, 7; Connelly 1993, 54; Elwain 1991, 17; Gregory 1992, 16; Minutes of Beverley and East Riding Golf Club, 1 November 1890 (Club Archives)).

NUMBERS AND NARRATIVES

Other fundraising efforts also relied predominately on members. A common method, usually one-off, was the bazaar. This could sometimes be of major proportions, as when Biggar raised over £1000 in 1907 and in 1905 when another Scottish club, Braemar, aiming to raise £600 to clear its debts, was so successful that in 1907 the fees for local members were halved and £80 was spent on a veranda for the clubhouse (Soulsby 2002, 13–15; Ward and Ward 1995, 56). At a lesser level, in terms of funds raised, were concerts, theatricals, dinners, smokers and dances and also minor forms of patronage from the donation of trophies and sponsorship of competitions.

Members also contributed via the bar. Golf differed from many sports in that its playing facilities were used all week and often all year round, especially with the technological contribution of lawn mowers for cutting the summer grass and rainproof playing attire to combat wet weather. Hence provision of clubhouse facilities could be justified on the grounds that they would not lie empty too often. Even when the course was shut the clubhouse could be open. The clubhouse itself could make a contribution to covering its cost by helping attract more members (and retain existing ones). It also provided a venue for revenue-raising social functions. But its main contribution was probably its bar facilities. Not all clubs indulged: at Fairhaven, noted by other local Lancastrian clubs as being for 'short drivers and Methodists', the sale of intoxicating liquors was prohibited (Chamberlain 1995, 3, 26). However for many golf club members alcohol was an integral part of golf's rituals and culture and, if consumed on club premises, drink could contribute to the viability of the club itself. In 1912 clubs petitioned Parliament against clauses in the Scottish Temperance Bill that would have closed golf club bars at the same time as other licensed premises (*Golf Illustrated*, October 11, 1912, 70). Golf literature, cartoons and anecdotes endorse the popularity of the 'nineteenth hole' for much of the sociability of the golf club centred around the provision and consumption of alcohol. In his evidence in 1929 to the Royal Commission on Licensing, the representative of the National Golf Club's Protection Association (formed in 1921 to protest against new restrictions on club opening hours) noted that many golfers might not care to play 'without the availability of intoxicating liquor' (Collins and Vamplew 2002, 51–54; *Report of the Royal Commission on Licensing 1932*, 106). Although this is for a later period, there is no reason to believe that it did not apply to earlier years. Brewers, but particularly distillers, were well aware of the market potential of the golf club. Whiteways offered clubs free samples of their 'sparkling Devonshire cider'; John Harvey of Bristol promoted 'Golf Blend Scotch Whisky'; and a regular advertisement in *Golf Illustrated* from the turn of the century featured Colonel Bogey Whisky, 'a most stimulating tonic for golfers' (*Golf Illustrated*, June 22, 1900, July 1, 1900, May 11, 1900).

Membership thus was vital to club finances. The key issue was to get sufficient members (of the right kind) to cover costs. Initial marketing was often by public advertisement in the local press or by word of mouth between potential players. Few, if any, clubs seem to have been satisfied with their beginning level of membership. Even clubs as large initially as Headingley (founded 1892 with 220 members), South Herts (1893 with 250) and Wirral Ladies (1894 with 263) had by 1914, respectively grown to 525, 450 and 325. Of clubs established before 1900 there was an average increase of over 230% in membership by 1914.

What might attract new members was not only the quality of the course but also its other facilities, particularly the clubhouse and the other activities offered such as tennis and croquet. Some might be deterred by the size of subscription and entry fee but others might see this as reflecting social standing. An opulent clubhouse offered a shop window effect.

Like appointing a leading tournament player as club professional or hosting a prestigious tournament or an exhibition match featuring leading players, a well-appointed clubhouse showed that this was an ambitious club.

Ease of access to the course was an important marketing feature and almost all entries in the golfing annuals stress the nearness of the local railway station. The railway was vital to the viability of most golf clubs and, as part of a symbiotic relationship, special fares for golfers were often negotiated.[4] Generally railways provided access for any member distant from the course and allowed golfers to play a number of courses, not just their local one. More specifically they helped clubs attract members from the great conurbations, especially London. Of the original 153 gentlemen members of North Hants, 54 of them gave a London club as their residential address (Littlewood 2004, 11).

Many clubs offered special rates for young players. Although this may have been primarily a concession to members who had children, it can also be seen as a sustainability policy, looking towards the next generation of members. Some clubs, especially those with other facilities, also offered membership to non-golfers. At North Hants they paid the same entry fee but a much reduced subscription. Most of the 104 such members (compared to 215 golfing members) in 1905, of whom 87 were women, joined for access to the tennis courts (Littlewood 2004, 11).

The limit to overall membership was set by clubhouse and, particularly, course capacity. When this was reached then waiting lists were opened and, often, entry fees raised. At Woking most candidates had to wait two-and-a-half years to join. If there was insufficient demand then a gamble on price elasticity could be undertaken by reducing or even dropping entry fees. By 1909 North Hants membership had fallen to 175 from the 215 of 1905. The response of getting rid of the entrance fee in 1910 helped raise the number to 352 by 1913. Many clubs accepted that a rise in subscriptions was a way to set the club's finances right, but at Ganton's AGM in 1901 the members rejected the Committee's proposal to increase subscriptions and set up a review panel which reduced the professional's wage from 35 shillings a week to 25 shillings, sacked one of the three groundsmen, and approached the landlord for a reduction in rent. The members then agreed to purchase more shares to put the club on a sounder footing (Connelly 1993, 55; Littlewood 2004, 14–15; Worthington 1991, 4). Generally, however, clubs faced rising demand as reflected in the 240% increase of entry fees and 175% in subscription rates by 1914 for clubs founded before 1900. A perennial problem in any circumstance was ensuring that subscriptions were paid. Aberfeldy and Seascale both adopted a 'name and shame' approach where a list of members was displayed in the pavilion and the date they paid noted besides their name. Blackburn for one actually took legal proceedings against some defaulters (Anderson 1993, 12; Rees 1994, 29; Smith 1994, 14).

There was another source of golf income available to the clubs: visitors. Initially some clubs did not charge visitors introduced by their own members, but soon they realized that green fees could make a useful contribution to club coffers, even if tax had to be paid (*Golf Illustrated*, March 11, 1910, 81). In 1911 at Crowborough Beacon they were more significant than membership subscriptions. Edgbaston first introduced such fees in 1901 at two shillings for a day and two shillings and six pence for Sundays, but shortly afterwards, in view of overcrowding, raised the Sunday fee to five shillings. Several clubs, seeing the value of visitors' fees, began to organize contests specifically for them in the summer months, particularly in holiday resorts. At Aberfeldy in Scotland club members gave up their own summer competitions to free up the course for visitors who paid a shilling a day, two shillings a week or five shillings for a month of play (Durie 2003, 109–128; Heath 1986, 14–15; Macdougall 1995, 13; Rees 1994, 57). National publicity, such as entries in the various golfer's handbooks, informed the world about the club and its course, and could attract visitors and their green fees; best of all was the exhibition match involving leading players as these virtually guaranteed coverage in the golfing press. Visitors were not necessarily holidaymakers; many would come as members of golf clubs and golfing societies which had no course of their own. Ranfurly Castle became a popular venue for former pupils' club outings, the Liberal Golfing Society and Glasgow University Golf Club (Crampsey 1989, 21). Yet visitor arrangements were primarily financial transactions not social interaction sessions and when membership lists were full visitors found themselves less welcome. However, clubs did not exclude them, possibly because their own members wished to continue having the opportunity to play with visiting friends, so they rationed them by price – with five shillings a day quite common though 'the exorbitant charge of half a sovereign is not unknown' – or by time with limits placed on how many times a visitor could play as at Rochdale where they were restricted to 3 days in any year (Deasy 1987, 16; Kinloch 1906, 677).

Other agencies did help. Seascale had half its rent remitted by the railway when in 1899 it ran into financial difficulties (Anderson 1993, 21). A need for revenue tempted some clubs to sell grazing rights but then came the need to keep animals off parts of the course, particularly the greens. But mainly it was the membership who funded the club and its activities. The financial relationship between a golf club and its members was not generally one of profit-seeker and customer. The members paid fees for their recreation, but were also willing to contribute to the club's expenditure for expanding the course and improving the facilities, or to assist the club out of economic difficulties. All clubs raised funds via entry fees and annual subscriptions and from members' spending in the bar and on clubhouse catering. Others also relied on members to purchase debentures, provide personal loans and sign up to special subscription lists. Even when money did not come directly from members, as with mortgages and bank loans, members were asked to stand as guarantors. Essentially the millions of pounds that went into golf club formation was raised by golfers self-financing their hobby. One reason that they were prepared to spend the money was that it could partly be regarded as an investment in cultural and social capital.

Cultural capital

Simply playing the game could contribute to personal cultural capital formation as it brought experience and a honing of skills, but for individual golfers cultural capital could be institutionalized by the awarding of a club-based handicap which showed their relative proficiency compared to other players. For women this could bring national status as, unlike men who did not adopt a national standardized system of handicapping until 1926, the Ladies Golf Union had introduced one in 1897 (*Golfers Handbook* 1954, 123). The donation of trophies might also bring, or more likely cement, a high status position within the donor's associativity group.

More generally cultural capital can be envisaged as an understanding not just of the rules of the game but the etiquette that accompanied the sport both on the course and in the clubhouse. Although individual clubs might develop their own cultures, golfers shared a set of values in their code of conduct. Here loss of cultural capital by those committing faux pas might be more significant than its actual accumulation. Golf was a character-building 'respectable' pastime in which players practised sportsmanship and fair play. Golf placed responsibility for policing on the players themselves, and maintained notions of honour and chivalry. Breaches of behavioural norms, such as driving into those in front, counting an opponent's strokes in a bunker or leaving divots, led not to the forfeit of a hole but to loss of social status and possible ostracism within the club (Hutchinson 1892, 257, 268, 272).[5]

There was a way in which the club itself could create its own cultural capital from which its members could benefit via aesthetic appreciation and skill improvement. The quality of the course and clubhouse resulted from the club's combination of physical and financial capital; and the atmosphere and level of service in the clubhouse and shop and the coaching offered by the club professional could be attributed to its policies relating to human capital formation. Then there was the matter of the membership itself where 'quality' could be self-sustaining.

Social capital

Social capital can be viewed as involving mutual support and obligations, social cooperation, trust and – of importance to a sporting organization – institutional effectiveness. Indeed the establishment and operation of a golf club is a prime example of how, by developing relationships and working together, people can achieve more than they could simply by acting as individuals. For this study the concept will be applied in the very basic sense of inclusion versus exclusion.[6] The core of the analysis focuses on Putnam's concepts of 'bonding social capital' and 'bridging social capital' (Putnam 2000, 22). Bonding social capital draws people together from a similar social niche and tends to reinforce exclusive identities, develop in-group loyalties and maintain homogeneity, whereas bridging social capital brings together people from diverse social divisions and tends to generate broader identities and wider reciprocities. The construction of bonding social capital infers the use of exclusionary practices to enforce a homogeneous group identity in contrast to bridging capital's more inclusive agenda that cuts across class, gender and other boundaries. What follows is an attempt to assess which type of social capital pertained at late Victorian and Edwardian golf clubs.

Membership

There is little published evidence on the composition of golf club membership. Many club histories give *some* detail on *some* of the early members, virtually all of them middle and upper-middle class, but this might simply reflect the fact that they could be identified more readily. Class here has been defined by occupation, a generally recognized proxy for class affiliation. Class is not the sole social indicator relevant to sports participation as people have multiple collective identities including those of neighbourhood, workplace, region, religion and nation, all of which can cut across class. Unfortunately such information is difficult to obtain with respect to golf club membership. Names and addresses, when they are available, require the expertise of a local historian and the application of census data to draw anything more from the material, which is beyond the scope of this study and its practitioner.

Some club historians have traced more information, but even in their histories generalization has subjugated detail, though there is a common suggestion of a dominant middle-class presence on most golf club membership lists. An exception to the lack of specification is Martin's examination of Minchinhampton members which showed that those accepted were mainly landowners, proprietors of the major local industries such as woollen mills and engineering works, members of the professions, doctors, lawyers and the clergy, as well as serving and retired officers of the armed forces (and their sons) (Martin 1989, 68).

Such social exclusivity was controlled both informally and formally. Informally the costs of playing club golf could restrict the economic group from which members would be drawn. If entry fees and annual subscriptions of 2–5 guineas were not enough of a deterrent, there were also the costs of travel, hiring a caddie, lunch and drinks, depreciation of clubs and the loss of balls which were estimated by one golfer at 17/6d for a day's play, no small sum when the average level of full-time earnings was 28/- a week (*Golf Illustrated*, June 20, 1906, 65). Uniforms were another cost. Initially red coats had often been donned to warn walkers on the course that golfers were about, but uniforms were also an overt way of displaying one's prosperity and of differentiating club members from others: it was a demonstration of who the wearer was (Hutchinson 1892, 276). Special sports clothing was an aspect of the new amateurism of late Victorian Britain and, although golfing attire did not share the white purity of athletics, tennis and cricket outfits, the golfing uniform, when worn with club tie, signified that the wearer belonged to a respectable and reputable organization (Holt 2006, 365). When the similarly discernable Norfolk jacket and plus fours became de rigueur, they served the same purpose. Although by 1914 club uniforms generally were reserved for formal occasions such as dinners and presentations, wearing an elaborate outfit was a means of group identification.

Even if they could raise the money potential members generally had to be nominated and seconded by existing ones, endure a listing period during which any member could raise objections, before facing election by the committee. Often a simple majority was insufficient as many clubs operated a blackball system of election in which one negative vote could outweigh all the positive ones. *Golf Illustrated* was adamant that 'the ballot boxes of clubs are quite sufficient to preserve social distinctions' (*Golf Illustrated*, May 30, 1913, 245). One way to ensure a desired social composition was to issue invitations to acceptable potential members. This was the procedure adopted at Liverpool by J. Muir Dowie, who, after friends asked him to 'endeavour to organize a golf club', sent a circular to those 'mentioned as a probable member' (Farrar 1937, 166).

Middle-class divisions of income and occupation were reflected in the local hierarchies that emerged between clubs. Lowerson has shown that Royal Eastbourne (1887) was for the aristocracy and gentry and nearby Willingdon (1898) for the professional classes (Lowerson 1995, 132). Despite the folklore claims of golf in Scotland being more accessible than in England, similar examples are easy to find north of the border. Around Dundee, Carnoustie became the province of the local gentry and professionals, Dalhousie was for businessmen, and the Mercantile served the rest of the middle class. At North Berwick the original club was a closed shop for gentry so the New Club was formed for local professional men (Lowerson 1994, 80; Seaton 1999, 3). A perusal of the clubs listed in *Nisbet's Golf Guide and Year Book* for 1914 suggests that this might have been happening elsewhere: in many areas several clubs co-existed but their entrance fees and subscription rates imply different clientele.

Clubs could also decide whom to invite to share their facilities. Matches were arranged with other clubs but, as these were not part of any league system, there was no compulsion to play against any clubs not of similar social standing. Committees were also cautious

NUMBERS AND NARRATIVES

Table 2. Occupational structure of committees and boards of directors (%).

Category	Committees	Boards	Overall
Manufacturers	8.2	14.9	13.6
Legal	12.9	13.2	13.2
Merchants	6.4	8.9	8.5
Other professionals	4.7	8.6	7.9
Higher administration	12.9	6.4	7.7
Medical	5.9	7.7	7.3
Gentry	5.9	7.3	7.0
Retailing	3.5	6.6	6.0
Financial	1.2	6.7	5.6
Lower administration	4.7	3.9	4.1
Industrial professionals	0.6	3.9	3.4
Tradesmen	2.9	3.2	3.1
Clerics	4.1	1.3	1.8
Military officers	5.3	0.8	1.7
Miscellaneous	4.1	3.3	3.5
Unknown	14.7	1.5	4.1

Source: See text.

regarding visitors. Although they offered a contribution to the coffers, green fees, like subscriptions, were usually set at a level to operate also as a filter mechanism. Additionally many clubs only allowed bonâ-fide members of other recognized clubs to play as visitors. Rather than trust to the selection policies of other clubs, some put their faith in the judgement of their own members and only authorized visitors introduced by them or who, as at Ricksmansworth, were 'friends of members' (Harmsworth 1914, 307).

Committees

Most clubs were run by honorary committees – a significant site of *male* voluntary activity – placing the control of assets and real estate worth millions in the hands of a few club officials, albeit generally elected from within the membership. Of more importance for many members was that these groups decided policies on membership, subscriptions and social relationships within the clubs. The committees made decisions on club uniforms, dress codes and other aspects of clubhouse behaviour, much of it ritualized symbolic practices of etiquette and civility.

Knowledge of the background of committee members can show the socio-economic groupings from which power emanated. Like membership, much information on committees in club histories is partial. However, 23 histories have been traced in which all, or nearly all, of the original committee members' occupations are identified, some 170 in total. Those clubs that adopted company status replaced the club committee with a board of directors. Here detail is easier to find as lists of the boards had to be returned by law, though the information relates to the committee at the time of becoming a company not necessarily the original committee. Material for 74 golf companies has been found covering a total of 735 board members. There are possible problems with the sample being both limited and non-random, the self-ascription of occupations, and the allocation of these into socio-economic categories by the researcher. Nevertheless, as shown in Table 2, they suggest a solidly middle-class power base within the British golf club. Possibly only tradesman could be regarded as working class and some of these may have been self-employed small businessmen.

Ladies' golf

There was a gender aspect to golf's social capital. Unlike many Edwardian sports golf was played by both sexes. In 1911 there were some 400 clubs with 50,000 members affiliated to the Ladies Golf Union (Stringer 1911). Nevertheless whilst the sport was not one of courage and overt masculinity like cricket, football and rugby it was still framed as a male-dominant activity and the history of women's golf is one of separate and often unequal development, though within the confines of social class.[7]

A substantial number of female golfers belonged to clubs specifically organized for women. The first properly constituted ladies' golf club was at St Andrews in 1867, soon followed by one at Westward Ho! in Devon. Both were established by male golfers for their female relatives and neither possessed a full-length course (Cossey 1984, 18; Davies and Brown 1989, 35). Most women golfers, however, became members of what was often labelled a 'ladies' club' but which was in reality a 'ladies' section' within a parent club. Many of the newer clubs of the 1890s onwards had allowed women membership from their foundation but they too moved to form separate ladies' sections (or even clubs) when numbers increased.

Many clubs imposed restrictions on when women could use the course. When the women at Burton-on-Trent asked about playing times in 1912 they were told 'keep clear of normal starting times in accordance with the established custom' (Owen 1984, 12). At most clubs this meant that the course was solely for men on competition days, on either all or part of Saturday (and Sunday in those clubs that allowed play on the Sabbath), and on local half days and Bank Holidays. Even when they shared playing times with males, female golfers were expected to give way to men on the course. The objections to women centred around slow play, attributable to them taking more strokes due to the lesser distances that they hit the ball. One way round the problem was to develop separate playing facilities for men and women. These tended to be of 9 holes (18 was often seen as too tiring), of much less yardage than those of men, and without serious hazards (Starkie-Bence 1898, 260–267). A sample from the 1914 edition of *Nisbet's Golf Guide and Year Book* of 29 women's clubs with separate courses shows that 25 of these had 9 holes or less This suited the bulk of female players who saw golf as 'an excellent means of combining fresh air, exercise and society, as a gentle form of healthy exercise that required skill rather than force and which allowed time on and off the course for social interaction' (*Ladies Field*, February 25, 1899, 493).

Separate but easier courses did not appeal to the better female players who wished golf to be challenging (Kerr 1896, 133). The club course then became a contested terrain. As Horace Hutchinson, a leading amateur golfer and golf journalist, noted in respect of the incursion on his own links:

> We used to hear at first: 'It's absurd, these ladies not sticking to their own course; they can't drive far enough to be able to appreciate the long course.' But then it very soon became evident that they could play better than a large number of the male members of the club, which rather knocked the bottom out of the argument. (Hutchinson 1899, 71)

The issue then became one of distinguishing between female social golfers and the more serious women players. Many clubs reduced the restrictions to those with low handicaps. Although St George's Hill demanded scratch, other clubs accepted handicaps within the range of 11–18 as fitting their quality control requirements. Nevertheless these women, like any that used the men's courses, played off advanced tees so as to shorten the length of the round, a device that reinforced the notion of golf as masculine.

There was less compromise off the course where the clubhouse generally remained a male preserve. At Beverley & East Riding the women were allowed to rent a room in the clubhouse but had their refreshments served through a hatch. Whilst Douglas Park allowed women to use the men's dining room for lunch and tea (though only during designated 'ladies' hours'), Dunbar was more typical in not admitting them to the clubhouse at all. Like the clubhouse, power too was generally not for sharing. As was openly specified at Olton and Douglas Park, and implicitly understood elsewhere, women joined 'on condition they took no part in the management of the [parent] club'. At almost every club women had no voting rights. Even within many ladies' clubs men held the power. At Eastbourne Ladies the five-person committee had no female representation and Edinburgh Ladies initially had a male president, secretary and both vice-captains, with 16 of the 20 committee positions going to men. At Rochdale, ladies were allowed to elect their own captain, secretary, treasurer and committee but all decisions had to be approved by the exclusively male main club committee. This, of course, followed the political thinking of the time with women often denied a say in the running of anything, except the household (Cadney 1991, 8; Deasy 1987, 35; Ironside 1977, 16; *Ladies Golf Union Year Book* 1897, 120; MacCabe 1981, 66–68; Milton 1993, 4; Ward 1990, 70).

Yet not all clubs were so dogmatic or discriminatory in their attitude to women. Barnehurst actually had a female secretary to run a club in which men and women had the same rights of membership, equal use of the links, and similar access to the clubhouse where certain rooms were reserved exclusively for each sex (*Bystander*, March 15, 1905). In contrast to the 230 clubs which stated in the 1914 *Nisbet's Golf Guide and Year Book* that they enforced restrictions on female members, another 45 clubs advertized that they had 'no restrictions for ladies' or even, as with Brighton's Dyke club, that 'ladies are always welcome'. As 34 of these clubs also charged reduced subscriptions for women this could almost be labelled positive discrimination.

Occupational groups

Another version of social capital comes from Bourdieu who suggested that membership of a golf club was a major modern indicator of social capital, a concept which he viewed instrumentally believing that individuals would intentionally build relationships within the club for their own benefit, especially the facilitation of business networks (Bourdieu 1997, 46–58). There was the occasional complaint of this happening in Edwardian times (*Golf Monthly*, August 1912, 462). The perquisite of the right to propose new members gave existing ones the opportunity to improve business relationships by introducing clients (of the proper social background) and professional colleagues. Out on the course two to three hours of walking, broken intermittently by a need to concentrate on a shot, and the relative physical isolation of the players could produce a scenario where pleasure and business negotiation or networking could co-exist and be cemented over drinks in the clubhouse. More common was the coming together of men from the same occupational group. In his detailed study of those men who founded golf clubs in Victorian England, Cameron suggests that occupational links may have been a vital ingredient in spreading the golfing gospel. He has identified doctors, clergymen, merchants, army and naval officers as missionary groups (Cameron 2010). Some clubs in the London area became recognized for membership by certain professional groups: Northwood, known as the 'Pill Club', was full of doctors; Woking replete with lawyers; stock exchange dealers played at Sunningdale; and the fourth estate could be found at both Raynes Park and North Surrey. Outside the metropolis 35 of 72 of shareholders of Rochdale's original shareholders were directly involved in the textile industry and jewellers were conspicuous on Handsworth's board of directors (Blackman 1990, 18; Deasy 1987, 34; *Golf Illustrated*, June 3, 1910, 215).

Even more occupationally homogeneous were many of the golfing societies, though they often termed themselves golf clubs, which virtually included only those with the same business interest. In 1913, one golfing journal claimed that 'numerous golfing societies are being formed every day by people belonging to particular classes, professions, and sets' (*Golf Illustrated*, January 31, 1913, 140). Such societies had in fact flourished from the late nineteenth century. In the years to 1914 Burnett and Lewis traced 375 golf societies, overwhelmingly city-based. Of these 52 were in London, 60 in Glasgow and 181 in Edinburgh, whose dominance might be attributable to the initial development of the sport on the east coast of Scotland. Overall in Britain some 57% of societies were occupationally based in that the members worked for the same employer, in the same trade or in the same profession. Within Edinburgh itself, 72 Societies were based on members working for one employer: 17 were for insurance companies, 8 for banks, 5 for printers and 8 for the related trades of papermakers, type-founders, stationers and publishers. Another 5 catered for local government employees. There were 20 trade group societies: 3 were for licensed victuallers with the others being mostly for self-employed shopkeepers. The 13 professional group societies included accountants, architects, members of the stock exchange and surgeons (Burnett and Lewis 1996–97).[8]

Artisans and others

A writer in *Golf Illustrated* of November 1906 maintained that 'prevailing opinion' was that golf was 'an expensive game suitable only for the moneyed and leisured classes'. The same journal in 1909, citing the *Westminster Review*, noted that 'golf is not a game for the poor man' (cited in *Golf Illustrated*, February 19, 106; Lewis 1995, 16). Yet there was working-class involvement.

A very few clubs accepted working men as members but usually with severe restrictions. Hawick was probably unique in allowing (from 1892) working men to join at half fee but with full membership privileges and by 1897 there were 45 of these compared to 147 ordinary members. Silloth allowed them to join at half subscription but without any voting rights or access to the clubhouse and they were reminded in writing that 'respect must be shown to the [full fee paying] members' (Barrie 1898, 32, 54; Pearson and Cusack 2002, 6, 18).

There were also the municipal courses, often partially aimed at a working-class market, from which few golfers were excluded as most operated on a 'pay-and-play' basis charging by the round, though this was very much a Scottish development with 12 of the 19 courses traced situated north of the border. Many councils may have been altruistic in the provision of golf facilities seeing them as part of the broader municipal socialism movement to improve the health and fitness of their electorates (*Golf Illustrated*, January 17, 1913, 103). For others, such as Eastbourne and Bournemouth, municipal investment in courses was specifically to entice visitors whose spending would impact beyond the fairways; as the mayor of Weymouth put it, a council-owned course open to visitors would 'improve the attractiveness of Weymouth as a spa town' (Ward 1984, 15). Even in Scotland Callander Town Council purchased land for a municipal course 'to maintain its status as a health resort and tourist centre' (Minutes of Callander Town Council, September 8, 1913). This dichotomy of approach was reflected in the style of management and the prices charged. The bulk of corporations opted for direct management in which they ran the enterprise, including employing a professional to organize playing times, hire out clubs and give lessons. Clearly this mode of management encouraged wider participation than the delegated form, as at Bournemouth, where the council provided the basic facilities which they leased to a private club. At Bournemouth a round of golf cost a shilling, six times the fee at Aberdeen or Edinburgh's Braid Hills where 'immense numbers of bonâ-fide working men [played] day after day'. In one week in September 1906 three Edinburgh municipal courses, Braid Hills, Saughton Park and Portobello, had a total of 3884 players including 306 women (*Golf Illustrated*, September 14, 1906, 223; Taylor 1902, 15). In Edinburgh too several businesses in the late nineteenth century organized golf clubs for their employees with outings and inter-firm matches being held on public courses. Ultimately this led to the formation of the Edinburgh Establishment Golf Club Federation, mainly comprising companies connected with the printing trade, who played a league tournament on the Braid Hills municipal course (Chalmers 1995, 5). Some municipal courses also had clubs attached often with relatively low subscriptions. Excluding Bournemouth and Brighton who respectively charged 3 guineas and 30 shillings, the average annual fee for the other 9 clubs for which there is data was just under 12 shillings which suggests they were aimed at the lower end of the socio-economic spectrum.

Other clubs were formed specifically for working men, usually by or with the assistance of a parent club. The first workingmen's golf club was established at Newbiggin near Newcastle in 1885 and by 1914 there were at least 21 others in existence. Many of these artisans' clubs, as they became commonly known, were part of a socio-economic transaction between the parent club and local workmen in which the latter gained playing rights, at greatly reduced fees, in exchange for undertaking maintenance tasks around the course. The 11 subscriptions known ranged from 0 at Northam to 10 shillings at Beverley with a mean of 3/6d. For some clubs this might have been a way of coping with a shortage of ground staff in an era of expansion of clubs which put pressure on local supplies of wage labour. Another reason for artisan club development stemmed from the parent club having its course on common or commonly used land. Integration of local working-class golfers lessened possible protests from the neighbouring community (Chape and Ogilvie 1984, 192).

The artisan organizations operated within parameters set by the parent club which imposed restrictions on who could join and when they could play. At Sutton Coldfield numbers were limited to 35, all of whom had to be 'working men resident in Sutton Coldfield, or persons residing near the links who are, or have been, in the employment of the Club'; all members of Northam Artizans (*sic*) who played at Royal North Devon had to reside in the Northam Parish; and the Cantelupe artisans had to live within five miles of the Forest Row course where they played (Davies and Brown 1989, 105; Minutes of Sutton Coldfield Golf Club, February 5, 1909 (Club Archives); Porter 2006, 39). At most clubs play by working men was restricted to early morning and late evening and at Cannock Chase they played only on Sunday afternoon, a day on which parent club members were not allowed on the course. Apart from the ritual regular match between parent club and artisans there was little mixing on the fairways. Indeed at Royal North Devon the artisans used a special gate to the first tee so that they did not cross in front of the clubhouse (Davies and Brown 1989, 119; Harmsworth 1914, 334).

Human capital

Player self improvement

Another reason why golfers were willing to finance their clubs was one of personal human capital formation. Golf was a 'rational' recreation, justifiable for the health benefits that it could bring. Golf differed from many late Victorian sports in that it was not solely for the young and male, but 'for players of all degrees and ages' (Hutchinson 1892, 30). Handicapping allowed the best to play with the worst, the young with the old, men with women. It could be played as part of a team, in foursomes both mixed and gendered, in singles and even by oneself against par and the environment. Golf was also multi-motivational. For some it offered excitement; for others escape from home and work. Some sought to demonstrate their individual skill and prowess; others looked to the companionship of the foursome. Some sought to beat their opponents; others just the handicapper. Some enjoyed the challenge of the elements; others preferred the sociability of the clubhouse. Yet some potential players might need more than the promise of pleasure. They sought external as well as intrinsic justification for walking around the countryside striking a ball with a stick. Ethically sound, physically demanding (but to a limited extent) and out in the open air, golf improved mind, body and health. It afforded 'sufficient exercise for all' without being 'too violent for those who are older or less robust' (Hutchinson 1892, 30). Thus it was a way of extending into middle age the cult of manly athleticism drilled into many of them at public school but without the physicality of lawn tennis, that other life-long sport that emerged in the late nineteenth century.

Holt has shown that poor urban air quality, new patterns of commuting that lessened daily walking, and growing sedentary office employment prompted a greater emphasis on outdoor exercise, which was increasingly regarded by the medical profession as beneficial to health. Younger men could push their bodies hard in football and athletics but older ones were better suited by more gentle recreations such as golf.[9] Health could be mental as well as physical. Concentrating their attention on the ball allowed players to forget their worldly cares, at least for a while. Hence for those who regarded golf as a 'healthy outdoor exercise', of value to 'any man whose duties confine him within doors for a considerable part of the day', playing the game was not merely a matter of consuming the golf product but of using it as an intermediate consumption good, as a means to an end of improving personal human capital (Pope 1909, 177; *Times*, December 30, 1908, 17). As one local newspaper summed it up, the golf club was 'a social meeting ground where the hard worked man of business may lay aside his everyday worries and anxieties; and friends meet in a healthful rivalry and enjoyment' (*Harrow Observer*, June 25, 1893).

The work force

While office workers and others used golf to improve personal human capital, the club itself was more concerned with that aspect of human capital formation involving its own workforce. Golf clubs were usually small business enterprises, generally employing perhaps a dozen or so outside workers and possible half that number in the clubhouse.[10] These were usually under the direct supervision of a head greenkeeper (or the professional) and a clubhouse manager, both of whom would be responsible to the club secretary and/or committee. Holt has compared the golf club to a country estate in that 'there is land to be worked, men to be hired as well as sport to be had'. But it was a country estate run on democratic principles (at least for the members) with a new captain often being elected every year, thus placing an onus on the club secretary who tended to have a longer term of office. He had to keep the members happy, balance the books, insure against damage by suffragettes, negotiate with landlords, local councils and railway companies, maintain the fairways and fabric of the club, and control a labour force of greenkeepers, professionals, caddies and stewards. In short he dealt with members' problems and problem members ("Concerning Golf Secretaries" 1909, 94; Holt 1993, 11).

This section will focus on two groups of employees – the caddies and the club professionals – whose skills can be regarded as specific to the golf sector rather than being transferable elsewhere in the economy. It was a natural progression for the middle-class golfers from employing servants in their homes to using them in their recreational activities. So they paid the local professional to repair their clubs and they hired caddies to carry their golfing equipment. At many golf clubs playing without a caddy was socially unacceptable, even when not specifically regulated against. Before the invention of the golf bag in the 1890s it was impractical, but generally there was the implication that the manual labour associated with a round of golf should be done by someone other than the player. Others felt that 'golf was a very difficult science which required extreme mental concentration and the labour of being one's own caddie was an objectionable and serious distraction' (*Times*, November 12, 1912, 16). Some caddies, generally designated 'first class', were employed as advisors not just bag carriers and others, the forecaddies at the bottom of the caddying pyramid, did no carrying at all but travelled ahead of the players to let them know when it was clear to play and, more importantly, where their balls had gone. In between were the 'second-class' caddies who, till the development of the golf bag in the 1890s, carried their employer's clubs under their arms, created tees from damp sand, and, after the round, cleaned the clubs with an emery board and linseed oil.

Club professionals made a living by making clubs, repairing clubs, selling clubs and other equipment, and 'the most important duty of giving instruction to the members' (Sherlock 1912, 173). They were very much small businessmen with a responsibility for training assistants and apprentices as well as running a workshop and sales department.[11] Outside the main clubs there might be other jobs to do such as organizing the caddies if there was no separate caddiemaster, acting as greenkeeper especially at the nine-hole courses and smaller clubs, working as a bar steward sometimes with mother or wife as cook, collecting fees, starting the monthly medal competitions, and even looking after the club horse as was the case with poor Thomas Winton at Muswell Hill (Minutes of Muswell Hill G.C., May 1, 1897). This was outside his formal working hours, but the horse was vital to course maintenance. It is ironic that professional golfers who gained their jobs because of their skill at playing the game then had little opportunity to play competitive golf because of other demands on their time.

Nature of the contract

The golf club was a small enough business enterprise to allow for a direct and personal relationship between those employed and the club committee or even individual club members. However, whether 'paternalism' is the most appropriate description of industrial relations at the club is conjectural (Fitzgerald 1988, 9–11). It is a concept used imprecisely by historians but having the essential ingredient of employers providing welfare with the expectation that workers could be subject to control outside their working lives

(Melling 1983, 56). Employee–employer relationships at the golf club resonated those of the landed estate where the provision of housing (albeit tied), sick pay and other acts of generosity gained the squire respect from the agricultural labourers. Yet the club administrators could not influence the non-working lives of the greenkeepers, professionals, stewards or caddies unlike the traditional paternalistic employers, both agrarian and industrial, who could insist on church attendance and specific voting patterns. What could be demanded were hierarchical deference, acceptable dress and appropriate behaviour.

The immediate employer of the caddie was the club member who paid the hiring fee, but the caddie did not obtain such employment directly. He was allocated his task by the caddiemaster, a servant of the club himself, who was also often responsible for recruiting caddies and it was, as the 1911 National Insurance Act made clear, the club that was the prime employer of the caddies. It was the club that set the hiring regulations including the fee and the club that disciplined the caddies. Most clubs had written expectations of caddie behaviour. At St Andrews the 1910 caddie regulations stated that the bag carriers should be 'tidy in dress, sober when on duty and civil to his man'. Bramall Park was not untypical in warning caddies that they could be temporarily demoted or even suspended if they broke the working rules. The ultimate sanction was dismissal which could occur, as specified at Axe Cliff for 'continued bad and obscene language'. If the St Andrews' Offences Register is any guide the caddie regulations were enforced as it records many instances of fines and suspensions (Knowles and Tait 1994, 72; Mackenzie 1997, 10, 32–33; Thomas 1993, 9).

Clubs paid their professional a weekly retainer but he was allowed to earn extra money from the shop, from teaching (though, as with caddie fees, the club set the price that the professional could charge), and often also from the fees paid for services of caddies. The retainer guaranteed a weekly income because revenue from sales and teaching could fluctuate and would certainly be lower in the winter months. There was a limit to earnings at a club which was set by the time allocated to particular tasks. If he was cutting the grass then the professional could not be making clubs; if he was in the workshop then he could not be out teaching; if he was out teaching then he had to pay for an assistant to cover for him in the shop (some clubs offered an allowance of five shillings a week towards this); and if he was supervising the caddies then he was unavailable for other work, so the penny or two from their fees – or the half-crown a week as given to Tom Fernie at Aldeburgh – was in essence compensation for lost income (O.F.T. 1982, 17).

According to J.H. Taylor, five times Open Champion and first chair of the PGA, the recipe for being a successful club professional combined several ingredients including 'clean living', 'acute technical knowledge which he imparts intelligently to his pupils' and, significantly, being 'courteous to his employers'. 'Impudence', 'ingratitude' and 'indiscipline' were all subjective concepts capable of being interpreted quite differently by player and club official or member, but power lay with the latter. Although the 1909 AGM at Bishop Auckland recorded that the engagement of J. Martin from Bathgate had been 'of great benefit to the Club', a year later he was asked to apologize to the Secretary about his language when asked to re-position some tees and also given a final warning to maintain the course in better order. He was given notice the following March over his poor timekeeping and insolence. James Gowans was fortunate to have a generous three months' notice clause in his contract with Flempton, as the majority of professionals had only a week or a fortnight's grace. Most club professionals would be aware that their employment was, even if not specified as clearly as in

James Cunninghame's contract with Coventry Hearsall, only 'as long as he gives satisfaction to the committee' (Minutes of Bishop Auckland Golf Club, September 14, 1909, October 6, 1910, March 1, 1911 (Club Archives); Newbould 1994, 21; Nunn 1995, 8; Taylor 1914, 22).

The changing labour market

The expansion of golf from the 1880s created a rising demand for caddies for, although some players carried their own bags, generally social status and even club rules (especially for competitions) dictated the employment of others for the task (*Times*, November 12, 1912, 16). The use of forecaddies declined as courses began to be laid out with less blind spots and better mown fairways. The remaining caddie market was one where children and adults competed. Adults had no great advantage in the competition for jobs as, unlike in most manual labouring positions, physicality did not necessarily raise productivity: ability and knowledge were the key employability factors. The majority of caddies were boys or young men with some adults and, at weekends, schoolboys to meet the peak demand (Agenda Club 1912, 4–5). However, state intervention in the form of compulsory national insurance for over 16s from 1912 and a raising of the school-leaving age led to conflicting pressures on the employment of younger caddies. The demand may have been rising but it was irregular depending on the time of the year and the day of the week. Hence most caddies were casually employed at piece rates with only a few, as at Sunningdale, on a wage. They tended to be engaged in the order that they arrived at the course and there was considerable waiting time. The club professional had to be available, as stated in Tom Chisholm's contract at Royal Eastbourne, 'from early morning until everyone had ceased to use the course for play' to perform the many tasks allocated to him (Milton 1987, 118). There was no real off-season for golf professionals. Although demands on their time might vary with the weather and holiday periods, few courses closed for the winter once effective drainage became affordable or for the summer as mowing equipment improved. Sunday play was a contentious issue at many clubs but by 1913, 40% of clubs in England (much less in the Celtic fringes) allowed it (Lowerson 1989, 190). As sabbatarian barriers came down the discussion shifted to the rights and wrongs of employing caddies on that day. The results were varied, ranging from a request to the Ashdown members not to employ caddies on a Sunday to Copthorne's Sunday ban on under 18s (Arnell 1988, 37; Minutes of Copthorne Golf Club, October 21, 1911). The situation was somewhat different for the club professional. Again he had no place in the discussion but once there was Sunday play there was Sunday work. Traditionally this had been his one day off in the week but increasingly, as was specified in James Bradbeer's contract at Porters Park, this now became Monday (Moreton 1999, 181).

The rise in demand for caddies was in specific local labour markets, often in areas where there had been no club before, and there is no evidence that the caddie fee was driven up. Whereas the railway brought clubs into competition for members, caddies did not travel by rail. The new clubs tapped fresh supplies from a reserve army of boy labour rather than competing against existing clubs in a limited market, so that generally clubs experienced 'no difficulty in keeping up the supply of regular caddies' (Agenda Club 1912, 27). Nevertheless, although some descriptions portray a horde of youngsters clamouring for work, the situation was probably not one of an oversupply of labour (Hutchinson 1892, 304). Pairs, trios and quartets of golfers setting out at regular intervals over a 18-hole course demanded a large supply of bag carriers. There was little move to bring in girls as caddies. The ones employed at Mid Herts because of a dearth of boys were an exception (Gregory 1992, 6–7). This possibly owed less to a regard for their physical well-being – members employed young girls to do physical labour in their houses – and more to a regard for their moral well being and a reluctance to have them mix with male caddies. Professionals were more mobile geographically than caddies. Although most professionals served only one club, over 20% of those who remained professionals for more than two years worked at a minimum of three clubs in their career. Some moved up the hierarchy of clubs to enjoy the enhanced status (and possibly money); others opted for larger clubs where they were likely to be concerned solely with teaching and running the shop. Some, of course, were fired.

Improving the labour force

In the work place human capital formation can be considered broadly as the treatment of the labour force in ways which can contribute to increased production and productivity. It should be noted, however, that human capital is embodied within the individual. The skills accrue to the person who then uses them for his employer. If he leaves the skills, experience and knowledge go with him. Hence in jobs where such talents were deemed important, it was in the employer's interests to have a loyal labour force. Healthier, self-disciplined and well-trained workers with the knowledge that they would be looked after in times of distress are likely to be better employees than a casualized work force subject to constant uncertainty and insecurity.

Disciplinary procedures were the stick but there could also be a carrot. Pay rises generally do not appear to have been a mode of rewarding the professional for good performance or behaviour. Perhaps this was simply expected as part of the job. Housing was often provided for the professional, particularly if he also had responsibility for the greens. Yet this also served the purpose of ensuring that he would be at work first thing. Naturally the accommodation was tied, a standard feature of rural employment. Clubs could be good to their pros. Those who suffered serious ill-health often had a subscription fund opened for them. In 1909 David Stephenson received £270 from such lists at both his former club (Hunterscombe) and his current one (Prince's, Sandwich) (*Golf Illustrated*, November 26, 1909). Clubs might pay for their professional to enter and travel to the Open Championship or allow the assistant professionals and clubmakers time off to play in local events. Winners of major tournaments could expect additional rewards from their home club. Harry Vardon received a 'purse of sovereigns' from Ganton after his 1896 Open Championship win. For his Open win in 1908 James Braid received £140 from Walton Heath and £60 more than this when he repeated the feat two years later (*Golf Illustrated*, November 5, 1909; Lewis 1995, 31). Nor was it unusual for a popular professional to receive a testimonial when he left his club for another. Ilkley Golf Club gave Tom Vardon £50 when he departed, while his successor, Douglas McEwan, was given £53 by Musselburgh Golf Club as a leaving present. On the occasion of his marriage, George Duncan received a clock, ornaments and a cheque from the members of his club at Timperley. It was not just the big names that fared well. When T.B. Whitehead, the Ilford professional, married, the members presented him with £9 and, when he emigrated to America six years later, over £20 was raised as a farewell gift 'in acknowledgement of his good services to the club' (Gregory 1992, 22; Lewis 1995, 31; Minutes of Ilford G.C., April 16, 1909, November 18, 1915 (Club Archives)).

Caddies were relatively well paid for what they did. At large clubs it was possible for caddies to earn 15 shillings a week though 10 shillings (exclusive of Sunday work) was more normal. Tips and food allowances could raise this by three shillings (*Golf Illustrated*, August 6, 1909,

173, August 13, 1909, 197; Agenda Club 1912, 7). To put this into perspective a school leaver in Dorset taking up caddying could earn almost as much as his agricultural labouring father for significantly less effort and time (*Times*, July 27, 1909, 19). However, the non-wage rewards such as provision of food, shelter and sanitary arrangements were generally inadequate (*Times*, November 12, 1912, 16).

Clubs did not formally invest in employee development. Skill enhancement for the professionals, including learning how to play with the new rubber-cored ball, was a matter of individual practice – if they could find the time – and of testing their temperament on the occasional (for most) venture into tournament competition. Their greenkeeping skills developed by experience as there was no formal training available. Most productivity gains came from labour specialization so that, unlike Bert Howell who at one time combined four jobs at West Sussex, – teaching professional, head greenkeeper, caddiemaster and club maker – the professional was able to focus his efforts more effectively (Sumpter 1997, 9). Such benefits were more likely to accrue at a larger club with the financial resources to employ more staff. The costs of labour-intensive site maintenance bore heavily on smaller clubs: 18 holes needed as many greens and fairways to be kept playable whether there were 50 or 250 members. Caddies learned their trade by doing it and over time accumulated knowledge of course intricacies. An ability to use this knowledge to advise their employer of the day could lead to promotion to first-class caddy status. Some caddies would learn playing techniques by observation and by practising with old clubs donated to them by members. Many clubs held an annual caddies' competition in which playing skills could be demonstrated and those who caught the professional's eye might secure an apprenticeship as a clubmaker or join the greenkeeping staff (*Golf Illustrated*, February 4, 1910, 133).

Two aspects of caddie life with implications for human capital formation were of concern to some golf club secretaries. First was the moral risk associated with the downtime while they waited for a bag: 'the regular caddie … has about five hours' leisure five days in the week, but nothing to do to fill them except idling or gambling' (Agenda Club 1912, 129). Some commentators saw possible health and moral problems in that the boys were often hanging round the club in all weathers waiting for employment, but, worse than this, was it might be done in the company of adult males who, except at long-established clubs, were regarded as men of dubious character. 'Loafing habits' could be acquired while waiting for employment 'under insufficient supervision and in an uncivilized environment' (Agenda Club 1912, 129). Second was their awareness that caddying was a dead-end job which might pay youngsters well but did not offer a reasonable income for an adult even if a club was prepared to employ those over 16, which became rarer with the introduction of employer national insurance payments for that age level. The perceived problems of such caddies were part of a wider issue in Britain. There was concern that a growing demand for child labour in occupations such as errand boys, machine minders and industrial packers was creating a pool of young workers, trained for nothing else and destined to swell the ranks of casual labourers as they became older and lost their jobs to younger and cheaper boys who in turn faced the same fate (Tawney 1909, 517–537). Hence some clubs took steps to improve the lot of their caddies both in the short term via the introduction of savings schemes, clothing clubs and recreational facilities and in the longer run by making employment conditional on attending evening classes. Yet most initiatives remained isolated ones dependent on altruistic individuals in a small number of clubs. Overall, efforts to ameliorate the condition of caddies were sporadic, uncoordinated, and far from comprehensive.[12]

Collective action

Part of human capital formation is the expectation that the time invested by the individuals will result in economic rewards, either in higher wages or other benefits. To achieve this sometimes necessitates collective action. For caddies this was the occasional unsuccessful wildcat strike. They never organized themselves into an association: generally they were too young, too ill-educated and too poor to pay subscriptions. They relied on paternalism for protection and the improvement of their working conditions and life chances. Professionals, however, formally established, in 1901, the first permanent trade union for sportsmen in the world, the PGA.[13]

The trigger was the growing practice of clubs offering the right to sell balls and repair clubs to the highest bidder rather than allow the resident professional to retain this customary privilege (Taylor 1910, 104). Specifically its objectives were: to promote interest in the game of golf; to protect and advance the mutual and trade interests of all its members; to hold meetings and tournaments periodically for the encouragement of the younger members; to institute a Benevolent Fund for the relief of deserving members; and to act as an agency for assisting any professional or club maker to obtain employment. Although this was a time of growing labour unrest in Britain and of increasing trade union membership, from the beginning it was emphasized that the organization had 'no desires of a revolutionary nature' and that they wanted 'to work in complete harmony with their patrons'. The PGA took pains not to label itself as a union and did not regard its primary function as 'wage raising' (*Golf Illustrated*, December 20, 1901, November 7, 1902). The professionals were well aware that whereas greenkeepers were indispensable professionals were not: clubs could organize their own sales of equipment, manufacturers could do repairs and golf schools could offer instruction. Hence the PGA never concerned itself with contract negotiations between a golf club and its professional. Instead it focused its attention on benevolent activities and establishing a quasi-labour exchange for professional golfers. Clubs seem to have respected its motivations and members often subscribed to the PGA benevolent fund, offered prizes for local PGA-organised tournaments and in return some of them received honorary membership of the PGA (*Golf Illustrated*, November 7, 1902; Minutes of PGA Western Section 1909–11 *passim* (PGA Archives)).

Moreover, the Association was generally able to persuade clubs to allow their professionals the exclusive right to sell balls at the club. This stemmed from its role in developing tournaments. In the eight years before the first PGA-organized tournament, professional golfers had about 13 tournaments a year in which they could play, with average prize money of just over £55. With the exception of the Open Championship these were mainly irregular events. By 1913 an incipient tour had been established with 31 tournaments averaging nearly £90 in prize money. Much of this development was attributable to the PGA who organized tournaments at the national, regional and local levels and actively sought sponsorship for them. Between 1902 and 1914 over half the professional tournaments played in Britain were national or regional ones sanctioned by the Association and 30% of the rest were district events run by branches of the PGA (Lewis 1995, 93–98). A key aspect of these tournaments was that with relatively few exceptions only PGA members were eligible to enter and a condition of being a member was to have the exclusive right to sell balls. The PGA was able to strengthen its position by bringing the star tournament players into its ranks. This may be attributable to the fact that both at the start and end of their careers the tournament players were club professionals and remained attached to a club even when participating extensively in elite activities. Clubs were keen to host tournaments and to have their professional play in them. For some this was a continuation of their traditional patronage of the professional, but it can also be seen as a means to establish a higher position within the hierarchy of golf clubs. Whatever the motive it led to clubs accepting the PGA demand that ball sales should be the prerogative of the club professional.

Conclusion

The application of five concepts of capital has helped explain the development of the golf club in Britain before 1914. It also suggests that any explanation requires an awareness of how the various forms of capital interacted with each other. Without the physical capital formation involved in obtaining and developing land there could have been be no golf, a space-extensive sport requiring as much land as a small farm. Most of the several million pounds of financial capital needed to pay for this came from the members themselves. They were willing to pay for their recreation for a variety of motives, including personal human capital formation as they sought to be physically and mentally healthy, cultural capital formation as they acquired the skills and etiquette of golf, and social capital formation in that they did so in company that they preferred. Golf's handicapping system gave all players an equal chance on the course but social equality was less of a consideration. The bonding rather than the bridging variety was the dominant form of social capital at the British golf club though, for some, social capital included making commercial connections, using the club as a forum for business rather than an escape from it. Generally the club was a site for males of a similar social standing to meet together in a homosocial environment. The clubhouse itself offered a masculine sanctum where men could dine, drink, play cards or billiards and read the papers, all free from female involvement save for the club servants. Female and working-class players were accommodated without breaking down the male, middle-class dominance by parent-club development of separate 'ladies' sections and artisan clubs. It was in the interests of the club to have a thriving ladies' section as, despite their lower subscriptions, they made a contribution to financial capital formation via purchases at the professional's shop, payment for lessons, hiring of caddies, and, when allowed, using the clubhouse for meals and refreshments. The artisan players also made a contribution, in their case to the maintenance of the club's physical capital. Nevertheless, restrictions on when and where women and artisans could play served to segregate them from the full-fee paying male club members; as did the clubhouse rules. The majority of club members still required another form of capital to ensure that they could play their game: the human capital embodied in caddies and the club professionals, the former to carry their equipment and the latter to supply balls and teach skills.

Notes

1. For another discussion on golf using a symbolic capital framework see Ceron-Anaya (2010, 339–358).
2. A beginning has been made (see Vamplew 2013).
3. See the chapters on architecture and course construction by H.C. Colt in Sutton (1912).
4. For a regional case study see Foster (2009).
5. See also Verner (2000).
6. For more on this see Vamplew (2010).
7. For more detail on women's golf in this period see George, Kay, and Vamplew (2007).

NUMBERS AND NARRATIVES

8. Later unpublished research by Lewis produced totals of 417 societies in Scotland by 1914 and 89 in England. Information supplied by Peter Lewis, 20 March 2000.
9. Holt (2006, 352–369); Lowerson (1995, 127) and Cameron (2010) have noted that many golf clubs were given impetus to their founding by local medical men.
10. At the top end of the scale in 1913 Walton Heath employed 83 full-time and 110 part-time workers (*Times*, October 23, 1913).
11. The Midlands PGA actually described its members as 'good, sound businessmen'. Minutes of Midlands PGA, 26 October 1905 (PGA Archives, The Belfry, Sutton Coldfield). For a more detailed study see Vamplew (2008b, 54–79).
12. For more details see Vamplew (2008a).
13. For the official history of the PGA see Holt, Lewis, and Vamplew (2002).

Disclosure statement

No potential conflict of interest was reported by the author.

References

Agenda Club. 1912. *The Rough and the Fairway: An Enquiry by the Agenda Club into the Problem of the Golf Caddie*. London: Heinemann.
Anderson, J. 1993. *Seascale Golf Club 1893–1993*. Seascale: Club.
Arnell, Henry. 1988. *A History of Royal Ashdown Forrest G C 1888–1988*. East Grinstead: Club.
Barrie, J. 1898. *Historical Sketch of the Hawick Golf Club*. Hawick: Edgar.
Blackman, Peter. 1990. *The Northwood Golf Club Centenary 1891–1991*. Northwood: Club.
Bourdieu, Pierre. 1997. "The Forms of Capital." In *Education, Culture, Economy and Society*, edited by A. H. Halsey, H. Lauder, P. Brown and A. Stuart Wells, 46–58. Oxford: Oxford University Press.
Brailsford, Dennis. 1996. "The Lord's Day Observance Society and Sunday Sport 1834–1914." *The Sports Historian* 16: 140–155.
Burnett, John and Peter N. Lewis. 1996–97. "Edinburgh City Golfing Societies and Their Prizes." *Review of Scottish Culture* 10: 113–125.
Cadney, D. 1991. *The Story of Olton Golf Club*. Worcestershire: Grant.
Cameron, Donald M. 2010. *Social Links: The Golf Boom in Victorian England*. Cambridge: Social Links.
Ceron-Anaya, Hugo. 2010. "An Approach to the History of Golf: Business, Symbolic Capital, and Technologies of the Self." *Journal of Sport & Social Issues* 34: 339–358.
Chalmers, A. 1995. *Torphin Hill Golf Club 1895–1995*. Edinburgh: Club.
Chamberlain, Alan. 1995. *A History of Fairhaven Golf Club 1895–1995*. Fairhaven: Club.
Chape, T., and W. Ogilvie. 1984. *Newbiggin Golf Club Limited*. Newcastle: Club.
Charman, Derek. 1990. *The Leicestershire Golf Club: A Centenary History 1890–1990*. Leicester: Club.
"A Chat about Golf." 1903. *Chambers's Journal*, 80: 268.
Clark, Peter. 2000. *British Clubs and Societies 1580–1800: The Origins of an Associational World*. Oxford: Oxford University Press.
Collins, Tony, and Wray Vamplew. 2002. *Mud, Sweat and Beers: A Cultural History of Sport and Alcohol*. Oxford: Berg.
"Concerning Golf Secretaries." 1909. *Golf Illustrated*, January 22, 94.
Connelly, J. 1993. *A Temple of Golf: A History of Woking Golf Club 1893–1993*. Woking: Club.
Cossey, R. 1984. *Golfing Ladies*. London: Orbis.
Crampsey, Robert. 1989. *Ranfurly Castle Golf Club: A Centenary History*. Bridge of Weir: Club.
Davies, E. G., and G. W. Brown. 1989. *The Royal North Devon Golf Club 1864–1989*. Westward Ho!: Club.
Deasy, E. 1987. *Rochdale Golf Club 1888–1988*. Rochdale: Club.
Durie, Alastair J. 2003. *Scotland for the Holidays*. East Linton: Tuckwell.
Edwards, L. 1973. *The West Lancashire Golf Club*. Liverpool: Club.
Elwain, W. 1991. *Bristol and Clifton Golf Club 1891–1991*. Bristol: Club.
Farrar, G. B. 1937. "The Royal Liverpool Golf Club." *Golf Illustrated*, March 6.
Fitzgerald, Robert. 1988. *British Labour Management and Industrial Welfare 1846–1939*. London: Croom Helm.

Foster, Harry. 2009. *Links Along the Line*. Chichester: Phillimore.

George, Jane, Joyce Kay, and Wray Vamplew. 2007. "Women to the Fore: Gender Accommodation and Resistance at the British Golf Club before 1914." *Sporting Traditions* 23: 79–98.

Golfer's Handbook. 1913. Edinburgh: Scottish Newspaper Publishing.

Gillmeister, Heiner. 2002. "Golf on the Rhine: On the Origins of Golf, with Sidelights on Polo." *International Journal of the History of Sport* 19 (1): 1–30.

Gregory, Brian. 1992. *The History of Mid-Herts Golf Club*. Wheatampstead: Club.

Hamilton, David. 1998. *Golf: Scotland's Game*. Kilmacolm: Partick Press.

Harmsworth, V. G., ed. 1914. *Nisbet's Golf Guide and Year Book*. London: Nisbet.

Heath, Peter. 1986. *Edgbaston Golf Club 1896–1986*. Droitwich: Grant.

Historian. 1966. *A History of Ashford Manor Golf Club*. Ashford: Club.

Hogan, Michael. 1991. *Betchworth Park Golf Club: A History of the Club 1911–1991*. Betchworth: Club.

Holt, Richard. 1993. *Stanmore Golf Club 1883–1993*. Stanmore: Club.

Holt, Richard. 1998. "Golf and the English Suburb: Class and Gender in a London Club, C.1890–C.1960." *The Sports Historian* 18: 76–89.

Holt, Richard. 2006. "The Amateur Body and the Middle-class Man: Work, Health and Style in Victorian Britain." *Sport in History* 26: 352–369.

Holt, Richard, Peter N. Lewis, and Wray Vamplew. 2002. *The Professional Golfers' Association 1901–2001*. Worcestershire: Grant.

Humphreys, Claire. 2011. "Who Cares When I Play? Linking Reputation with the Golfing Capital and the Implications for Golf Destinations." *Journal of Sport & Tourism* 16: 105–128.

Hutchinson, Horace G. 1892. *Golf*. London: Longmans Green.

Hutchinson, Horace G. 1899. *The Book of Golf and Golfers*. London: Longmans Green.

Ironside, B. 1977. *Dunbar Golf Club*. Dunbar: Club.

Kerr, J. 1896. *The Golf Book of East Lothian*. Edinburgh: Constable.

Kinloch, F. 1906. "Golf of Yesterday and Today." *Chambers's Journal* 83: 677.

Knowles, Freddie, and Graham Tait. 1994. *The Bramall Park Golf Club Centenary 1894–1994*. Bramhall: Club.

Leach, Henry. 1906. "The Golfer and His Millions." *Fry's Magazine* 6, 422.

Lewis, Peter N. 1994. "The Growth of Golf in Great Britain." *Golfiania* 6 (1): 11–14.

Lewis, Peter N. 1995. *The Dawn of Professional Golf*. Ballater: Hobbs & McEwan.

Littlewood, John. 2004. *North Hants Golf Club Centenary History 1904–2004*. Worcestershire: Grant.

A London Golfer. 1909. "Golf and the Budget." *Golf Illustrated*, May 14, 243.

Longstaff, J. R. 1994. *The First Hundred Years of Bishop Auckland Golf Club 1894–1994*. Bishop Auckland: Club.

Lowerson, John. 1982. "Joint Stock Companies, Capital Formation and Suburban Leisure in England, 1880–1914." In *The Economic History of Leisure: Papers Presented at the Eighth International Economic History Congress, Budapest*, edited by Wray Vamplew. Adelaide: Flinders University.

Lowerson, John. 1989. "Golf." In *Sport in Britain*, edited by Tony Mason, 187–214. Cambridge: Cambridge University Press.

Lowerson, John. 1994. "Golf and the Making of Myths." In *Scottish Sport in the Making of the Nation*, edited by Grant Jarvie and Graham Walker, 75–90. Leicester: Leicester University Press.

Lowerson, John. 1995. *Sport and the English Middle Classes 1870–1914*. Manchester: Manchester University Press.

MacCabe, J. O. 1981. *Douglas Park Golf Club: The First Eighty Years*. Glasgow: Club.

MacDonald, Alistair. 1985. *The History of Langley Park Golf Club 1910–1985*. Beckenham: Club.

MacDonald, John. 1986. *Crail Golfing Society 200 Years 1786–1986*. Crail: Club.

Macdougall, A. 1995. *The Life and Times of Crowborough Beacon Golf Club 1895–1995*. East Sussex: Club.

Mackenzie, Richard. 1997. *A Wee Nip at the 19th Hole*. London: Collins Willow.

MacLean, John. 1987. *Coventry Golf Club 1887–1987*. Coventry: Club.

MacPhee, P. 1992. *Ballater Golf Club 1892–1992*. Ballater: Club.

Martin, D. 1989. *Minchinhampton Golf Club Centenary History 1889–1989*. Minchinhampton: Club.

NUMBERS AND NARRATIVES

Melling, J. 1983. "Employers, Industrial Welfare, and the Struggle for Work-place Control in British Industry, 1880–1920." In *Managerial Strategies and Industrial Relations*, edited by H. F. Gospel and C. R. Littler, 55–81. London: Heinemann.

Milton, J. T. 1987. *A History of Royal Eastbourne Golf Club 1887–1987*. Eastbourne: Club.

Milton, R. 1993. *A History of Ladies Golf in Sussex*. Brighton: Sussex County Ladies' Golf Association.

Moreton, J. 1999. *Porters Park Golf Club*. Hertfordshire: Club.

Newbould, D. 1994. *Coventry Hearsall Golf Club 1894–1994*. Coventry: Club.

Nunn, P. H. 1995. *One Hundred Years of Golf at Flempton: A History of the Flempton Golf Club 1895–1995*. Flempton: Club.

O.F.T. 1982. *Aldeburgh Golf Club: The First Hundred Years 1884–1984*. Ipswich: Club.

Owen, Colin. 1984. *A History of the Burton Golf Club 1894–1984*. Burton: Club.

Pearson, John. 1990. *York Golf Club 1890–1990*. York: Club.

Pearson, John, and P. Cusack. 2002. *Golf at Silloth 1890–2000*. Silloth: Club.

Pope, W. R. 1909. "Golf as Exercise." *Golf Illustrated*, February 19.

Porter, Roger. 2006. *The Forest Row Golf Club*. Forest Row: Club.

Putnam, R. 2000. *Bowling Alone: The Collapse and Revival of American Community*. New York: Simon & Schuster.

Report of the Royal Commission on Licensing (England and Wales) 1929–1931. 1932. London: HMSO.

Rees, J. 1994. *Never an Old Tin Hut: A Centenary Celebrated*. Aberfeldy: Club.

Scott, P. W. 1992. *Huntley Golf Club 1892–1992*. Huntly: Club.

Seaton, D. C. 1999. *Bass Rock Golf Club 1873–1998*. North Berwick: Club.

Sherlock, J. 1912. "From the Professional's Point of View." In *The New Book of Golf*, edited by Horace G. Hutchinson, 171–206. London: Longmans Green.

Smith, Garden B. 1909. "The Caddie Question." *Golf Illustrated*, July 23.

Smith, R. B. 1994. *Blackburn Golf Club 100 Years*. Blackburn: Club.

Soulsby, Eve M. 2002. *Braemar Golf Club: The Story of the First 100 Years*. Braemar: Club.

Starkie-Bence, A. M. 1898. "Golf." In *The Sportswoman's Library*, edited by F. E. Slaughter, 260–267. London: Constable.

Stringer, M. 1911. "Women's Golf in 1911." *Golfing*, December 28.

Sumpter, D. 1997. *West Surrey Golf Club: The First Sixty Years*. Godalming: Club.

Sutton, Martin H. F. 1912. *The Book of the Links*. London: W.H. Smith.

Tawney, R. H. 1909. "The Economics of Boy Labour." *The Economic Journal* 517–537.

Taylor, J. H. 1902. *Taylor on Golf*. London: Hutchinson.

Taylor, J. H. 1910. "A Plea for the Professional Golfer." *Golf Illustrated*, January 21.

Taylor, J. H. 1914. "Aims and Aspirations of a Professional." *Golf Magazine*, 22.

Thomas, Jack. 1993. *Axe Hill Golf Club 1894–1994*. Seaton: Club.

Vamplew, Wray. 2005. "Sporting Innovation: The American Invasion of the British Turf and Links, 1895–1905." *Sport History Review* 35: 122–137.

Vamplew, Wray. 2008a. "Child Work or Child Labour? The Caddie Question in Edwardian Golf." www.idrottsforum.org

Vamplew, Wray. 2008b. "Successful Workers or Exploited Labour? Golf Professionals and Professional Golfers in Britain 1888–1914." *The Economic History Review* 61: 54–79.

Vamplew, Wray. 2010. "Sharing Space: Inclusion, Exclusion, and Accommodation at the British Golf Club before 1914." *Journal of Sport & Social Issues* 34: 359–375.

Vamplew, Wray. 2013. "Theories and Typologies: A Historical Exploration of the Sports Club in Britain." *The International Journal of the History of Sport* 30 (14): 1569–1585.

Verner, Monica K. 2000. "American Golf and the Development of a Civilized Code of Conduct." PhD diss., Oklahoma State University.

Ward, Peter. 1984. *Came Down to Golf*. Weymouth: Ellesborough.

Ward, J. M. G. 1990. *One Hundred Years of Golf on Westwood*. Beverley: Coxton.

Ward, P., and A. Ward. 1995. *A History of Biggar Golf Club through 100 Eventful Years 1895–1995*. Biggar: Club.

Worthington, G. 1991. *The First Hundred Years of Ganton Golf Club 1891–1991*. Scarborough: Club.

Playing together: towards a theory of the British sports club in history

Wray Vamplew

ABSTRACT
This article brings together theories and extant analysis to assist in a better understanding of the theoretical complexities of establishing, organising, operating, and sustaining the sports club. It explores theoretical perspectives on the origins of the club; various levels of associativity; capital formation particularly that involving social capital; conviviality; the life cycle of the club; and aspects of third sector theory, the economics of the firm and invention and innovation.

Whilst a major discussion on the origins of the sports club revealed disagreements and differences internationally, it showed an acceptance that the club was central to the development of modern and, in some instances, pre-modern sport (Krüger 2008, 39–48; MacLean 2008, 49–56; Riess 2008, 33–38; Szymanski 2008a, 1–32; Nathaus 2009, 115–122). Clubs emerged from the desire of people to collectivize their leisure activities. They enabled people with a common purpose to come together, provided a basis for agreeing common rules and regulations, created a framework for competitive interaction, and secured a location for participation and sociability. Sports clubs offer more than sport and perhaps that is their attraction for many people. It is not just conviviality and the creation of social capital but also the binding together of a membership by a community of interest. A detailed search of the British sporting press has shown that by the late eighteenth century, the club was the major sporting institution in Britain, often possessing distinctive uniforms and with the vast bulk operating some form of restriction to ensure social homogeneity of membership (Harvey 2004). In more modern times, with due regard to school sport, there is substance in Allison's claim that the club was 'the form of organization through which most people were introduced to amateur sport' (Allison 2001a, 51). The club has become the basic unit of much grass-roots sport; a key and ubiquitous institution in the development of British sport. Sports clubs benefit individuals, communities and society. By facilitating access to sport, they can contribute to health and fitness (including reduced obesity) – lifelong depending on the sport – as well as to happiness and well-being; by providing a means for people to meet, they can assist social capital formation, both bonding and bridging, and promote community cohesion; and by encouraging volunteers to assist in club affairs, they help individuals take a positive social role from which they, the club and the community can gain (Andreff 2006, 219–224; Coalter 2007, 537–559; Guerro, Kesenne, and Humphreys 2011). Nevertheless 'the significance of voluntarism in leisure should not be romanticized. Men can simply reconstruct tyrannies on a smaller scale in clubs' (Tomlinson 1979, 39).

The sports club has a special place in sports history. It is an unacknowledged 'long residual', the term applied by Hardy and his colleagues to behaviours and beliefs that tie the sporting present to the past (Hardy, Loy, and Booth 2009, 131–132). They drew on the ideas of Braudel, a central figure in the Annales School of historical practice, and Williams, a cultural sociologist. Braudel defined his 'longue durée' as 'old habits of thinking and acting, the set patterns which do not break down easily and which, however illogical, are a long time dying' while Williams considered experiences and values as 'residual' if they were 'formed in the past but … [were] still active in the cultural process' (Braudel 1980, 30, 75; Williams 1977, 122). Although Hardy's list never mentioned clubs, given their long tradition it can be argued that sports clubs deserve categorization as a further long residual. Additionally the sports club might be considered an example of transnational history, the spread of an ideology and institution across national boundaries. Transnationalism is a fuzzy concept though the editors of *The Palgrave Dictionary of Transnational History,* published in 2009, were 'interested in links and flows, and want[ed] to track people, ideas, products, processes and patterns that operate[d] over, across, – through, beyond, above, under, or in-between polities and societies' (Iriye and Saunier 2009, xviii). In Britain, the club as a social institution preceded the widespread development of sport, but the promoters of the latter quickly adopted the idea as a mechanism of organization. When sport was exported from Britain in the late nineteenth century to its formal and informal empires, the club went with it as associated cultural baggage. This international diffusion of the club concept can be seen as early transnationalism. However, recent research has argued that sport also emerged independently within other cultures (Tomlinson and Young 2011, 487–507). More work is required on the nature of the clubs that developed around them; and on the interchange of ideas of organization as sports of all kinds became internationalized.

To date, there has been relatively little to explain the origins and existence of the sports club itself historically. What follows is an attempt to bring together theories and some extant analysis to assist in a better understanding of the theoretical complexities of establishing, organising, operating, and sustaining the sports club, bearing in mind that such clubs are not homogeneous identities.[1] When starting a club, there has been no legal requirement to establish it in a particular way. This has led to a variety of structures and organizational frameworks. Moreover, clubs can have different cultures: they can be more or less regimented; have varying levels of sociability; be full of cliques or open; and play sport at different levels of competitiveness.

Theoretical perspectives: origins of the sports club

Eisenberg has suggested that the organization of early modern sport in Britain led to 'cursory social relationships'. This was due, she argues, to sports competitions being open to all thus making the role of the athlete culturally unattractive with a consequent low social status. Rich landowners and leisure industry entrepreneurs offered cash prizes but had little interaction with the competitors and 'as a rule sporting social relationships ended with the handing over of the cash prize, and the parties involved went their own ways, mostly never to be seen again' (Eisenberg 2011, 202–203). This analysis, however, ignores the issue of sports clubs and their membership where social relationships did develop and indeed which actually could have initiated the formation of a club.

Informal games did not need clubs, but once a formal level of organization was required then clubs developed. When organising themselves into institutions for the purpose of playing, sportspersons had a long tradition of 'the club' to draw upon as British provincial and metropolitan life had a strong associational culture into which sport slotted relatively seamlessly. Clark, the authority on British clubs and society before 1800, sees voluntary organizations emerging in significant numbers out of English social and economic development from the time of the English Revolution to the late eighteenth century. Indeed, he argues that 'the special pressures of the early modern period moulded the distinctive characteristics of British clubs and societies, and so their role in modern society' (Clark 2000, viii).

Building on the pioneering work of Buchanan, Szymanski propounded an economic theory of the sports club based on individuals making rational choices (Buchanan 1965, 1–14; Szymanski 2010, 71–82). The premise was that participation in sport is generally a voluntary activity. People choose to play sport and they choose to join sports clubs: there is no compulsion involved. Buchanan's study was the first attempt to develop a formal theoretical structure to cover collective ownership-consumption arrangements. Much of his argument centred on theorizing the optimal size of a club which was reached when the marginal benefit of an additional member reducing the subscription costs to individual members equalled the marginal cost brought about by pressure on facilities. His work applied to any institution with cooperative membership, not sports clubs in particular, and did not consider the theoretical problems consequent on many sports clubs having two sets of facilities, one for playing and one for socialising. In economic terms, a club good exists on an intermediate point between fully private goods (which can exclude some buyers and are rivalrous in that consumption by one person precludes consumption by another) and fully public goods (which can do neither). The club can set entry requirements designed to exclude some aspiring members, but the use of its facilities by one member does not impinge on their use by others until congestion occurs.

Individuals make organizational choices but within constraints set by the state. Szymanski (2008a, 1–32) has argued that modern British sport emerged from new forms of associativity that developed autonomously in Britain during the European enlightenment following the retreat of the state from the control of associative activities. Clark (2000, 16) too has emphasized this passive role of the state in encouraging the expansion of clubs of all kinds as part of civil society. The situation was in contrast, Szymanski contends, to that in countries such as France and Germany where club formation continued to require the explicit or implicit approval of the state. There modern sports developed in ways consistent with, or even in the service of, the objectives of the state, most notably the need to maintain military preparedness. Britain as an island nation relied on naval power and did not require a large standing army or conscription.

Szymanski's critics acknowledge the ambition of the analysis but suggest missing elements and alternative causal factors (Krüger 2008, 39–48; MacLean 2008, 49–56; Riess 2008, 33–38; Nathaus 2009, 115–122).[2] They argue that more evidence is required to support the hypothesis; that he should have looked further back in time for his European material; that he failed adequately to address the issue of class; and that he understated the role of commercialization. Collins (2013, 10–11) actually claims the creation of sports clubs was a consequence of the commercialization, organization and growth of sport, rather than its cause as maintained by Szymanski. He argues that sporting clubs emerged mainly after the commercialization of sport in the eighteenth century, basing this on the virtual absence of such clubs in Clark's study of associations formed before the nineteenth century. This, of course, presumes that Clark actively sought information on sports clubs, but, in any event, Clark did state that by the end of the eighteenth century traditional sporting activities were increasingly run by clubs (Clark 2000, 123). Harvey's (2004) research seems to confirm this view. Collins acknowledges the growth of golf clubs in Scotland in the eighteenth century as an exception without explaining their absence from Clark's survey.

Theoretical perspectives: levels of associativity

Although Szymanski based his ideas on consumer choice, his was essentially a generalization about sports clubs with participation in sport as the sole function for membership, what elsewhere has been labelled the first level of associativity (Vamplew 2013, 1576). Certainly playing sport is at the core of sports club activity, but simultaneously it can offer social goods such as health and camaraderie. Hence people can join for pluralistic motivations. Following Hardy's (1981, 193–198) pioneering arguments, the task is to differentiate between the instrumental and expressive functions of sports clubs. The instrumental function is that of promoting a sporting activity – often outlined in the club's constitution as its primary goal – by the membership working together to acquire playing space, erect clubhouses and purchase equipment. Although instrumentality led to the establishment of clubs, the expressive functions of many clubs often became the cement that held the membership together via social capital creation, reinforcing a sense of identity and enhancement of status.

Vamplew (2013, 1575–1579) has proposed three levels of associativity that could be examined. The first level was the result of a desire to participate in sport. He suggests that research could be done on whether team sports had a different club structure from individual sports, whether field sports varied from other rural sporting activities or what the difference was between land-extensive and more space-confined urban sports. A second level of institutional collectivity was associated with the feeling of community or group solidarity that it offered. Among such collectives were clubs involving the workplace, political affiliation, educational background, religious faith, a residential or military connection, and those catering for the disabled, a specific age range, gender, ethnic or racial group, or sexual orientation. Sub-sectors of the second level of associativity groups can be labelled as the third level of associativity; for example, the education group could cover school sport, former pupil clubs, university clubs, clubs restricted to the teaching profession, etc.

What are being identified are broad categories that appear to cross-temporal boundaries (and possibly spatial ones), though it is not asserted that the same motivations were apparent at different points in time. Workplace sport, for instance, might be attributed to paternalism in one factory at one time but elsewhere, in another period, perhaps to trade unionism. The typology does not specify an ideal type of club within each category, except in the sense of suggesting the shared significant characteristics of those clubs in each classification. Other qualities possessed by clubs in the same category may not be similar. Hence, for example, Catholic and Protestant sports clubs were based on religious affiliation (the prime characteristic of a particular secondary associativity), but they may have varied in their willingness to play clubs of different denominations, their promotion of sport for females, or the types of sport which they embraced.

Theoretical perspectives: capital formation

Vamplew (2012, 299–231) has developed a theoretical construct in which sports clubs embody forms of capital. He argues that an approach focussing on varying definitions of capital, in particular physical, financial, human, cultural and social, can help our understanding of club formation and development. He suggests that preliminary investigations can employ user-friendly definitions which could be made more sophisticated, if necessary, at a later stage. Hence physical capital formation can be considered as those improvements made to natural resources to create productive assets that help procure revenue. Financial capital can be regarded as the money source such as share purchase, debentures, loans, and even donations that pay for these fixed assets and also the working capital that covers operating costs. Human capital formation embraces those aspects of the labour force that enhance productivity such as the acquisition of skill, competencies, knowledge, and experience as well as improved physical and mental health. It can also encompass self-improvement for non-economic reasons such as simply wanting to be fitter or more culturally aware. Economic forms of capital do not explain everything and researchers need also to look at cultural capital which can be considered as reputation- or status-enhancing activities and social capital in the form of the development of networks between individuals that can benefit them socially and economically.

Indeed, the aspect of capital theory that has featured most in academic discussion of the club is that of social capital. However, as Coalter (2007, 539) has warned, the concept is 'diffuse and contested'. Those using the term have tended to provide their own definitions, often vague and suited primarily to the views they were advancing. For example, Nichols, writing for the Central Council for Physical Recreation, argues that voluntary sports clubs make a substantial contribution to social capital, but does so simply by asserting that sports clubs provide a structure and opportunity for active citizenship and social interaction, while Driscoll and Wood in their exploration of Australian rural sport define social capital as 'a collective term for the ties that bind us' (Driscoll and Wood 1999 cited in Coalter 2007, 548; Nichols 2003 cited in Coalter 2007, 545).

In the context of any analysis of sports clubs, two major social capital theorists have relevance. Although Bourdieu and Putnam have differences in their approaches and arguments, there is broad agreement that social capital refers 'to social networks based on social and group norms which enable people to trust and cooperate with each other and through which individuals or groups can obtain certain types of advantage' (Coalter 2007, 540). In particular, Bourdieu defined social capital as 'the aggregate of the actual or potential resources which are linked to a durable network of more or less institutionalized relationships of mutual acquaintance and recognition'; and Putnam felt it referred to 'connections between individuals [and the]social networks and the norms of reciprocity and trustworthiness that arise from them' (Bourdieu 1997, 51; Putnam 2000, 18). Neither of these authors – despite Putnam's book title – specifically focussed on sport; yet both have relevance to sport.

Social capital can be viewed as involving mutual support and obligations, social cooperation, trust and – of importance to a sporting organization – institutional effectiveness. Indeed, the establishment and operation of a golf club is a prime example of how, by developing relationships and working together, people can achieve more than they could simply by acting as individuals. Bourdieu actually suggested that membership of a golf club was often taken for instrumental purposes with both course and clubhouse providing the opportunity for business networking (Bourdieu 1997, 46–58; Coalter 2007, 540). There was

NUMBERS AND NARRATIVES

the occasional complaint of this happening in Edwardian times, though historical evidence to support Bourdieu's view tends to be anecdotal rather than documented (*Golf Monthly*, August 1912, 462). The perquisite of the right to propose new members gave existing ones the opportunity to improve business relationships by introducing professional colleagues and clients (of the proper social background). Out on the course two to three hours of walking, broken intermittently by a need to concentrate on a shot, and the relative physical isolation of the players could produce a scenario where pleasure and business negotiation or networking could co-exist and be cemented over drinks in the clubhouse. More common was the coming together of men from the same occupational group. In the London area, for example, Northwood, known as the 'Pill Club', was full of doctors, Woking of lawyers, and Sunningdale of stock exchange dealers (Blackman 1990, 18; *Golf Illustrated*, 3 June 1910, 215). Even more occupationally homogeneous were many of the golfing societies which virtually included only those with the same business interest. In 1913, one golfing journal claimed that 'numerous golfing societies are being formed every day by people belonging to particular classes, professions, and sets' (*Golf Illustrated*, 31 January 1913, 140). In the years to 1914, Burnett and Lewis traced 375 golf societies, some 57% of which were occupationally based in that the members worked for the same employer, in the same trade or in the same profession (Burnett and Lewis 1996/97). Whether Bourdieu's argument might hold for clubs in other sports is problematic. Cementing business relationships while playing would certainly be restricted to very few sports due to the nature of the activity. Golf is almost unique in having 'idle time' for conversation during a game. However, both post match for players and at any time for spectators, advantage could be taken of hospitality facilities provided by many clubs.

Putnam is particularly relevant as he is interested in the role of organized voluntary associations and collective outcomes. His concepts of 'bridging' and 'bonding' social capital perhaps have most relevance to sports clubs (Putnam 2000, 22). Bonding social capital draws people together from a similar social niche and tends to reinforce exclusive identities, develop in-group loyalties and maintain homogeneity, whereas bridging social capital brings together people from diverse social divisions and tends to generate broader identities and wider reciprocities. The construction of bonding social capital infers the use of exclusionary practices to enforce a homogeneous group identity in contrast to bridging capital's more inclusive agenda that cuts across class, gender and other boundaries. Much contemporary government policy (actual and proposed) relating to sports clubs assumes that bridging capital is preferable to the bonding kind: indeed, the latter is often castigated as discriminatory in that by creating strong ingroup loyalty, it can also produce strong outgroup antagonism, an intolerance of diversity and non-conformity, and exclusion of outsiders (Coalter 2010, 1383; Spaaij and Westerbeck 2010, 1359).

Few, if any, studies of sport in the contemporary world have identified clubs as creating beneficial social capital – except to a restricted and selective membership. The evidence points to the domination of bonding social capital over bridging. Similarly, although there are no detailed social surveys to support the view, it would appear that this was also the experience of the past. Historical examples of clubs restricting membership to specific social groups are not difficult to find. In the late eighteenth century, the original 12 members of the Royal Caledonian Hunt Club included four dukes, three earls and three baronets (Kay 2000/01, 32). More generally, hunting literature contains many claims that the sport unified rural society. Most were along the lines promulgated in 1808 by John Hawkes, friend of famous huntsman Hugo Meynell, that 'The Field is a most agreeable coffee-house, and there is more real society to be met with there than in any other situation of life. It links all classes together, from the peer to the peasant' (Quoted in Iztkowitz 1977, 24). The hunting field was open to all. Foxes were vermin and hence there were no game law qualifications to be met and land belonging to others had to be traversed with appropriate sporting compensation. However, although the farmer or tradesman was welcome to ride alongside the hunting gentry, fraternization – if it can be labelled as such – ended there. There were no invitations to the hunt balls, dinners or races: here social distinctions were emphasized and reinforced (Itzkowitz 1977, 26–27). Off horseback the social capital created was of the bonding variety: as Sir Christopher Sykes put it in 1792

> When the pleasures of the chase can be made the means of calling the gentlemen of the country together, they become really useful and beneficial to society. They give opportunities of wearing off shyness, dispelling temporary differences, forming new friendships and cementing old, and draw the gentlemen of the country into one close bond of society. (Quoted in Itzkowitz 1977, 19)

These lend support to the generalizations of, among others, Harvey who, on the basis of a detailed study of contemporary sporting magazines though with only isolated information, concludes that most late eighteenth- and early nineteenth-century sporting clubs were socially exclusive (Harvey 2004, 191).

The same scenario of social exclusivity can be found in the nineteenth and early twentieth centuries when sport clubs descended the socio-economic scale. Mid-nineteenth-century Bolton bowling clubs were mainly subscription-only, drawing on the local commercial and industrial elite (Swain 2013, 153). Vamplew's (2010, 359–375) study of Late Victorian and Edwardian golf clubs notes that while golf's handicapping system gave all players an equal chance on the course, social equality was less of a consideration. Hansen's (1995, 300–324) examination of the Alpine Club's Registers (from 1859–1890) reveals a membership overwhelmingly dominated by the professional middle classes. Yet in itself this does not mean that others were deliberately excluded. Until we turn to the club's stated objective of facilitating 'association among those who possess a similarity of taste'. To be eligible, aspiring members had to possess experience of climbing in the Alps or 'provide evidence of literary or artistic accomplishments relating to mountains'. Moreover, the very existence of clubs catering primarily for adherents to particular faiths or former pupils of particular schools and universities suggests some form of social exclusivity was being applied.

It appears that Tranter (1998, 41) was correct when he hazarded that 'for most of the social elite sport was an opportunity for social differentiation not conciliation, and was used to restrict rather than expand contact with social inferiors'. Other historians agree. Lowerson's (1995, 98) view on leisure clubs for the urban middle classes in the early twentieth century was that 'their ostensible purpose was a particular sport. But often far more significant and far less easily constructed by historians was their role as instruments of relatively fine social differentiation and arbiters of public custom'. Huggins (2004, 99) sums up the situation as 'some clubs were formed to ensure and demonstrate members' social exclusivity; others were formed because they were excluded'. Hence, Jews excluded covertly from the golf clubs around Leeds in the 1930s reacted by establishing their own Moor Allerton Golf Club and in Middlesex West Indians and Asians respectively set up 29 and 65 of the 334 cricket clubs affiliated to the Club Cricket Conference in 1999 because of an unwelcoming attitude by white cricket clubs (Wigglesworth 1996, 129; Williams 2001, 173–298).

Historically, it is difficult to find examples of clubs supplying bridging capital. The *Vereine* in London actually had more English members than German, perhaps thus fulfilling its objective 'to introduce and encourage German gymnastics in England, and by closer intercourse to bring about a better mutual understanding between two ancestrally related nations' (Westaway 2009, 571–604). Possibly, though there is no evidence, there was more bridging capital apparent in the post-match conviviality in league and cup competitions where clubs were not free to choose their opponents as was common when fixture lists comprised mainly friendlies as in much early southern club cricket and rugby union. It could also be speculated that proselytizing clubs who used sport to spread the gospel might be more likely to create bridging capital than those who looked to cement existing second- and third-level associativity relationships.

There is no need to fully accept Bordieau's explanation of the relationship between sporting practice, corporeal engagement and social position to recognize that certain sports appealed more to different groups on the socio-economic hierarchy.[3] The basic premise argued here is that essentially people prefer to play sport with like-minded individuals: they are perhaps social animals first and sportspersons second. They generally sought to exclude rather than include and brought together people with similar socio-economic backgrounds rather than acting as agencies of social integration. As Szymanski (2010) has noted 'people may join clubs as much because they know who is excluded as who is included'. Even those who formed their own clubs because they felt they were discriminated against set up exclusionary barriers; so, in the 1970s and 1980s, West Indians from different Caribbean islands formed separate cricket clubs and Asian cricket clubs often represented different religious and language groups within the Asian population (Williams 2001, 176).

Theoretical perspectives: conviviality

In his early exploration of the club Buchanan acknowledged that his theory applied only to the economic motivations for joining and was not relevant where 'individuals join clubs for camaraderie' (Buchanan 1965, 2 note 12). One aspect of this, possibly associated with social capital formation, is conviviality: indeed it has been described by Holt (1989, 347) as being 'at the heart of sport'. Examples across time and sport are easy to find. Kay's (2000/01, 30, 36) examination of the Royal Caledonian Hunt's early minute books shows 'a distinct lack of enthusiasm for both the field and the turf' in contrast to the 'emphasis on drinking and dining'. In Irish cricket in the late nineteenth century, military bands played every Tuesday at the North of Ireland Cricket Club in Belfast and the post-match events on the I Zingari tour of Ireland in 1875 had 'the most attractive dances, the best of music, and the best of suppers' (Reid 2012, 152. Quote is from *John Lawrence's Handbook of Cricket in Ireland 1875–6*). In the early twentieth century, the Public Schools Alpine Sports Club advertised itself as 'a congenial society of people interested in Alpine sports' (Anon 1913, 9). Yachtsmen may have joined the Royal Cruising Club primarily for access to its navigational charts or the chance to win one of its annual awards, but it was an implicit condition of membership that they undertook 'to mix with fellow members whenever they meet afloat' (Underhill 1930, n.d.). At the other end of the social spectrum most working-class angling clubs met in public houses and, as was explained to a Parliamentary Committee in 1878, 'had a jollification afterward', though the witness was careful to add 'without exceeding the bounds of temperance' (Quoted in Lowerson 1988, 109).[4] Alcohol was not always a necessary accompaniment: one member of the Glasgow Ladies Cycling Club in 1900 was 'totally unashamed' to admit that, in her view, 'the great event of a ladies club run is tea' (*Scottish Cyclist*, 24 October 1900 XIII, 713). Interviews with former Pegasus players suggest that restoring the glory days of the Corinthians was less important to them than 'enjoyment from playing in congenial company at the highest level of the amateur game' (Porter 2002, 2). In her study of Banbury in the mid-twentieth century Stacey (1960, 88) concluded that most sports clubs in the town existed less to enable the populace to 'engage in sport as an exercise in competitive athleticism but as an occasion for social intercourse'. Today in the lower sporting reaches there is Sunday public house football where teams such as Real Ale Madrid play prior to indulging in a lunchtime drink (Vamplew and Collins 2002, 123–124). Conviviality served to create bonding social capital via friendship and enjoyment. When reported in the press, social gatherings could act as an image creators for the club, both in demonstrating approved, respectable behaviour to the outside world and in showing potential members how friendly and convivial the club actually was. Telfer (2004, 198) suggests that the quality of its socials and smokers did more for the reputation of a harrier clubs than any of its cross-country runs. Moreover in their study of leisure organizations in the 1980s Bishop and Hoggett (1986, 123) suggest that what should be the substantive leisure pursuit might actually be of secondary importance to the social side of a club's activities.

Nevertheless Holt's simple assertion requires elaboration as, outlined in the following typology, the sociability of the sports club could take several organizational and beneficiary forms. First, and perhaps most common, was the simple hospitality of the club bar used for informal socializing. Not all clubs possessed their own drinking facilities and pub landlords often seized the opportunity to gain trade. In the interwar years a guide to pub management noted:

> ... the golden rule for achieving popularity – the popularity that pays in bigger profits: interest yourself in those sports and pastimes in which your customers are interested ... Encourage the formation of clubs which will naturally make your house their headquarters; and if, as in the case of a cricket or football club, you cannot provide the ground, you can still place a room at the team's disposal for changing in, and encouraging the holding of the committee meetings at your house. (Capper 1925, vol. 3, 22)

Second, gatherings could be organized by the club exclusively for its members such as the annual dinner. Third, hospitality could be organized by the club for its members and the opponents of the day. This became a customary post-match expectation and could serve to reduce any animosity from the onfield activities. As one Scottish observer noted in the early 1890s, 'there is barely a football match played but some disagreeable incident happens. The players at such a meeting [the after-match social] have an opportunity of mending matters and with songs and sentiment forgetting the field squabbles' (*Kilmarnock Standard*, 7 January 1893). Fourth, there were events organized by the club but open to the public (or a restricted section such as friends of members) with proceeds going to the club itself. Edinburgh Northern Harriers declared a profit of £200 from its smokers and dances in 1897 (Telfer 2004, 202). The fifth category was a variant of this with proceeds going to a third party, usually a charity. Gregson and Huggins (1999, 83–84) maintain that smoking concerts were common ways of fundraising for the club itself or for a charity, the latter often involving the appearance of music-hall performers as guest artists. Finally there were events hosted and organized by others for the benefit of the club.

Theoretical perspectives: a life-cycle approach

A life-cycle approach to clubs brings in the idea of the club as a dynamic institution; one that can grow or fail, cope or not cope with internal and external change. Such an approach would begin with the origins of clubs. Vamplew (2012, 300) has suggested that most private golf clubs started in one of three ways: on a small scale by a group of friends and neighbours with a basic course and few, if any, facilities; on a larger scale with invited local members, a clubhouse and an architecturally-designed layout; or as limited liability companies usually offering high quality facilities. Whether clubs in other sports followed the same models remains to be researched.

Early clubs often began in isolation; matches were 'inhouse' between 'marrieds' and 'singles' and other practical groupings. A minority stayed like that, providing recreational sport for their members. Others sought to play 'friendly' fixtures against (socially?) suitable opposition. Yet others responded to a demand from their membership for more meaningful competition and entered cups and joined leagues. For some clubs survival may have been the basic institutional motivation, achieving a steady state rather than growth. Reasons for this probably varied. Physical and financial limits to the expansion of playing facilities would be one factor. Limits may also have been set by the size of the local meeting place: angling clubs were often fixed around the 40 mark by the space available in the local public house (Lowerson 1988, 109). Some clubs may just have preferred to remain small, social gatherings.

Associational vitality cannot be assumed. As Tomlinson (1979, 17) stated 'leisure groups do not have to go on. They are not obligatory'. Not all clubs succeed and a life-cycle analysis must also consider the death of clubs and reasons for their demise. Clubs had to deal with an external economic environment that was not always propitious. Wigglesworth (2007, 109–118) has documented examples of clubs feeling the effects of economic recession from the late eighteenth century onwards. Some were engulfed by the financial problems; others survived via retrenchment or occasionally amalgamation. It is important to apply a time dimension to club history. Some clubs faced problems because they were formed at a time of boom for their sport which ultimately led to too many clubs chasing potential members. Inevitably this led to rationalization by extinction and amalgamation. A case in point is rugby in Kendal. Introduced to the area in 1871 a decade later there were eight teams which eventually merged to form two clubs – 'Hornet' and 'Town' – which in turn joined together in 1892 to form Kendal Thursday Football Club (Wigglesworth 2007, 118).

In a pioneering study of the life cycles of golf, tennis and bowling clubs, Kay (2013) has argued that sports historians have tended to focus on club origins and devoted much less attention to their later years, despite the problems they faced in adapting to changing social and economic circumstances. Based on an analysis of almost 100 clubs and regional sports association histories, she suggests that life cycles should be examined via three, often overlapping, categories of membership, finance and social matters. Her research identified patterns in club development in that at some point all clubs had to make decisions about the admission of female and junior members, about changing subscription rates, upgrading facilities, holding fundraising events, about Sunday play, and about selling alcohol. She points out that the point at which these issues were faced may have been dependent on the club's specific individual circumstances or the general social and economic circumstances in which it operated. Kay also notes that decision-makers were important and researchers need to discover those who were the driving forces in the establishment and development of the club and how the institution dealt with their departure. Clubs could become hidebound by tradition.[5] Their autonomy meant that they could become static institutions maintaining practices that might be regarded as inappropriate in the wider community. Indeed social legislation designed to reduce discrimination and improve equality has tended to exclude private clubs from its provisions (Allison 2001b, 64).[6] Another useful historical study but limited to clubs of a specific type in a particular geographic area is Williams's (1995) research into church-based cricket clubs in Lancashire between 1900 and 1939. He shows that such clubs grew significantly in the 1920s years before collapsing in the 1930s in face of better facilities provided by works teams, house builders taking over playing areas, and the desire of members to play at a higher standard in open clubs.

A life-cycle approach would require a study of published club histories and, where possible, club archives. What could be adopted overall is an institutional version of prosopography, the idea first outlined by Stone (1971) as a means to understand the historical development of power elites. Essentially it seeks to investigate common characteristics of a historical group, whose individual biographies may be largely untraceable, by a collective study of their lives. This has been done for elite French sportspeople and some athletic trainers but, instead of human biography, commonalities could be sought among clubs and their memberships (Erard and Bancel 2007, 67–79; Oldfield 2012, 35–60).

Theoretical perspectives: other approaches

Given that sports clubs have much in common with voluntary groups, theories of the third sector may have relevance. Until the late twentieth century economists tended to ignore the non-profit sector, dismissing it as an unproductive use of resources and outside the realm of rational economics because it was not profit focussed. Generally they now accept that non-profit institutions exist because of market failures in the private sector and voids left by government agencies in the public one (Rose-Ackerman 1996). New models of institutional behaviour have been developed covering non-economic institutions such as churches, political parties, charities and clubs. The third sector is differentiated from the private (business) one in that revenue is not an end product but a resource and from the public (government) one as it cannot raise revenue by taxation. This has allowed the voluntary sector to provide 'social risk capital' as it was sufficiently free of both the profit constraint of business and the political feasibility often required for government action (Ott 2001, 50). Many policy documents referred to clubs as 'the voluntary sector in sport' and even sports themselves acknowledge that 'the voluntary sector has a fundamental role to play in the provision of sport' (Allison 2001b, 21; Northern Council for Sport and Recreation 1993, 1). Yet sports clubs usually promote self-interest and focus on enthusiasms rather than the mutual help and welfare favoured by much of the voluntary sector, leading to a suggestion that the voluntary sector label should be abandoned for sports clubs and that they should occupy a defined space as 'amateur sports organisations' (Allison 2001b, 32).

The economic theory of the firm may have some relevance to sports clubs, particularly commercially-focussed clubs such as those in the fitness industry. Moreover even not-for-profit organizations have to face many of the problems encountered by small profit-oriented businesses such as paying staff, selling a product, and balancing the books. Other aspects might also apply to commercially-minded clubs in professional sport catering for a mass spectator market, though here care must be taken to determine towards which end of the profit-maximization/utility – maximization spectrum their motivations lay.

Finally Rogers's (2002) concepts of invention and innovation (and distinguishing between the two) might prove useful as a means of interpreting the development and diffusion of clubs, particularly within a specified sport. It emphasizes the role of opinion leaders and change agents who can perceive advantages in innovations and influence others to adopt them. He identifies four groups of innovators: the pioneers, the early majority of adopters, the late adopters and the laggards. For an example of such an application within football as the game became professionalized see the work of Lewis (2010) which, while primarily a response to critics of his work, does suggest that this might be a useful way forward in club analysis. It would also be a way of assessing whether the early sports clubs took their ideas from non-sport organizations and to what extent later sports clubs borrowed from earlier ones and from each other.

Are clubs really necessary?

Today the sports club is under threat on several fronts. The financial crisis, economic recession, cutbacks in public spending, and rising unemployment, all potentially undermine the existence of the sports club, as does increased legislation on matters of liability, health, safety, disclosure and disabled access. This raises an interesting research issue of whether sport needs clubs.

Clearly sport has existed without the club as an organizational unit. Many, if not most, traditional rural sports were scarcely organized at all as they were essentially local games and pastimes played on an ad hoc basis when competitors felt like it (Collins, Martin, and Vamplew 2005). Those that were bigger events do not appear to have used the club as a fulcrum. Historically none of the folk football events studies by Hornby (2008, 11) relied on clubs to supply participants: although players usually represented a particular area, teams were decided by birthplace, residence, family ties and sometimes marital status.

A counterfactual approach would suggest that had sports clubs not existed, sport would have developed very differently. Team sports would probably have remained annual or irregular events with no leagues or knockout cup competitions. Sports for individuals might well have progressed – gamblers would have seen to that – but perhaps less so the conviviality side of the sport, though landlords and publicans would still have sponsored competitions and provided facilities to attract a drinking clientele.

Notes

1. For a discussion of the quagmire that definitions of the sports club can lead us into see Vamplew 2013, 1570–1573.
2. See also Szymanski, (2008b, 57–64).
3. For a synthesis of Bordieau's views see DeLuca 2013, 343–4.
4. In the later nineteenth century angling clubs were generally located in public houses. By 1900 few northern pubs were without an affiliated angling club and London's 620 clubs were almost all pub-based. The landlords offered rooms for moderate rents as the clubs provided regular custom and temperate behaviour (Lowerson 1989, 19).
5. In their study of female involvement in club administration, White and Kay (2006) have suggested that newer clubs were more innovative in this regard.
6. Only when lottery funds and government grants have been sought have clubs been forced to come to terms with the real world.

Disclosure statement

No potential conflict of interest was reported by the author.

References

Anon. 1913. *The Public Schools Alpine Sports Club Year Book*. London: Horace Marshall.

Allison, L. 2001a. *Amateurism in Sport*. London: Frank Cass.

Allison, M. 2001b. *Sports Clubs in Scotland*. Edinburgh: Sportscotland.

Andreff, W. 2006. "Voluntary Work in Sport." In *Handbook on the Economics of Sport*, edited by W. Andreff and S. Szymanski, 219–224. Cheltenham: Edward Elgar.

Bishop, J., and P. Hoggett. 1986. *Organizing Around Enthusiasms: Mutual Aid in Leisure*. London: Comedia.

Blackman, P. 1990. *The Northwood Golf Club Centenary 1891–1991*. Northwood: Club.

Braudel, F. 1980. *On History*. Chicago, IL: University of Chicago Press.

Bourdieu, P. 1997. "The Forms of Capital." In *Education, Culture, Economy and Society*, edited by A. H. Halsey, H. Lauder, P. Brown and A. Stuart Wells, 46–58. Oxford: Oxford University Press.

Buchanan, J. M. 1965. "An Economic Theory of Clubs." *Economica* 32: 1–14.

Burnett, J., and P. N. Lewis. 1996–97. "Edinburgh City Golfing Societies and Their Prizes." *Review of Scottish Culture* 10: 113–125.

Capper, B., ed. 1925. *Licensed Houses and their Management*. London: Caxton.

Clark, P. 2000. *British Clubs and Societies 1580–1800: The Origins of an Associational World*. Oxford: Oxford University Press.

Coalter, F. 2007. "Sports Clubs, Social Capital and Social Regeneration: 'Ill-defined Interventions With Hard to Follow Outcomes'?" *Sport in Society* 10 (4): 537–559.

Coalter, F. 2010. "Sport-for-development: Going Beyond the Boundary?" *Sport in Society* 13 (9): 1374–1391.

Collins, T. 2013. *Sport in Capitalist Society*. Abingdon: Routledge.

Collins, T., J. Martin, and W. Vamplew, eds. 2005. *Encyclopedia of Traditional British Rural Sports*. Abingdon: Routledge.

DeLuca, J. R. 2013. "Submersed in Social Segregation: The (Re)Production of Social Capital Through Swim Club Membership." *Journal of Sport and Social Issues* 37 (4): 340–363.

Driscoll, K., and L. Wood. 1999. *Sporting Capital: Changes and Challenges for Rural Communities in Victoria*. Melbourne: Centre for Applied Social Research RMIT.

Eisenberg, C. 2011. "Playing the Market Game: Cash Prizes, Symbolic Awards and the Professional Ideal in British Amateur Sport." *Sport in History* 31 (2): 197–217.

Erard, C., and N. Bancel. 2007. "Prosopographical Analysis of Sports Elites: Overview and Evaluation of a Seminal Study." *The International Journal of the History of Sport* 24 (1): 67–79.

Gregson, K., and M. Huggins. 1999. "Sport, Music-hall Culture and Popular Song in Nineteenth-century England." *Culture, Sport, Society* 2 (2): 82–102.

Guerro, P. R., S. Kesenne, and B. R. Humphreys, eds. 2011. *The Economics of Sport, Health and Happiness*. Cheltenham: Edward Elgar.

Hansen, P. H. 1995. "Albert Smith, the Alpine Club, and the Invention of Mountaineering in Mid-Victorian Britain." *Journal of British Studies* 34 (3): 300–324.

Hardy, S. 1981. "The City and the Rise of American Sport." *Exercise & Sports Sciences Review* 9: 183–219.

Hardy, S., J. Loy, and D. Booth. 2009. "The Material Culture of Sport: Toward a Typology." *Journal of Sport History* 36 (1): 129–152.

Harvey, A. 2004. *The Beginnings of a Commercial Sporting Culture in Britain*. Aldershot: Ashgate.

Holt, R. 1989. *Sport and the British*. Oxford: Oxford University Press.

Hornby, H. 2008. *Uppies and Downies: The Extraordinary Football Games of Britain*. Swindon: English Heritage.

Huggins, M. 2004. *The Victorians and Sport*. London: Hambledon and London.

Iriye, A., and P.-Y. Saunier. 2009. *The Palgrave Dictionary of Transnational History*. Basingstoke: Palgrave MacMillan.

Itzkowitz, D. C. 1977. *Peculiar Privilege: A Social History of English Foxhunting 1753–1885*. Hassocks: Harvester.

Kay, J. 2000-01. "From Coarse to Course: The First Fifty Years of the Royal Caledonian Hunt, 1777–1826." *Review of Scottish Culture* 13: 30–39.

Kay, J. 2013. "'Maintaining the Traditions of British Sport'? The Private Sports Club in the Twentieth Century." *International Journal of the History of Sport* 30 (14): 1655–1669.

Krüger, A. 2008. "Which Associativity? A German Answer to Szymanski's Theory of the Evolution of Modern Sport." *Journal of Sport History* 35 (1): 39–48.

Lewis, R. W. 2010. "Innovation not Invention: A Reply to Peter Swain Regarding the Professionalization of Association Football in England and its Diffusion." *Sport in History* 30 (3): 475–488.

Lowerson, J. 1988. "Brothers of the Angle: Coarse Fishing and English Working-class Culture, 1850–1914." In *Pleasure, Profit, Proselytism: British Culture and Sport at Home and Abroad 1700–1914*, edited by J. A. Mangan, 105–127. London: Cass.

Lowerson, J. 1989. Angling. In *Sport in History*, edited by T. Mason, 12–43. Cambridge: Cambridge University Press.

Lowerson, J. 1995. *Sport and the English Middle Classes 1870–1914*. Manchester, NH: Manchester University Press.

MacLean, M. 2008. "Evolving Modern Sport." *Journal of Sport History* 35 (1): 49–56.

Nathaus, K. 2009. "The Role of Associativity in the Evolution of Modern Sport: A Comment on Stefan Szymanski's Theory." *Journal of Sport History* 36 (1): 115–122.

Nichols, G. 2003. *Citizenship in Action: Voluntary Sector Sport and Recreation*. London: Central Council for Physical Recreation.

Northern Council for Sport and Recreation. 1993. *Spare a Thought for the Volunteer: An Action Plan*. NCSR.

Oldfield, S.-J. 2012. "Narrative, Biography, Prosopography and the Sport Historian: Historical Method and Its Implications." In *Sports Coaching: Pasts and Futures*, edited by D. Day, 35–60. Crewe: MMU Institute for Performance Research.

Ott, S. J. 2001. *Nature of the Non-profit Sector*. Oxford: Westview.

Porter, D. 2002. "Amateur Football in England, 1948–63: The Pegasus Phenomenon." *Contemporary British History* 14 (2): 1–30.

Putnam, R. 2000. *Bowling Alone: The Collapse and Revival of the American Community*. New York: Simon & Schuster.

Reid, S. 2012. "Identity and Cricket in Ireland in the Mid-nineteenth Century." *Sport in Society* 15 (2): 147–164.

Riess, S. A. 2008. "Associativity and the Evolution of Modern Sport." *Journal of Sport History* 35 (1): 33–38.

Rogers, E. M. 2002. *Diffusion of Innovations*. New York: Simon & Schuster.

Rose-Ackerman, S. 1996. "Altruism, Nonprofits, and Economic Theory." *Journal of Economic Literature* 34 (2): 701–728.

Spaaij, R., and H. Westerbeek. 2010. "Sport Business and Social Capital: A Contradiction in Terms?" *Sport in Society* 13 (9): 1356–1373.

Stacey, M. 1960. *Tradition and Change: A Study of Banbury*. Oxford: Oxford University Press.

Stone, L. 1971. "Prosopography." *Daedalus* 100–1: 46–71.

Swain, P. 2013. "Bolton Against All England for a Cool Hundred: Crown Green Bowls in South Lancashire, 1787–1914." *Sport in History* 33 (2): 146–168.

Szymanski, S. 2008a. "A Theory of the Evolution of Modern Sport." *Journal of Sport History* 35 (1): 1–32.

Szymanski, S. 2008b. "Response to Comments." *Journal of Sport History* 35 (1): 57–64.

Szymanski, S. 2010. "Economists and Sports History." *Journal of Sport History* 37 (1): 71–82.

Telfer, H. 2004. "Ludism. Laughter and Liquor: Homosocial Behaviour in Late-Victorian Scottish Harrier Clubs." In *Disreputable Pleasures: Less Virtuous Victorians at Play*, edited by M. Huggins and J. A. Mangan, 185–203. London: Cass.

Tomlinson, A. 1979. *Leisure and the Role of Voluntary Groups*. London: Sports Council.

Tomlinson, A., and C. Young. 2011. "Towards a New History of European Sport." *European Review* 19: 487–507.

Tranter, N. 1998. *Sport, Economy and Society in Britain, 1750–1914*. Cambridge: Cambridge University Press.

Underhill, A. 1930. *A Short History of the First Half-Century of the Royal Cruising Club*. London: Roworth.

Vamplew, W. 2010. "Sharing Space: Inclusion, Exclusion, and Accommodation at the British Golf Club Before 1914." *Journal of Sport & Social Issues* 34: 359–375.

Vamplew, W. 2012. "Concepts of Capital: An Approach Shot to the History of the British Sports Club Before 1914." *Journal of Sport History* 39 (2): 299–231.

Vamplew, W. 2013. "Theories and Typologies: A Historical Exploration of the Sports Club in Britain." *The International Journal of the History of Sport* 30 (14): 1569–1585.

Vamplew, W., and T. Collins. 2002. *Mud, Sweat and Beers*. Oxford: Berg.

Westaway, J. 2009. "The German Community in Manchester, Middle-class Culture and the Development of Mountaineering in Britain, c.1850–1914." *The English Historical Review* CXXIV: 571–604.

White, M., and J. Kay. 2006. "Who Rules Sport Now?: White and Brackenridge Revisited." *International Review for the Sociology of Sport* 41 (3–4): 465–473.

Wigglesworth, N. 1996. *The Evolution of English Sport*. London: Cass.

Wigglesworth, N. 2007. *The Story of Sport in England*. Abingdon: Routledge.

Williams, J. 1995. "Cricket and Christianity in Lancashire, 1900–1939." *Local Historian* 25 (2): 95–108.

Williams, R. 1977. *Marxism and Literature*. Oxford: Oxford University Press.

Williams, J. 2001. *Cricket and Race*. Oxford: Berg.

Index

Abercorn FC 41
Aberdeen FC 35
Abington, 'Squire' 87
Adair, Daryl 6, 12
Adelaide Oval 6
agency, role of 53
agents 95, 99
air travel 93
Aitken, John 109
Alcock, Charles 74
alcohol consumption 100–1, 124–5, 168–9
Allison, L. 161
Alpine Club 167
Amateur Football Association 66
amateur riders (of horses) 87, 91, 125
amateur status in sport, definition of 106–7
amateurism 144
Anderson, David 109
Anderson, Willie A. 117
Andreff, W. 28
angling clubs 55, 168, 170
apprentices in horseracing 96, 98, 124
Apsley and District Charity Competition 76
Archer, Fred 84, 88, 94–5, 98
Armstrong, Lance 15
Armstrong, Sam 96
artisans' golf clubs 149, 157
Ashton-under-Lyne Charity Competition
    Committee 75
Association Football Players' Union (AFPU) 62,
    68, 74, 108, 119, 122–3
associativity and associational culture 163–4
Aston Villa FC 72, 74
Athletic News 64, 76
Auchterlonie family 110–11, 117
Australia 6–8, 21, 165
Ayton, L.B. 119

Baird, James 110
Bale, J. 52
Ball, Thomas 111, 118–19
Banbury 169
Banks, John 100
Barbezat, D. 20, 22, 84

Barnes, S. 90
Barnsley FC 78–9
Barrett, George 88
Bass (company) 69
Batley, James B. 109, 114
Bechhofer, Frank 5
benefit matches 33, 68, 123
benevolent funds 68, 74
Bennett, Captain 91
Bentley, J.J. 80
Betchworth Park Golf Club 132–3
Biddlecombe, Terry 90
Bilsborough, Peter 28
Bishop, J. 169
blackballing 144
blood sports 48
Booth, Douglas 3–4, 23
Bourdieu, Pierre 147, 165–6, 168
Bourg, J.-F. 48
bowling clubs 167
Bradbeer, James 111, 153
Braid, James 111, 114–19, 154
Brailsford, Dennis 49
Braudel, F. 162
Breasley, Scobie 85–6, 101
British Racing School 96
British Society of Sports History (BSSH)
    11, 14
British sporting culture 16, 48
Britt, Edgar 85–6, 96–7
Brookes, Charles 114
Brookhouse Mills, Blackburn 55
Brookshaw, Tim 91
Brown, Harry 87
Brown, Ray 8
Bryant and May (company) 56
Buchanan, J.M. 168
Bullock, Frank 85–6
bureacracy in the academic world 8–9
Burnett, John 134, 148, 166
Burnley 58, 69, 75
business activity associated with sport 51
business community's support for sport 35;
    see also sponsorship of sport

INDEX

Cadbury Brothers (George and Richard) 55–7
caddies 53, 106, 109–10, 134–5, 151–7
Cambridge University Press 7
Cambuslang FC 78
Cameron, Donald M. 147
capital: concepts of 131, 133, 157; forms of 165; *see also* social capital
Carr, Jack 109
Carslake, 'Brownie' 85–6, 88
Carson, Willie 88, 95, 98, 101
cartels 52
Carter, N. 53
Cashman, Richard 6
Cass, Frank 11
Catlin, Arthur 119
Caulfield, Michael 99
Cauthen, Steve 88, 100–1
Cecil, Henry 94
Celtic FC 27–42, 73, 76–80
Central Lancashire, University of 9, 13
Chalenor, Tom 88
Chamberlayne, J. 28
change agents 172
character-building through sport 8, 142–3
charitable activity 1, 20–1, 35–6, 62–81
Charlton, John 88
child labour 155
child riders (of horses) 88–9, 91
Chisholm, Tom 111, 153
Chisholme, T. 114
chivalry 48
Clapton, Eric 3
Clark, P. 163–4
class distinctions 47, 49, 54, 118, 124, 143–8; *see also* social relationships and social distinctions
clothing for sport 144
clubs 67–8; effects of economic recession on 170–1; life-cycle approach to 170–1; limits to the expansion of 170; origins of 170; role of the state in relation to 163; *see also* angling clubs; bowling clubs; cricket clubs; golf clubs; harrier clubs; sports clubs
Coalter, F. 165
Coalvile Charity FA 75
Coates, David 96
Coburn, George 109
codes of conduct in sport 8, 142
collectivity, institutional 164
Collins, T. 12, 163–4
Colonel Bogey Whisky 140
Colt, H.S. 133
commercial widening and *commercial deepening* 51
commercialization of sport 29, 43, 48, 50, 62, 79, 163–4
Commons Preservation Society 135–6
company status for sports clubs 30–1, 35, 139, 145
Connell, R.M. 29
consultancy work 10
consumption standards 47
Contemporary British History (journal) 84

conviviality 168–9, 172
Corinthians Club 77–8, 169
corporate social responsibility (CSR) 62–3, 67
corporate welfare 55–6
corruption 99–101, 125
counterfactual history 4, 172
Covick, Owen 28
Crewe, S. 57
cricket 23–4, 43, 51–2, 107–8, 120–7, 168; residential qualifications 123
cricket clubs 54, 167
Cronin, M. 21–2, 25, 48
cultural capital 133, 142–3, 157, 165
'cultural turn' in history 21
Cumani, Luca 93
Cunninghame, James 112, 152–3
cup competitions 36, 51
cycling 32

Dabscheck, B. 32–3
Daphne tragedy (1883) 64
Davis, Richard 90
Dawson, A. 28
Day, Dave 13
debentures, issue of 139, 142
Dejonghe, T. 28
De Montfort University 9–11, 19
Denny, William 56
Dettori, Gianfranco 96
Dettori, Lanfranco ('Frankie') 85–7, 90–102
Dewar, Sir Thomas 68–9
Dicey, Richard 96
disaster funds 63–6, 81
dividends, payment of 34
Dixon, P. 20
Donaghue, Steve 96
Douglas Park Golf Club 132, 147
Dowie, J. 5, 144
Downward, P. 28
Driscoll, K. 165
drugs, use of 100–2
Duckworth, L. 54
Dumbarton FC 35, 40–1, 64
Duncan, George 109–12, 115–19, 154
Dundee 41, 73
Dunwoody, Richard 94
Durr, Frankie 96–7, 101
Dyreson, Mark 14

Eagley Mills, Bolton 55
East Lancashire Charity Cup 75, 79–80
Economic History Review 27, 107
economic history of sport 16
economic theory of the firm 171
Eddery, Pat 87, 95–6
Edgar, John Douglas 119
Edgbaston cricket ground 53–4
Edinburgh Establishment Golf Club Federation 149
Edinburgh Northern Harriers 169
Edinburgh University 6

INDEX

Eisenberg, C. 162–3
Ellan Vannin sinking 64
Elliott, Charlie 95
empiricism 15
Encyclopaedia of British Horseracing 11
enlightenment thinking 49
entrepreneurship 29, 43
Essex, Lord 137
etiquette in sport 142
Everton FC 64, 72, 79
exhibition matches 141–2

factory system 48–9
Falkirk FC 34
Fallon, Kieren 93–4
Farrell, Paddy 91
Fernie, Tom 114, 152
Fernie, William 111, 117–18
Ffrench, Royston 96
field sports 62, 164, 166–7
First World War 65, 75
FItzgerald, R. 55
Flatman, Nat 92
Flinders University 6–10, 28
Flinn, Michael 6
folk football 172
Foord, Fred 111
football 122–7, 169; clubs' income sources 31;
    employment of professionals in 107–8; played
    for charity 62–81; players' wages 33, 36, 52, 77,
    107, 122–5; transfer system 52, 123–4; women's
    75, 77
Football Association (FA), English 34, 63–71,
    75–81, 122–3; Charity Shield 66–7, 80–1; *see
    also* Scottish Football Association
Football League, English 51, 54, 64–5, 122–3; *see
    also* Scottish Football League
Football National War Fund 74
football stadiums 28, 51–3
Fordham, George 88, 125
forecaddies 151, 153
Foucault, Michel 4
Fox, Kate 98
France 163, 171
Francome, John 90, 98–101
Frawley, S. 21
French, Tom 88
friendly matches 32, 35–6, 51, 63, 67, 77, 170
Fujak, H. 21
Fulford, Harry 118, 120

Gallier, Susan 87
Gamage's (outfitters) 53
gambling, prohibition of 125
Garnham, N. 20
George, Jane 12, 107
Germany 163
Gibson, O. 108
Gibson, William 132
Gilmore, Orla 107

Glasgow Association 65–6
Glasgow Charity Cup 28, 63–81
Glasgow Rangers FC 27–8, 32–3, 37–42, 64, 76–7, 80
Godolphin Racing 94, 102
golf 20–1, 25, 106–27; compared with other sports
    123–5; elite players of 110–18, 121, 125–7,
    156–7; multi-motivational nature of 150;
    organ-isation of tournaments 121–2, 156;
    women's 135, 146–7, 157; working-class
    participation in 148–9, 157; *see also* caddies;
    handicapping system
golf balls: manufacture and sale of 126, 156–7;
    rubber-cored 137, 155
golf clubs (equipment), manufacture, repair and
    sale of 108–10, 114, 151, 156
golf clubs (institutions) 1–2, 11, 107, 118, 131–57;
    bar facilities 140; clubhouses 137–43, 147, 157;
    committees of 145; development of 54, 57, 132,
    164, 170; employment relationships at 150–2;
    enhancing the skills of professionals 155;
    estimates of number in Britain 134–5; financing
    of 139–40, 157; land occupied by 135–7, 157;
    laying out of courses 137; membership of 52,
    140–6, 165; nomination and seconding of
    potential members 144; professionals at 53,
    108–14, 117–18, 123–6, 135, 141, 143, 151–4,
    157; reasons for moving 137; secretaries of
    150–1; setting-up costs of 138–9, 142; visitors to
    141–5; waiting lists, entry fees and subscriptions
    141–4, 147–8
Golf Illustrated (journal) 118–22, 134–5, 140, 144,
    166
golfers, estimated number in Britain 135
Golfers' Handbook 106, 108, 137
Golfing Annual 134–5
golfing societies 148, 166
Gouguet, J.-J. 48
Gowans, James 112, 152
Grant, Davie 110
grants to scholars 7
Gray, Ernie 109
Greaves, Alex 86, 97
green fees 141–2, 149
Gregson, K. 169
guarantors of sports clubs 139, 142
Guttmann, Allen 11–12, 49

Hall, W. 73
Hamilton Academical FC 32
handicapping system in golf 142, 146, 150, 157,
    167
Hansen, P.H. 167
Hanson, Sir Reginald 66
Hardman, Edward 109
Hardy, Stephen 21, 25, 50, 164
harrier clubs 169
Harvey, Adrian 24, 48–50, 164, 167
Harvey's of Bristol (company) 140
Hawes, Alexander Travers 132
Hawkes, John 166–7

INDEX

Hay, Stan 100
Haynes, Jonathan 101
Heart of Midlothian FC 32–8, 42, 53
Hemsworth Grammar School 3
Hess, Rob 14
Hibernian FC 36
Hide, Eddie 86–90, 93–4, 96–8
Hill, J. 58
Hills, Percy 108, 114
Hoad, Roger 100
Hobsbawm, Eric 4
Hoggett, P. 169
Holt, Richard 12, 137, 150, 168–9
Hood, Tom 114
Hornby, A.N. 78
Hornby, H. 172
Horserace Betting Levy Board 91
horseracing 5, 11–12, 19–21, 24, 50–4, 62, 107, 120–7;
    American style of riding 97; *see also* jockeys
Howell, Bert 131, 155
Howell, R. and M. 15
Hudson, Don 3
Huggins, M. 19, 53, 67–8, 167, 169
Hughes, J. 20, 22, 84
Hughson, John 13
human capital 131–3, 150–1, 154–7, 165
Humphreys, Claire 131
Hunt, T. 20
Hutchinson, Horace 146, 150
Hutchinson, John 28
Hutchinson, Ron 85–6
hypothesis testing 21

industrial sport 54–8; definition of 54
industrialization and the Industrial Revolution 1,
    46–50
Inglis, S. 52
Injured Jockeys' Fund 91–2
injured players 74
International Centre for Sports History and
    Culture 10–11
International Journal of the History of Sport (*IJHS*)
    13–14
International Society for the History of Sport and
    Physical Education (ISHPES) 11, 14
international students 8
Irish cricket 168
Irish Football Association 69

Jackson, A. 20, 107–8
Jackson, N.L. ('Pa') 66, 70, 77–8
Jersey, Earl of 136
Jockey Club 20, 24, 86–91, 96–8, 100–1, 120
jockeys 20, 22, 62, 84–102, 122–4; earnings 93–7;
    fining and suspension of 98; injuries sustained
    by 89–92; malpractice by 99–101; power
    relationships experienced by 97–9; retirement
    for 101–2; skills of 96–7; supply of and demand
    for 85–7; travel undertaken by 92–3; weight
    watching by 87–9

Jockeys Association 99, 101–2
Johnson, Richard 95
Johnstone, Rae 85–6
joint authorship 12
joint stock companies 139
Journal of Sport History (*JSH*) 12–13, 131
journalists 9–10
Juvenal 16

Kay, Joyce 11–12, 24, 55, 63, 84, 107, 168, 170
Kendal 170
Kilmarnock FC 78
King, Jeff 98
King, Tom 119
Kirkcaldy, Andrew 117
Korr, Chuck 7–8, 28, 56

Ladies Golf Union 142, 146
ladies' sections of golf clubs 135, 146, 157
Ladlow, Anna 95
Lean, Michael 101
legislation, social 171
'Leicester school' 5
Leicester University Press 7
leisure time and leisure activities 47–9, 161
Leitch, Archibald 52–3
Lever Brothers 55–7
Levich, Frank 68
Lewis, G. 90, 100
Lewis, Geoff 96
Lewis, Guy 94
Lewis, Peter N. 12, 107, 115, 134–5, 148, 166
Lewis, R.W. 172
life-cycle approach to clubs 170–1
links golf courses 137
'little Kitchener' 88
Littlewood, John 134
Llewelyn, Carl 91
Loates, Sammy 92
Loates, Tommy 92, 125
Longrigg, Roger 5
'longue durée' 162
Lowe, William 111
Lowerson, John 136, 139, 144, 167

Macaulay, Lord 21
Macbeth, Jessica 107
MacDonald, Rory 95
MacKenzie, Donald 15
magazines, sporting 52, 167
Magdalene Asylums 73
Maguire, Adrian 95
Maher, Danny 85, 88
Malcolm, D. 23–4
Manchester 48, 55
Manchester Metropolitan University 13
Manchester United FC 67
Mangan, J.A. 13, 22
Mankell, Henning 15
Manley, Jonathan 13

INDEX

Marlow, Charles 100
Marriage, John 96
Martin, D. 143–4
Martin, J. 119, 152
Martin, 'Skeets' 85
Marylebone Cricket Club (MCC) 120, 125
Mason, Tony 5
Massy, Arnaud 115
Maynard, J. 84
Mayo, Charles 117–18
McAndrew, John 109, 114
McCoy, Tony 89–90, 94, 97, 100–1
McDowell, M.L. 57
McEwan, Douglas 119, 154
McKernan, Michael 6
McKinley, W. 112
McNeil, Simon 101
Mercer, Joe 96
Meredith, Billy 68, 125
middle-class morality and attitudes 47, 49, 54
Middleton, Iris 12, 19
military preparedness 23, 163
Mitchell, Abe 115
Mitchell, Alexander 136–7
Mitchell, Sophia 86
Moore, George 85–6
Morgan, Ernest 108
motivations of sports promoters and organizers 1
municipal golf courses 148–9
municipal transport and utilities 54
Munting, R. 56
'muscular Christianity' 56

National Football Museum 13; *see also* Scottish
    Football Museum
National Golf Clubs Protection Association 140
National Hunt racing 84–93, 96, 100–1
Neale, W.C. 51
New Zealand 24
Newcastle United FC 67
Nichols, G. 165
Nicholson, David 95
Nicholson, Frenchie 96
Nicolls, David 86
Nisbet's Golf Guide and Year Book 134, 144, 146–7
non-profit institutions 171
Norfolk jackets 144
Norfolk and Norwich Hospital Charity Cup
    Committee 76
North American Society for Sport History
    (NASSH) 7, 12
North Hants Golf Club 132–3, 137–8, 141
Northampton Town FC 67
Northern Ireland 6
Northern Racing College 96

Oke, J.H. 109
Olympic medals 15
O'Neill, Jonjo 95, 100–1
Open Championship 118–23

opinion leaders 172
Orr-Ewing, Alexander and John 55, 57
outdoor exercise, value of 150
Oxford Handbook of Sports History 46

Paddick, Bob 6
Paisley Charity Cup 59
Palgrave Dictionary of Transnational History 162
Paramio, J.L. 52
Park, Willie 110–11, 117
participant sports 131–2
Partick Thistle FC 33
paternalism 151–2, 156, 164
patrons and patronage 68–70
Paxton, Peter 112
Pay Up and Play the Game 7, 16, 22, 25, 55
philanthropic employers 55
Phillips, F.S. 133
pigeon shooting as a sport 15
Piggott, Lester 87–91, 95–6, 101–2
Pilkington's (company) 55
Pinkerton, D.Y. 111
'plus fours' 144
post-modernism 23
price maintenance 31
print media 52
prize-fighting 51
product improvment and *product development* in
    sport 51
Professional Footballers' Association 108
Professional Golfers' Association (PGA) 54, 62,
    106–8, 119–23, 126, 134, 156–7; objectives of
    120, 156; organization of tournaments by
    121–2, 156
Professional Riders Insurance Scheme 92
professionalism in sport 1, 28, 76, 81, 125;
    definition of 106
profit maximization 27–33, 36, 40–3, 51–2, 171
prosopography 171
psychic income 70, 81, 124
public schools 23, 48
Public Schools Alpine Sports Club 168
Putnam, R. 143, 165–6

Quaker industrialists 56
qualitative research 20–4
quantitative research 21–5; *see also* statistics, use
    of
Queen's Park Rangers FC 32, 67, 76–7

racecourses 53
Racehorse Owners' Association 99
Racing Calendar 24, 85, 89, 92
railways, impact of 19–20, 92, 141–2
Randall, Jonathan 108–9
Ray, Ted 109–10, 117
Reid, John 88, 100
Reiff, Johnny 85
Reiff, Lester 85, 97
religious affiliations 164, 167–8, 171

INDEX

Rendlesham Benevolent Fund 91
Renouf, Thomas 114
Renton FC 40–1
research quality exercises 7, 10, 12–13
research students, supervision of 10
reserve funds 36
retainers: paid to golf professionals 113, 122, 126, 152; paid to jockeys 95
Richards, Eric 6
Richards, Gordon 101
Richards, Huw 9
Richmond and Gordon, Duke of 136
Rickaby, Bill 98–9
Roberts, Michael 86
Robey, George 68
Robinson, R. 77
Rogers, E.M. 172
Rolland, Douglas 117
Rosebery, Earl of 73
Routledge (publisher) 11, 13–14
Routledge Companion to Sports History 21
Rowntree's (company) 57
Royal & Ancient Golf Club 106, 120–3
Royal Caledonian Hunt Club 166–8
Royal Cruising Club 168
rugby 24, 168
rural sports 172; *see also* field sports

St Mirren FC 34
Salt, H.S. 62
Sandiford, Keith 12
Saturday afternoon sport 49, 51, 112
Saul, Berwick 6
Sayers, Ben 110
Schultz, J. 15
Scott, Bill 100
Scottish football 27–43
Scottish Football Annual 79
Scottish Football Association (SFA) 28–32, 35–40, 63–5, 68, 70–5, 78
Scottish Football League (SFL) 27–31, 36–43, 65, 71–2
Scottish Football Museum 28
Scottish Sport (newspaper) 72, 75
Scudamore, Peter 87, 99, 101
Senghennydd colliery explosion 64
shareholders 34–5, 53
Sheffield 66
Sheffield United FC 78
Sheffield Wednesday FC 76, 78–9
Sinclair, Gus 8
Sissons, R. 123, 125
Sloan, Ted 85
Smirke, Charlie 97, 101
Smith, Doug 96, 100
Smith, Eph 96
Smith, Garden 118, 135
Smith, George 73
smoking concerts 169
Smout, Christopher 6

Sneyd, Major 96
Snowden, Jem 100
Soccer and Society (journal) 63
sociability of sport 137, 140, 150, 161–2, 169
social capital 131, 133, 143, 147, 157, 161, 164–9; *bonding* and *bridging* types of 143, 157, 166–9; definition of 165
social relations and social distinctions 54, 132, 140, 144, 146, 150, 157, 162–3, 167–9; *see also* class distinctions
source material for historical research 24
Southern Counties Football Association 69, 73
spectator facilities 52
spectator sports 49–50, 62, 69
sponsorship of sport 99, 142–3, 156; *see also* business community's support for sport
Sport in History (journal) 14
sport history as an academic subject 14–15
sport as an industry 50–4
Sporting Traditions (journal) 6
sports clubs 1–2, 25, 29–31, 49; cultures of 161–2; *instrumental* and *expressive* functions of 164; membership of 162–3; need for 172; origins of 162–4; pluralistic motivations for joining 164
sports equipment manufacturers 52–3
sports products 50–1; *packages* of 51; *see also* golf balls; golf clubs (equipment)
Stacey, M. 169
stakeholders 65–70
statistics, use of 1, 3, 20–5
steam power 49
Stephenson, David 118, 154
stewards 30
Stirling University 11–13
Stoddart, Brian 13
Stone, L. 171
Sunday sport 47–8, 93, 111, 136, 146, 149, 153, 169
Swain, P. 55
Swinburn, Walter 88, 100–1
Sykes, Sir Christopher 167
synthesis in academic work 6
Szymanski, S. 28, 49, 164, 168

Taylor, John Henry ('J.H.') 114–21, 152
Taylor, Josh 114, 117–20
Taylor, M. 122, 124
team sports 48, 164, 172
Telfer, H. 169
Al Thani, Sheikh Joaan 102
theory, use of 3–4
Third Lanark FC 77
'third sector' economics 1, 171
Thompson, F. 73
Thompson, Jimmy 91
Thorner, Graham 100
Titanic and the *Titanic* Relief Fund 63, 81
Tolson, John 12, 19
Tomlinson, Alan 16, 49, 162, 170
topophilia 52

INDEX

Tottey, F. 112
trade unionism 55–6, 119–20, 156, 164
transnationalism 162
Tranter, Neil 48, 50, 53, 167
Tribble, Alan 109
Turner, Michael 87–8, 101

'uncertainty' hypothesis 52
uniforms, wearing of 144
urbanization 50
utility maximization 27, 29, 32–3, 43, 51–2, 171

Vale of Leven FC 40–1, 72
Vardon, Harry 20, 110, 114–19, 154
Vardon, Tom 117–19, 154
Vereine, the 168
Vertinsky, Patricia 13
violence in sport 8
voluntarism and the voluntary sector 162, 171

Walker, W. 111
Walsall FC 64
Walton, John 5
Walvin, James 5
Weaver, Jason 92
Weir, Alex 108
welfare facilities provided by employers 55–6
Wells, John 88
West, E.J. 71
Weston, Tommy 93
Wharncliffe Cup 66, 76–80
'what if history' 4

Wheatley, Elijah 95
whips, jockeys' use of 97
Whitcombe family 110
White, Jack 110, 115–17
Whitehead, T.B. 114, 119, 154
Whiteway's Cider (company) 140
Wigglesworth, N. 170
Williams, J. 171
Williams, R. 162
Williamson, Bill 85–6
Williamson, Tom 108
Wilson, John 111
Wilson, Reginald 109
Wingate, Charlie 112–13
Winton, Thomas 109, 151
women's sport 58, 75, 77, 86, 135, 146–7, 157, 168–9
Wood, L. 165
Wootton, Frank 85–6
working hours and work patterns 47, 49
workplace sport 58, 164; *see also* industrial sport
Wright, J.R. 88
Wylie, Alexander 56–7, 77

yachting 168
Young, Arthur 47
Young, Christopher 16, 49
Young, D.C. 16
Younger, William 53

'Zulus' 54, 77